To the Ends of the Earth

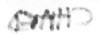

To the Ends of the Earth

The Globalization of Christianity

Kenneth Hylson-Smith

Paternoster:
thinking faith

LONDON ● ATLANTA ● HYDERABAD

13 12 11 10 09 08 07   7 6 5 4 3 2 1

First published in 2007 by Paternoster
Paternoster is an imprint of Authentic Media
9 Holdom Avenue, Bletchley, Milton Keynes, Bucks, MK1 1QR, UK
285 Lynnwood Avenue, Tyrone, GA 30290, USA
OM Authentic Media, Medchal Road, Jeedimetla Village
Secunderabad 500 055, A.P., India
www.authenticmedia.co.uk/paternoster

Authentic Media is a division of Send the Light Ltd., a company limited by guarantee
(registered charity no. 270162)

British Library Cataloguing in Publication Data

A catalogue record for this book is available from
the British Library.

ISBN-13 978-1-84227-475-0

Designed by James Kessell for Scratch the Sky Ltd. (www.scratchthesky.com)
Print Management by Adare Carwin
Printed in Great Britain by J.H. Haynes and Co., Sparkford

This book is dedicated to Isla Mhairi and Iona Clare, my much loved granddaughters

Contents

Preface

This book is a response to the many historians, sociologists, theologians, atheists, agnostics and media pundits who in recent decades have declared Christianity, or at least the institutional Church, to be in retreat and even suffering from terminal illness. After all, such purveyors of pessimism argue, the evidence is there for all to see. Declining church membership throughout Continental Europe and Britain, both absolutely and as a proportion of the population, empty pews, and the frequent apparent irrelevance of the Church and all that it does and says to twenty-first century secular life, seems to point unmistakably and irrefutably to a parlous condition. Apathy towards the churches and any form of organized religion seems to be widespread. There has been much talk about 'the death of God' even within the Church itself, and atheists and agnostics have attracted a sympathetic hearing as never before. The gloom mongers have largely set the tone concerning Christian belief and practice, the condition of the churches and their likely future, and morale is low in many quarters, both within the churches and among their well-wishers. So often the attackers seem to be winning the day and the upholders of Christianity appear to be on the defensive. Of course, Christ said that Christians would be in a minority, but this beleaguered state goes beyond a mere counting of heads. A significant body of commentators give the impression that the faith itself is facing annihilation and that this is the culmination of a long-drawn-out, at least two centuries-long, process of impairment. The USA may appear to defy this dismal picture and prognosis, but the situation there is frequently dismissed as the exception that proves the rule. It is also said by some analysts that even this one remaining stronghold of Christianity will sooner or later, and most probably sooner rather than later, succumb to the inexorable march of modernism, atheism and agnosticism.

The present work challenges this whole interpretation of both recent history and the contemporary state of health of Christianity. It asserts that the detractors and prophets of doom have misinterpreted both the historical and present situation. Seen within the perspective of the last three hundred years or so, and with an awareness of the current worldwide Christian scene, the analysis of past trends and the prognostication being made by the various jeremiads are a gross distortion of the facts. They are seriously warped assessments. Far from being a saga of decline and imminent demise, the story of the post seventeenth-century global Church is one of unparalleled progress and expansion. Worldwide Christianity has undergone a period of unprecedented vitality and growth during the last three centuries, and is currently more prominent, vibrant and influential than ever before.

In writing a book on such a wide-ranging topic, I am greatly indebted to a host of scholars, as indicated by the notes and the extensive bibliography. I have very much appreciated the helpfulness and encouragement of Dr Robin Parry, the Acquisitions Editor of Paternoster Publications.

Introduction

The fifteenth- and sixteenth-century Renaissance and the six-teenth-century Reformation were each, in their own right, epoch-making events. The one gave birth to the 'new learning' and the other to Protestantism. Nevertheless, as if these two achievements were not enough, the two movements together had a further unrealized result of massive long-term significance. They inaugurated an unprecedented departure from Christian orthodoxy – a paradoxical outcome for the Reformers, if not for many Renaissance men and women. There had been those before that revolutionary era who had expressed doubt in relation to certain specific Christian doctrines, or who had totally rejected the fundamental tenets of the Christian faith. But people in general had regarded such non-conformists as heretics, who were worthy of severe punishment for their impertinent stepping out of line. The Renaissance and the Reformation unconsciously changed all that. At first, it was a small, hardly discernable or noticed, process. Even so, what had been set in motion continued and grew. There was a sustained, relentless, escalating and momentous denial of basic Christian teaching, either in part or in total, and an under-mining of Christianity of a type and to an extent that had not pre-viously been encountered by the Church. It was one of the most stupendous unintended consequences of intended human action ever experienced by any culture or religion.

The rediscovery of the works of the ancient Greeks and Romans 'brought about a shift of interest to the affairs of this world as opposed to the next, and to the individual as opposed to the Church or state'.[1] Literate Europeans were exposed to a corpus of ancient classical texts which, although not specifically religious, quite typically had an agnostic or even atheistic flavour. These treasures from the long-distant past implicitly or explicitly enshrined opinions that were not reconcilable with core Christian dogmas. At best, from the Christian point of view, there was a belief in a pantheon of gods. At worst, as with the highly popular *Natural History* of Pliny the Younger, which went into 38 editions in Western Europe between 1469 and 1532, there was more than a hint that there may be no God at all.

It all amounted to a massive intrusion of distinctly non-Christian perspectives that could, and sometimes did, give encouragement to attitudes that were decidedly antipathetic to the creeds of the Church. By 1551 the English humanist Roger Ascham reported that Italy was rife with atheists.

To supplement and compound these inherently anti-theistic or polytheistic influences, the Reformation itself had an unplanned, unmeant secularizing tendency. In retrospect, it can be seen as having initiated a very tentative yet perceptible 'retreat of religion from the public space'. It triggered off the steady transformation of institutions, and set them on the path 'toward religious and ideological neutrality'.[2] They began to shed their religious identity. It was but the beginning in modern Western history of the process by which sectors of society and culture were 'removed from the domination of religious institutions and symbols'. The lessening of religious influence was not confined to the specialist religious institutions, and to those who were involved in their life. It affected 'the totality of cultural life and of ideation, and may be observed in the decline of religious contents in the arts, in philosophy, in literature and, most important of all, in the rise of science as an autonomous, thoroughly secular perspective on the world.'[3]

The sixteenth and seventeenth centuries most significantly provided the seedbed for this latter aspect of 'secularization' – the establishment and growth of modern science and the accompanying emergence of a more pervasive scientific attitude to life by people as a whole. It was a transformation in the way men and women viewed themselves and nature. The new orientation gradually replaced one in which, speaking very generally, 'man found his identity, meaning and purpose, both as an individual and as a member of society, in terms of a sacred world-view. It was a world-view which located the place and purpose of man within a comprehensive divine plan.'[4]

Out of the Renaissance and Reformation there emerged the first signs in modern church history of what Max Weber identified as the *disenchantment of the world*.[5] By this he meant the elimination of magic as a salvation technique, but the concept can legitimately be broadened to cover 'the impoverishment of the reign of the invisible'. Here we are witnessing an erosion of the very conceptual framework of religious thinking. It took place in a mostly subtle, unelaborated and little articulated manner, but it was as important as many of the more obvious cultural movements in that era of transformations. It represented the initial tentative move in a profound 'revolution in relations between heaven and earth, which decisively reconstructed the human abode separate from the divine'.[6]

Of course, the sixteenth- and seventeenth-century Protestant reformers were unaware of what they were doing in this particular respect. They may well have been horrified if they had appreciated what their new approach to the Bible and its teaching entailed. Underpinning the theology of Protestantism was the stress on the individual person standing alone before God and finding the way of salvation and sanctification in and through the Bible, which itself was made widely available with the invention of movable-type printing. Increasingly, Scripture was read literally, like any other text, for the information it imparted. 'Silent, solitary reading would help to free Christians from traditional ways of interpretation and from the supervision of the religious experts. The stress on individual faith would also help to make the truth seem increasingly subjective – a characteristic of the modern Western mentality.'[7] Luther thought that reason by itself was inimical to faith and could only lead to atheism, and his rejection of it actually contributed to the secularization of religion. His antagonism to any form of what would later be called 'natural religion', his intense focus on God as mysterious, hidden and only accessible through faith, had a perhaps unrealized consequence of emptying the physical and rational world of the divine. Luther also secularized politics as a result of his passionate conviction that the mundane order was diametrically opposed to the spiritual; and the two should be kept apart.

It was, perhaps, the development of science that provided the hammer blow to what was generally accepted as the biblical picture of a God-created world. Although the astronomer Nicolaus Copernicus (1473–1543) was convinced that his science was 'more divine than human', his theory of a heliocentric universe appeared to undermine the earth-centred depiction of the cosmos that was seemingly at the heart of the biblical view of creation. Confirmation of the Copernican theory by Johannes Kepler (1571–1630) and Galileo Galilei (1564–1642) only added fuel to the already raging fire. The final and devastating contribution to this sequence of scientific discoveries was the use by Galileo of his perfected telescope. 'All over Europe, people made their own telescopes and scanned the heavens for themselves.'[8] The world was increasingly becoming disenchanted.

Francis Bacon (1561–1626) added his weighty authority to reinforce the process of rationalization that lay behind much of the scientific developments and theories. He insisted that all truth, including the most sacred doctrines of religion, must be subjected to the highly rigorous and stringent critical methods of empirical science.

The elevation of science, and its ever-increasing impact on philosophy, was made more explicit and evident as a result of the work and outlook of Sir Isaac Newton (1642–1727). His deep involvement in the world of scientific method and experimentation left him with little appreciation of intuitive forms of perception that could offer people a different mode of truth, which was real to them. He longed for Christianity to be purged of its mythical doctrines, and he used his very considerable influence in an attempt to subject Christian dogma to rational scrutiny.

The Baconian and Newtonian perspectives were echoed in the late seventeenth century by the forthright demands of some radical philosophers and others who pressed for greater liberalism and 'freethinking'. 'From the moment that European opinion decided for toleration, it decided for an eventual free market in opinion . . . A free market in some opinions became a free market in all opinions.'[9]

The eighteenth century

The eighteenth century produced a surge in overt Enlightenment denials of the existence of God, or at least the God of orthodox Christianity. Various waves of new thinking contributed to this, in addition to those already indicated. First, there was the 'science of religion'. In this we see the emergence in Western thought of the concepts of 'religion' and 'religions' as we now understand them. 'The great revolutions in science and religion which took place in the sixteenth and seventeenth centuries thus paved the way for the development of a secular study of religions, and equally importantly, of a concept of "religion" which could link together and relate the apparently disparate religious beliefs and practices found in the empirical "religions".'[10] Westerners for the first time were exposed in a major way to the belief systems of the main world religions, and for many people this undermined their previous, possibly unchallenged, acceptance of Christianity as a unique faith, and their assumption that there was but one true God. At the very least, the question of the relationship of Christianity to other world faiths was brought to the fore and made a pressing issue. Acute awareness of the claims of other religions was a salutary and challenging experience. Questions not even previously asked were somewhat anxiously and apprehensively raised.

Then there was deism. This asserted that 'God' was merely the 'first of all causes', who had no ongoing relationship with nature or man. He was an absentee landlord; a clockmaker who wound up the world at the beginning and left it to tick away on its own, without any further attention or adjustment. It was a model that was widely and rapidly embraced by leading figures in the early years of the United States, including the nation's third president, Thomas Jefferson.

In the second half of the century there were yet further changes in the evolving corpus of opinion antipathetic to Christianity. This whole Age of Reason, was dominated by 'the assertion that reason and logic were the only keys to unlock the truth about the universe and everything in it', by 'a belief in human autonomy', and by 'the conviction that individuals and society at large could be brought to perfection as a result'[11] of such non-theistic means.

A new age for atheism was dawning. 'Paris boasted what medieval Oxford and ancient Athens did not command: a band of thinkers who celebrated their denial of anything which one could call "god".'[12]

The nineteenth century

In the nineteenth century Ludwig Feuerbach gave a final twist to the philosophical line of development just indicated, and suggested that religion could be explained in completely human terms. There were two main components introduced: biblical criticism and the so-called conflict of science and faith. The shaking of the theological foundations was typified by H.H. Milman who, in his *History of the Jews*, in 1829, depicted Abraham as an Arab sheikh, and little more, and who tended to rationalize some of the miracles; and by Friedrich Strauss, who in his *Das Leben Jesu*, portrayed Jesus as a mere Galilean teacher of pure and holy life.

Charles Darwin made 1859 a key date in the whole process being described when he issued a work that succinctly encapsulated his main theses in its title: *On the Origin of Species by Means of Natural Selection, or, The Preservation of Favoured Races in the Struggle for Life*. The excitement and discussion aroused was extensive and intensive.

It was the renowned scientist and enthusiastic Darwinian T.H. Huxley who coined the word 'agnostic' to describe his opinions, which, no doubt, were shared by countless others. He did not deny God's existence, but he could not concur with Christians in purporting to know anything about the character of such a deity, for that type of knowledge was in his view unattainable. 'His doctrine was ontologically neutral.'[13] His 'religion belonged to the realm of feeling, while science was part of the realm of intellect'.[14]

During the second half of the nineteenth century atheism mushroomed, vastly extended its influence, and assumed a greater and more pronounced public image. It came into the open as never before, and was more daringly and audaciously owned and declared than in any former age.

From Friedrich Nietzsche to the present day

It was Friedrich Nietzsche more than anyone else who set in motion the most recent phase in the unfolding saga of atheism and agnosticism.[15]

If Nietzsche gave the initial thrust to the modern non-theistic view of life and of the world, Sigmund Freud provided a psychological and psychiatric in-depth rationale for discarding the very notion of a supreme supernatural being. By doing so, he made a massive contribution to the advancement of atheism in the twentieth and twenty-first centuries. He regarded religion as an illusion, which, with the advance of human knowledge and more especially science, would gradually be whittled away.

The twentieth century was peppered with a most distinguished and impressive galaxy of atheistic academics. The atheistic existentialist philosophers Martin Heidegger and Jean-Paul Sartre were of particular and considerable importance, primarily among fellow intellectuals.

Albert Camus helped to communicate the atheistic existentialist message at a popular level, largely through his literature, which won him the Nobel Prize in 1957.

His fundamentally pessimistic outlook became a recurring theme in the succeeding decades, shared and incorporated into the works of Tennessee Williams, who assented to the view that there is both a horror and meaninglessness in existence. Bob Dylan and the Beatles introduced pure existentialism into some of their songs, as did the pop idol Bruce Springsteen in the 1980s, and the best-selling author Arthur Koestler.[16]

The 'death of God' theology

A unique feature of the twentieth-century Christian scene in the Western world was the appearance of a 'death of God' theology within the portals of Christianity itself. When it emerged in the 1960s it took the public by surprise. 'Surely the decision to be a theologian implies, if it means anything at all, that the reality of God is taken for granted!'[17] Such was the reaction of many bewildered, bemused and often angry people. The average churchperson, or

xviii   *Introduction*

even those with ill-defined, imprecise conceptions of God, and of what Christian theologians were in business for, responded in amazement. They were staggered that Christian theologians, whose most basic task was assumed to be the defence of belief in God, and the exposition of what that entailed, for the benefit of a less well-informed 'lay' audience, should disclaim belief in the very God they were supposed to be upholding and championing. To deny that God exists, or to give serious consideration to the emptiness of the term 'God' within a Christian world-view, seemed to many incredulous observers to be blatant hypocrisy and a confusion of roles on a massive scale. What was going on when, for example, one of these radical academics could declare with evangelistic zeal that 'the message the Christian is now called to proclaim is the gospel, the good news or the glad tidings, of the death of God'?[18]

Those at the forefront in purveying this teaching were mainly eminent US academics. They did not constitute a single, undifferentiated, 'movement' in which they all shared the same convictions and spoke with one voice. Perhaps the lowest common denominator that gave them a semblance of unity and coherence was the belief that the Christian God, as traditionally conceived, as described in the official creeds of the churches, and as proclaimed from countless pulpits throughout the Western world, had no meaning or relevance to modern man. But even the phrase 'death of God' was given a great range of meanings.

Gabriel Vahanian may be credited with having triggered off the debate when, in 1961, he published a work entitled, *The Death of God*. The death of God for Vahanian was a cultural fact. It was 'the loss of a transcendental or supernatural realm as the necessary context for understanding man and his world'. For him it meant 'the substitution of a purely immanental perspective as the only meaningful framework for dealing with the problems and questions of human existence. In such a setting God is simply not necessary.'[19] The apparent flourishing of Christianity in the USA at the time, Vahanian considered mere religiosity, a 'desperate caricature' of Christian faith, and the most convincing indication that culturally speaking God is dead. 'The difficulty is not so much that men have lost their faith as that it has ceased to inform their lives or to condition in any significant way the culture of which they are a part.'[20] Because he spoke in such cultural terms, he was able to argue that Western civilization had entered a post-Christian phase in which, perhaps paradoxically, the real God was and remained 'wholly other'.

Paul Van Buren claimed that science and technology had invalidated the old mythology of God acting in the world. He dismissed theism 'on the logical positivist's premise that statements about God, who is beyond empirical experience, are meaningless'.[21]

In 1966 Thomas Altizer made one of the most forthright and uncompromising statements on the whole issue of the death of God in *The Gospel of Christian Atheism*. When he burst onto the scene, 'there was something breathtaking about his speculative boldness'.[22] To him, the death of God spelt freedom from slavery to a tyrannical transcendent deity: 'Only by accepting and even willing the death of God in our experience can we be liberated from a transcendent beyond, an alien beyond which has been emptied and darkened by God's self-alienation in Christ.'[23] Altizer spoke in his book of 'the necessity of a Christian atheism'.[24] He favoured some form of Christian belief, but was strongly of the opinion that this should not be traditional Christianity.

William Hamilton was as explicit as Altizer in pronouncing that his generation was facing 'a loss which is not simply a loss of idols or of the God of theism',[25] but a real loss of transcendence. It was a genuine and palpable loss of God. It was impossible to believe in the biblical God in the old way.

In *The Secular City* (1965), Harvey Cox particularly addressed what he accepted as the valid sociological assertion that religion had limited prospects of survival except in a highly modified form.

Honest to God and its consequences

Although the death of God theologians were based almost entirely in the USA, their theology had international repercussions. It was also part of a wider radical trend that had emerged from the time of the Second World War onwards. In England, it was in 1963 that the general public suddenly, and in many cases for the first time, became aware of the nature, force and form of radical theology. John A.T. Robinson's *Honest to God* 'set all the fireworks and thunderings of the long-pent storm free to rage in fury'.[26]

In writing his book, Robinson was inspired by three theologians: Rudolf Bultmann, Dietrich Bonhoeffer and Paul Tillich. Bultmann, with his concern to 'demythologize' the gospel, was a challenge to the 'biblical' theologians. Bonhoeffer, with his vision of a 'religionless' Christianity, was a challenge to Christian escapism and undue pietism. Tillich, with his philosophy based on faith as 'ultimate concern' with the 'ground of our being', was a reminder of the call of the Church to embrace all humankind in its concern.

Robinson was motivated by a strong desire to communicate Christian doctrine to people he regarded as alienated from the current Church and its teaching. He believed that the Church was being called not merely to a restatement of traditional orthodoxy in modern terms and language, but to a more radical recasting 'in the process of which the most fundamental categories of our theology – of God, the supernatural, and of religion itself – must go into the melting'.[27] The lay world, he said, found traditional orthodox supernaturalism largely meaningless.

Man, Robinson asserted, had come of age, and the old images of God were no longer adequate. Pictures of God 'up there' or 'out there' were unhelpful. More appropriate was the terminology of depth psychology, in which God was thought of as 'the ground of our being'. Jesus was the 'man for others', who is united with 'the ground of his being' because of his utter concern for other people. The test of worship is how far it makes us more sensitive to the beyond in our midst, or to Christ in the hungry, the naked, the homeless and the prisoner. In the sphere of morals the radical 'ethic of the situation' was advocated, in which nothing was prescribed except love. Such teaching certainly caused consternation and quite widespread trauma. It was but part of the questioning of inherited Christian belief, and modes of expressing such belief, that agitated the churches of Western Christendom in that eventful decade.

In England, the theological climate that this created helped to provide fertile soil for the works of John Hick, Maurice Wiles, Don Cupitt and others, all of whom questioned the received faith of Christianity. This was especially so within the Church of England. Writing in 1986, one observer noted that since '*Essays and Reviews*

(1860), which first signalled the fact that the methods of German biblical criticism had penetrated the Church of England, there' had 'been a steady broadening of permitted theological opinion' until his own generation had 'reached the point where there' existed 'a diversity of fundamental Christian world views within a single church.'[28] The Church of England continued to pride itself on its ability to bring a range of theological convictions within its very ample umbrella. Nonetheless, there were many who questioned whether there was a limit to such a policy of tolerance. 'It is', one commentator remarked in 1989, 'stretching credulity beyond reasonable limits to maintain that such a diversity is an expression of comprehensiveness understood in terms of complementarity. Such diversity is not an expression of multi-faceted complementarity. It is an example of pluralism. The contemporary Church of England consists of a number of different Anglicanisms.'[29]

As we move into the latter part of the century perhaps the best representative in the English-speaking world of extreme theological radicalism was Don Cupitt. He described himself as 'a thoroughgoing Christian heretic and dissident' who 'cannot endure any attempt to control interpretation or finalize truth'.[30] Cupitt rejected any creed or set of beliefs to which he was asked to conform, and replaced such general statements of belief by his own formula. 'The only truly religious God is and has to be a man-made God. Your God has to be, let's be blunt about it, your own personal and temporary improvisation.'[31] For him, man would no longer accept beliefs to which he was asked to agree. 'The trouble with believing today, then, is that the churches persist and our own psychology persists in clinging to ideas of fixed meaning, authoritative interpretation, orthodoxy and final Truth. In an age when language has become completely enhistorized and humanized these ideas are no longer tenable, but we hold on to them because of our obsession with power, our desire to be governed and our reluctance to grow up.'[32]

Sociologists, historians and the secularization thesis

Statistics give considerable support to those sociologists and historians who attempt to make a case for the decline of the churches in

Continental Europe and Britain. Take the Church of England as an example. In the 1960s the number of Easter Day communicants fell by 24.5 per cent in England. In 1957 in a Gallup Poll survey 14 per cent of the people questioned said that they had been to church the previous Sunday, but by 1958 this figure had dropped to 12 per cent, and by 1963 it was down to 10 per cent.[33] The number of people on Church of England electoral rolls had declined from 3,638,000 in 1925 to 3,423,000 in 1940, to 2,959,000 in 1950, 2,862,000 in 1960 and 2,692,000 in 1964. As a rate per 1,000 of the total population of the country this represented 143 in 1925, 120 in 1940, 96 in 1950, 89 in 1960 and 81 in 1964.[34] Writing in 1980, Alan D. Gilbert could only report what appeared to be a tale of drift downwards. 'Since 1960', he said, 'declining membership, attendance, Sunday-school participation, baptisms, confirmations, and numbers of candidates offering themselves for the professional ministry have presented a consistent picture of massive crisis.'[35] By 1999 Church of England attendance had declined to 980,000, which was the result of a fall of 24 per cent during the 1980s and 23 per cent during the 1990s.

The numerical decline was equally alarming for the Free churches. Taken as a whole, they lost about one third of all their membership in England and Wales in the period 1914 to 1970.

In the discussion of secularization,[36] the USA has always been acknowledged as an exception, for whatever reasons. The combined Jewish, Buddhist, Muslim and Hindu adherents in that country number only about 4 or 5 per cent of the population. The overwhelming majority of the inhabitants give at least lip-service to a Christian allegiance, and for a great proportion this goes much deeper, and results in church or chapel attendance, often with a strong evangelical emphasis. It can categorically be said that the United States is in all essentials a Christian country at the present time, and that Christian predominance will probably be still more marked in decades to come. Out of all the Western nations, the United States will be the last to retain this status and role in the twenty-first century. But the proponents of the secularization theory do not allow this to detract from their main thesis. The USA is treated as an abnormality, to be explained historically and socially.

The end result of the 'secularization' debate, whether intended or unintended, is to add academic verification to the notion that the Church has been 'declining' and continues to undergo 'decline'. In other words, the cumulative effect of the persistent and insistent stress upon secularization is to reinforce a pessimistic reading and tone regarding the recent, say post-seventeenth-century, history of Christianity, the present health and the future prospect of the churches and of Christianity as a whole in the Western world. Some of the scholars involved extend such a gloomy analysis and forecast more generally and more globally than that. To this extent, the pessimists and the opponents of Christianity are strengthened and encouraged, while members of the churches, and those who wish Christianity well, are disheartened by what the proponents of the secularization theory have to say.

Although they differ among themselves in certain, sometimes important, respects, there is a core of consensus among the sociologists and historians concerned. Secularization is seen as the inevitable result of the rise of industrial society and the modernization of culture.

> It is argued that modern science has made traditional belief less plausible; the pluralisation of life-worlds has broken the monopoly of religious symbols; the urbanization of society has created a world which is individualistic and anomic; the erosion of family life has made religious institutions less relevant; and technology has given people greater control over their environment, making the idea of an omnipotent God less relevant or plausible. [37]

The media

It is, of course, the sensational and the unexpected that attracts the attention of the media, and reaction to the life of the churches is no exception. Thus, the death of God pronouncements, or any hint of theologians or church leaders holding views that question orthodoxy, soon produce headlines and editorial comment. And the very reporting of such material, often with an accompanying pessimistic, and not infrequently critical or even antagonistic, comment on it, tends to produce or reinforce mindsets. The constant publicity given to issues and topics that seem to be detrimental to the well-being of the churches is, in itself, harmful to the public perception of those religious bodies. The medium is the message. This is especially so if, as is frequently the case, there is little balancing prominence given to the untold signs of vitality in the Christian life of the nation and of Christianity worldwide. A distorted and biased view can easily be created. It is but one more factor in the cultivation of a widespread perception that the churches in general, and the Christianity that they represent and embody, are in retreat, if not at the stage of final decline.

The progress of Christianity since *c.*1700 and its present unparalleled healthiness

The foregoing account has painted a bleak scene from the vantage point of the churches and Christian believers. It has depicted an unfolding and seemingly relentless saga of erosion and an apparently relentless, unstoppable downwards slide, at least in Continental Europe and Britain. It has charted the emergence of many prophets, with their dire prognostications, foretelling a dismal future for the churches. It has highlighted the emergence and growth in the number of often highly intelligent and articulate atheists and agnostics, and the emergence of theologians who also seem to be exceedingly pessimistic about the prospects for traditional Christianity.

It may seem an impertinence to take issue with such an array of distinguished academics and others who are able to express their views with erudition, eloquence and persuasiveness. It may at first sight appear to be flying in the face of the 'facts', not only to contest some of the arguments raised, but to question underlying theories, assumptions and interpretations that are so prevalent. Nonetheless, this book does just that. It suggests that the two main premises underpinning most of the opinions that have been reviewed in this Introduction – that traditional Christian doctrine has increasingly become unacceptable to modern men and women, and is currently being discarded by people en masse, and that the post-1700 period has witnessed the alarming deterioration of Christianity, which is now in a parlous condition

– are ill-founded. To propose, as is done in this book, that since 1700 Christianity has undergone its greatest period of expansion ever, and is currently more vigorous, healthy and widely embraced than at any previous time, may seem to be untenable and absurd. It may seem to be at best whistling in the wind, and at worse evidence of some mental derangement. It may appear to represent an excessively optimistic response to a situation that should more appropriately be met with pessimism and defensiveness by any committed Christian. Nonetheless, that is the picture of the globalization of Christianity, and that is the revolutionary change in the worldwide Christian landscape, that will be depicted in the rest of this book.

Of course, all has not been well with Christianity during the last three hundred years and there are many causes for concern at the present time. This should be borne in mind in recounting something of the high points, the more commendable aspects, and the causes for Christian rejoicing in both the history of the faith, and in the contemporary situation. Triumphalism must not be allowed to replace despondency. The case must not be exaggerated. But, it must also not be ignored, downplayed or undervalued. The global advance of Christianity, and its current buoyancy, needs to be stated clearly and with conviction. New and more accurate perspectives are urgently required. The historical record and the interpretation of it, and the analysis of the present condition of worldwide Christianity, as presented by some academics and media commentators should be radically corrected. The present work is a small contribution to such a process of reappraisal.

1

Vibrant Christianity in Europe, Britain and North America

The first stirrings in Continental Europe

The various eighteenth-century and nineteenth-century evangelical revivals and awakenings in Continental Europe, Britain and North America, together constitute what was the principal, most dynamic and significant feature in the Protestant world of their day. Not only so, but they had incalculable medium- and long-term repercussions which reached out to the far corners of the world. And it all began with the emergence of Pietism and Moravianism in central and eastern Germany at the end of the seventeenth century and the early part of the eighteenth century.[1]

Pietism owed much, if not its foundation, to Philipp Jakob Spener who, from the late 1660s, championed a 'highly personal form of religion, with a strong emphasis on the individual's direct relationship with God and the need for a "New Birth" to cement that relationship'.[2] New birth became a hallmark of the Pietists, 'not because it was peculiar to them but because of the prominence they gave it. The essence of the matter was how best to realize the priesthood of all believers.'[3] The movement was not intended to be separatist, but integral to the Lutheran Church, and many pastors supported it.

In certain respects August Francke was the organizing genius of Pietism. At Halle he skilfully combined the proclamation of distinctive Pietist teaching with the promotion of the educational policies and the practical ambitions of the university. An orphan house had places for 3,000 people and was by a great margin the largest such institution in Europe. The schools and the teacher-training colleges were tangible expressions of Francke's 'system of state education which had Pietist teaching on conversion and the cultivation of the interior life at its centre'.[4] There was a Bible institute and a dispensary; and the press at Halle soon became one of the leading printing houses in Germany, producing an untold quantity of Bibles and other Christian literature for wide distribution in a range of languages. Although he followed Dutch models, the scale of Francke's enterprise was staggering, and unparalleled for his day. It 'gave a shape to charitable activity all over the Protestant world'.[5] The total complex must have been unbelievably impressive.

As we move into the third and fourth decades of the eighteenth century it is one of Francke's pupils, Count Nicholas Zinzendorf who assumed centre stage in this rapidly unfolding story of evangelical Protestantism. He allowed persecuted refugees of the ancient Protestant Church of Bohemia and Moravia to establish a settlement on his land, which became known as Herrnhut.

In 1727 the community itself experienced a remarkable revitalization. A revival had originated in Silesia and had spread to Upper Lusatia. The residents at Herrnhut were transformed from a band of quarrelling nomads into a body of dedicated evangelists; and soon missionaries from the renewed community were going to the West Indies (1732), Greenland (1733), the Indians of Surinam (1734), the Hottentots of South Africa (1737), and the Gold Coast and Ceylon (1737). It was not long before they exercised a vital influence in Britain and North America in the early years of the evangelical revival, especially in the 1730s. Between 1738 and 1740 in particular, Moravians played a crucial part in the birth and extension of the English and North American evangelical revivals. The 'events in the Hapsburg territories set off a chain reaction which extended to the edges of Europe and beyond.'[6]

Revival in England, Wales and Scotland

The details of the English revival are too well known to justify close scrutiny in the present work.[7] It is sufficient to note that it began in a quiet, unheralded way with the ministry of the young, energetic and charismatic evangelist George Whitefield, who preached with astonishing results, first in churches and then, because he was excluded from such ministry by the opposition of priests, and because he wanted to go where the people were to be found, to vast crowds in the open air. The brothers John and Charles Wesley joined him in what soon became a national crusade. Thousands of men, women and children were converted, and they were knit together in fellowship locally by means of small groups, called classes, and by the larger gatherings of all those who had come to faith, or who were seeking salvation. The movement had an immensely transforming effect on individuals, and it stirred up great reactions in towns, villages and hamlets alike. It provided a body of believers who were a power in the land. In fact, by the time of John Wesley's death in 1791 there were in excess of 500 Methodist preachers in the British dominions and the United States of America, and over 130,000 Methodist members. The movement also helped to create a climate of opinion that greatly contributed to the generation and continuation of a worldwide missionary enterprise of gigantic proportions in the course of the next century and a half.

By a highly predictable process, the revival developed not only as a distinct movement, but into the separate Methodist Church and the Countess of Huntingdon's Connexion, and subsequently into a number of other churches in the early part of the nineteenth century as a result of schism and secession.

While all this was taking place, evangelicalism became a potent force within the Church of England itself. All over England Church of England men and women, and most importantly Anglican clergy, underwent the same conversion experience and came, often without any obvious assistance or persuasion from anyone else, to preach the same gospel as their more famous Methodist contemporaries. The pioneers included such stalwarts as Samuel Walker of Truro, the eccentric but highly effective William Grimshaw of Haworth in Yorkshire, the erudite William Romaine in London, and the extraordinary ex-slave ship captain, John Newton, in Olney and then in London.

Although the evangelicals continued to be a maligned minority within the Church until well into the nineteenth century, by
their example and by their teaching they had, according to
W.E.H. Lecky, 'gradually changed the whole spirit of the English
Church. They had infused into it a new fire and passion of devotion, kindled a spirit of fervent philanthropy, raised the standard
of clerical duty, and completely altered the whole tone and tendency of the preaching of its ministers'.[8] Sir James Stephen
described the evangelical fathers as 'the second founders of the
Church of England'.[9] In the view of William Gladstone, the evangelical clergy were 'the heralds of a real and profound revival, the
revival of spiritual life'.[10]

Meanwhile, there was a revival in Wales.[11] In fact it pre-dated,
and was initially independent of the events so far described in
this chapter. Its genesis and progress were closely associated with
the concurrent but largely unconnected labours of three men,
Howell Harris, the Revd Daniel Rowlands, and the Revd Howell
Davies. It was only after they had independently achieved much
that they to an extent joined forces.

The revival at Cambuslang and Kilsyth[12] in Scotland in 1742
owed much to the interest ignited by Whitefield, but it rested
heavily on the ordinary work and life of the minister, William
McCulloch. When Whitefield arrived, there ensued scenes that
probably had no previous parallel in Scottish history. The nearby
parish of Kilsyth, under the ministry of James Robe, experienced
a not dissimilar revival. There was also a ripple effect, and hundreds of conversions were reported in surrounding parishes.

Conversions came not only from the preaching of ordained
men, but through the spoken word of teachers in the classroom,
through the Christian teaching of parents, and through the witness of ordinary people as they went about their daily tasks. The
ministers of the parishes helped to guide and control the activities, and the people looked to them as the leaders in spiritual
matters, but the work did not depend on them. In this revival
there was, typically, a largely spontaneous upsurge of spiritual
energy from within the small Christian fellowships, and an inner
momentum and generation of spiritual power and effectiveness,
which may be seen as distinctive characteristics, in varying
degrees, of all revivals.

Revivals and awakenings in North America

The Great Awakening

The eighteenth-century revivals were not confined to Continental Europe and Britain. They were transcontinental.

The Great Awakening, which reached its height between about 1740 and 1743, was one of the most significant, powerful and influential religious events in the whole of North American history. It had immense consequences at the time, and its knock-on consequences were profound and long lasting. It helped to colour not only the religious, but also the political, social and cultural life of America from then until the present day. Its effects were woven into the very fabric of the country's corporate political, social, cultural and economic, as well as religious, life to a degree that has only recently started to be appreciated in all its subtlety and pervasiveness.

From as early as the 1630s and 1640s, New England experienced revivals in which many 'gathered' churches ended up filled with new communicants. But then there was a drying up of this rich spiritual life, and 'the flow of new members into churches slowed to a trickle'.[13] By the late seventeenth century, however, there had been a measure of recovery.

Theodorus Jacobus Frelinghuysen, who arrived in the country in 1720, made a particularly valuable contribution to the preparation of the ground prior to the Great Awakening. One historian even claims that 'it is through his activities in central New Jersey that the colonial awakenings began'.[14]

William Tennent made a distinctive contribution to the establishment of an evangelical culture, and to the spreading of the evangelical message throughout the colony largely through the founding of his Log Cabin at Neshaminy in Pennsylvania in 1726. In that humble setting he educated pupils, among whom the most outstanding were his three sons William, John and Gilbert, and Samuel Blair. The college 'trained a whole school of practical evangelists and created a new party within the Presbyterianism of the Middle Colonies'.[15] Frelinghuysen introduced Gilbert Tennent to pietistic traditions, disciplines and techniques, and Tennent in turn carried the message throughout the Middle Colonies and to New England during his several sorties there.

To supplement the work of these itinerants, much was going on within local churches. For instance, there was a proliferation of religious societies in New England in the last part of the seventeenth century under the leadership of Cotton Mather, in imitation of the *collegia pietatis* and the Church of England societies.

Most importantly, a group of preachers centred in Boston, and led by Mather, gradually moved away from the traditional Puritan emphasis on formal reason and logic and increasingly stressed the kind of piety described in August Francke's writings. It was a shift, as was the creation of religious societies, that gave a more central role to the emotions, alongside, and in addition to the use of reason, in coming to a faith-commitment.

Before the Great Awakening there were a number of local revivals that arose out of the work of resident pastors. They were both a foretaste of what was to come and a preparation for the main drama. Most notably, they occurred in Solomon Stoddard's Northampton church in Massachusetts, which had such 'harvests' of religion in 1679, 1683, 1696, 1712 and 1718.

The most famous of the revivals was that at Northampton under Jonathan Edwards.[16] It has achieved fame not so much because of its magnitude, for it was not on a grand scale, but largely because of the distinction and renown of its pastor; the descriptions he gave of the events in three very widely distributed and much read publications, *A Narrative of Surprising Conversions* (1736), *Distinguishing Marks of a Work of the Spirit of God* (1741), and *An Account of the Revival in Northampton in 1740–42 in a Letter* (1743); and the immense enhancement of the revival, and dissemination of news about it, that occurred as a consequence of the involvement in it of George Whitefield.

The Northampton revival not only resulted in changed lives. The whole moral tone of the community was affected. 'This work of God, as it was carried on, and the number of the true saints multiplied', Edwards declared, 'soon made a glorious alteration in the town; so that in the spring and summer following, in the year 1735, the town seemed full of the presence of God.'[17]

The revival also comprehensively covered the immediate surrounding district, and the region as a whole. In Connecticut in the

1740s both the number of churches that admitted more new members and the volume of such additions, were greater than for any other similar period for which there are records. There were many examples of churches that filled up with new converts with astonishing speed, in several instances gaining more than a hundred extra communicants in less than a year. In over half the churches of the colony, 'more people became members than at any other five-year period in their history'.[18]

George Whitefield continued to be a pivotal figure.[19] He landed at Newport, Rhode Island, on 14 September 1740. Repeatedly during the succeeding few weeks his preaching attracted vast crowds, and there was an enthusiastic response from among those present. His achievement was colossal, but there was an innate drive and thrust in what had been started, and other evangelical leaders fanned the fire Whitefield had helped to kindle.

The Second Great Awakening

The Southern colonies were relatively untouched by the First Great Awakening. There were a few, isolated and uncoordinated local signs of increased religious fervour, but nothing more. Nothing occurred that can in any way be compared with the upsurge of religious life in the North.

What is often called the Second Great Awakening, which came in the latter part of the eighteenth century and continued into the early years of the nineteenth century, started as a Presbyterian movement. Initially, it was based on two backwoods colleges, Hampden-Sidney and Washington, both of which were in Virginia. To these was added Jefferson College in Western Pennsylvania, after its foundation in 1801, and Princeton. All three of them were Presbyterian foundations for the training of men for the ministry. The onset of this new infusion of spiritual life can be pinpointed to 1786, when there was a quite sudden and pronounced religious concern among the students, who until then had shown a characteristic lethargy and lack of zeal.

A second phase of this late eighteenth-century revival was also centred on colleges, but in this case they were Congregational. Yale was of particular importance. Despite the fact that there were other focal points for the Congregational 'outpouring of the

Holy Spirit', Yale under the leadership of President Timothy Dwight assumed a pre-eminent role of national significance. It soon became evident that 'what Hampden-Sidney, Washington, Jefferson, and Princeton colleges were for Presbyterianism, Yale and Andover particularly were for the Congregationalists – training schools for revivalists. It was but natural, therefore, that Yale and Princeton colleges furnished the pattern for practically all the early frontier colleges.'[20]

Among the distinctive characteristics of the Second Awakening that had not featured in the First Great Awakening, none was more pronounced than the camp meetings. These were inspired, and probably inaugurated, by James McGready, the first great frontier revivalist in the West.[21] Such was the number of people attending his meetings in Logan County, Kentucky, around 1800, that it became necessary to hold them out-of-doors. Although, from the beginning, they were well organized and administered affairs, it has to be recognized that the nature and demands of frontier life, and the kind of rugged and extrovert character it produced, may help to explain the often somewhat extravagant, enthusiastic, physical and emotional displays that accompanied the deep religious experiences of many who attended these gatherings.

It is difficult to quantify the success of the camp meetings, which were concentrated in the few years up to 1805, after which there was a marked tailing off in their importance and centrality, at least for some years, before they once again assumed a key role in revivals. It is evident that the attendances were absolutely stupendous for a rural region. 'Revivalists, rigid opponents, unconcerned travelers, laymen, all reported crowds that seemed to average between four and ten thousand.'[22] The estimates for the most spectacular and well publicized of the meetings at Cane Ridge, Kentucky, in August 1801, place the number at almost 25,000. The figures were undoubtedly inflated, and there was considerable duplication, with the same people on the crawl from one such assembly to another. Nonetheless, even with a halving of the quoted numbers, which may be more realistic, the crowds were outstanding, especially for that day and age and in those thinly populated territories.

The records for church growth are fragmentary, incomplete or non-existent, but they are enough to indicate a significant spurt in church membership. Between 1800 and 1802 the six Baptist associations in Kentucky grew from 4,766 to 13,569. In the five years immediately after the revival started, the Western Conference of the Methodist Church, which comprised the districts in Kentucky and Tennessee, expanded from 3,030 members to 10,158. In the course of the same period, the number of Methodist ministers tripled, from eleven to thirty-three. In South Carolina, where the camp meetings only appeared in 1802, between then and 1805 the Methodist membership more than doubled, from 7,443 to 16,089. In South Carolina, in the three years following the inception of camp meetings, the Bethel Baptist Association increased from 2,690 to 4,029. Georgia's Separate Baptist Association membership leapt from 797 in 1800 to 2,903 in 1804. Taking the whole of the South, Methodist membership grew from approximately 30,000 in 1800 to 59,000 in 1806.[23]

Frontier religion overall was

> much more solidly based than is usually pictured. The long lists of catechisms, Bibles, testaments, hymn books, disciplines, and other religious books, which were sold by the Methodist circuit riders to the people on their circuits are evidence of the religious instructions afforded. The fact that almost all the early Presbyterian preachers in the West were also school teachers is evidence that theirs was a teaching as well as a preaching ministry.[24]

It is also highly relevant that what was taught touched upon the very foundational convictions and orientations of a people who were experiencing the birth of a nation. The decade from 1740 to 1750 was 'a watershed in American thought';[25] and the beliefs that underpinned the revival were an essential element in that transitional process. The Second Great Awakening consolidated this nation-building ideology and extended its impact to the southern states.

Summary

Evangelism was an integral component of the international, intercontinental, eighteenth-century revival, and it was perhaps always possible that this would take the form of a global missionary thrust. What started off as an evangelistic movement in a particular area, or number of areas concurrently, always had the potential to widen its scope of activity. What was good for home consumption was good for worldwide consumption. The need for, and practice of, evangelism in one part of the world, logically could not be contained and restricted geographically to such circumscribed territories.

Vibrant Christianity in nineteenth-century Britain

In the latter years of the eighteenth century and the first few decades of the nineteenth century Britain experienced a further 'extraordinary flowering of evangelical religion'.[26] This second Christian resurgence persisted for about 100 years, and it was not confined to evangelicals. W.R. Ward has most usefully commented that: 'Like those other good products of the eighteenth century, Enlightenment and political economy, religious revival was to be far more influential in the nineteenth century than ever it was in the eighteenth.'[27] The eighteenth-century revival was unique because it inaugurated the modern evangelical movement. But its importance in this particular respect was immensely augmented by what followed. The dynamic, which was essential to the impending worldwide missionary outreach, came in Britain first of all from evangelicals, and then from High Churchmen.

Pre-Victorian Britain – the evangelicals

The strength of British evangelicalism in the closing years of the eighteenth century and the opening decades of the nineteenth century is widely acknowledged. Nineteenth-century historians and others recognized its pertinence and potential. Eugene Stock said that it was 'indisputedly the strongest force in the country'.[28] John Stoughton concluded that despite being a small minority within the Church, and despite their evident imperfections, the evangelicals at the beginning of the nineteenth century 'did what no other band of clergymen were doing at the time'. Few, he said, would deny that they were an 'immense power', and 'that they were the very salt of the Church of England, during a period when influences existed threatening decay and corruption'.[29] Two nineteenth-century High Churchmen gave a similar judgement. H.P. Liddon declared that

> The deepest and most fervid religion in England during the first three decades of this century was that of the Evangelicals. The world to come, with its boundless issues of life and death, the infinite value of the one Atonement, the regenerating, purifying, guiding action of God the Holy Spirit in respect of the Christian soul, were preached to our grandfathers with a force and earnestness which are beyond controversy.[30]

William Gladstone, a High Churchman, but brought up among evangelicals, said of the evangelical clergy, 'Every Christian under their scheme had personal dealings with his God and Saviour. The inner life was again acknowledged as a reality, and substituted for the bare, bald compromise between the seen and the unseen world which reduces the share of the "far and more exceeding and eternal" to almost nil.'[31]

It is true that the evangelicals 'did not cover all the ground, because there were not very many of them, and there were some matters which their limited range did not enable them to reach'. Nonetheless, 'they were in deadly earnest, and wherever their influence penetrated at all it penetrated very deep'.[32]

During the Napoleonic era evangelicals in the Church of England acquired a greater theological sophistication and comprehensiveness. They combined their former earnestness regarding basic Christian doctrines with a much increased concern to express their faith in practical measures for the relief of the poor and needy, and with a general desire to give assistance to disadvantaged groups in society. Evangelical leaders thus married the eighteenth-century evangelical emphasis upon spiritual new birth with a new awareness of their moral and social responsibilities.

The foremost example of evangelicals in action in the late eighteenth century and the early nineteenth century was provided by the activities of a small group of reformers under the leadership of William Wilberforce, the so-called Clapham Sect.[33] From 1787 onwards this small band of Christians, together with a wider supporting body of fellow believers, was dedicated to the 'glorious enterprise', as John Wesley dubbed it, of abolishing the slave trade, and to other reforms of national and international importance. A few of them were Members of Parliament, where they were collectively designated 'the Saints'. There were other Members of Parliament who were 'occasional Saints', who gave support to the core group on vital votes in the House of Commons.

The bill for the abolition of the slave trade was introduced, debated and defeated eleven times before its final success in 1807. It was left to another evangelical, Thomas Fowell Buxton,[34] to complete the work the Clapham men had begun by making slavery itself illegal. Victory was finally achieved in 1833.

Associated with the issue of slavery was the founding of Sierra Leone as a refuge for freed slaves; and the members of the Clapham Sect were almost entirely and independently responsible for this.

High Churchmen

The so-called Hackney Phalanx, like the Clapham Sect, was a tightly knit group of friends, but in their case united theologically by their High Churchmanship. At the top of its agenda, and that of its leader, Joshua Watson, was the need to provide more and better education and to supply new churches and clergy for the deprived, poorer, parts of London and for the rapidly expanding new industrial towns. In these places masses of people were growing up in ignorance, illiteracy and lack of Christian nurture, and Watson longed to be of assistance in remedying such a dire lack of facilities. These were objectives shared by the other 50 to 100 laymen and clergy of the Phalanx. They were impressively successful in helping to realize both of their dreams.

The Hackney Phalanx members also, like the evangelicals, did not restrict their visionary outlook to the domestic scene. Their global missionary interests were acute. They were instrumental in reviving and re-energizing the Society for the Promotion of Christian Knowledge (SPCK) and the Society for the Propagation of the Gospel (SPG), just in time for these bodies to play a part in the great missionary outreach that was to characterize the Victorian era, as will be seen in the next chapter.

The Phalanx epitomized and expressed the concern of many within the Church of England to hold fast to the best in its High Church tradition, and to meet the demands of a rapidly changing society. But it was the Oxford Movement that did most to embody and champion High Church ideals and expectations. It burst upon the church scene in the 1830s; and it quickly drew attention to deficiencies in the Church of England. It as promptly offered a way forward.[35]

The story of the movement is too well known, and too complicated, to rehearse in detail. Suffice it to say that in the period between John Keble's Assize Sermon on 14 July 1833 and John Henry Newman's dramatic reception into the Roman Catholic Church on 9 October 1845, and despite many failures and difficulties, Keble, Newman, Richard Hurrell Froude, Professor E.B. Pusey, Charles Marriott, J.B. Mozley, W.R. Ward and others defended and proclaimed their views with unmistakable clarity and forthrightness.

By one measure, pronouncement, written statement and action after another the message that burnt in the hearts and minds of the Oxford Movement members was communicated within Oxford, and to an extent outside the city bounds. After the devastating blow of Newman's defection, the movement did not shrivel up and die, but rather continued and widened its geographical spread. The new phase it entered in 1845 was in fact part of a flourishing of Christianity in the country from about the 1840s to the end of Victoria's reign.

The Dissenters

The Church of England was not alone in displaying signs of vitality. For Protestant Dissent in Britain generally, the period from about 1790 to about 1850 was pivotal. 'The late eighteenth century represented the crucial stage in its development; the process of change from contemptible insignificance to the full flower of Victorian Nonconformity.'[36] The leap forward appears to have been due mainly to the fact that Dissent made advances where the

Church of England did not. Overall, Anglicanism declined numerically relative to the increase in population, whereas, at the same time, Dissenting denominations were making progress. Thus, in 1791 the Wesleyan Methodist membership was announced in the Conference to be 72,476, although this did not include a number of hearers and helpers and those abroad. By 1800 it had risen to 90,619, and thirty years later to 248, 592. By 1841 it was about 328,000.

Although the Methodists enjoyed massive gains in membership, as with other Dissenting denominations, account should be taken of quality as well as quantity. 'Without its deep sense of religious commitment and conversionist zeal, no expansion would have taken place.'[37]

Enormous growth was a characteristic feature of all the dissenting bodies. The Congregational connexion grew from 35,000 members in 1800 to 127,000 in 1837, and in the same period the two main Baptist denominations almost quadrupled from 27,000 to just under 100,000.[38] Whereas in 1773 a list compiled by the Baptist pastor Josiah Thompson shows 1,685 Nonconformist congregations in England, including Monmouthshire, the 1851 census puts the figure at 17,019. Such figures reveal not only a gigantic absolute numerical growth, however measured, but also a significant improvement in membership as a percentage of the total population in a period of population explosion. Taking a wider time span, it was estimated by Dr John Evans in 1715–18 that Dissenters in England, again including Monmouthshire, accounted for 6.21 per cent of the population; but this had leapt to 17.02 per cent by the time of the 1851 census.

The 1851 religious census was in fact a surprise to many people, among other reasons for the progress of Nonconformity that it disclosed. Out of a total population for England and Wales of 17,927,609, those attending churches on 30 March 1851 were stated as: Church of England, 5,292,551; the main Protestant Nonconformist churches (Presbyterian, Methodist, Congregationalist and Baptist), 4,536,264; and Roman Catholics 383,630. The areas of greatest Dissenting strength were, perhaps unsurprisingly, the great revival regions, and those denominations that showed the most growth were the ones that had responded most readily and fully to the tide of revival.

The outstanding expansion of all the Nonconformist denominations was achieved in some measure because of the partial lifting of restrictions placed upon them as corporate bodies. Legislation in 1828, 1829, 1832 and 1835 established them more securely in the political, social and religious life of the country than ever before, and this encouraged waverers to join them.

The vibrancy of the Nonconformists was publicly and visibly demonstrated in a continuous and powerful way in the ministries and preaching of such stalwarts as Joseph Parker, John Clifford, Robert William Dale, Hugh Price Hughes and Charles Haddon Spurgeon. They commanded widespread respect and kept the Nonconformists prominent in the national public consciousness.

Outstanding numerical growth was also a feature of Roman Catholicism in the first half of the nineteenth century. The Parliamentary 'Papist Returns' of 1767 revealed a Catholic population of 69,376 for England and Wales; although this figure should probably be inflated to 80,000 to allow for all the rural communities. But whatever the precise number it starkly and dramatically contrasts with the estimated three-quarters of a million by the time of the 1851 census. This astonishing increase proportionately far outstripped the rate of increase of the population of the country as a whole. By the mid-nineteenth century Catholics accounted for about 3.5 per cent of England's population.

Thus, despite many differences in what they had to offer, and partly, no doubt because of these dissimilarities, the Church of England, the Nonconformists and the Roman Catholics all showed signs of being very much alive and healthy in the early decades of the nineteenth century. Their shortcomings, such as their dismal failure to have any significant impact on the mass of the new unskilled labouring classes, especially in the new industrial towns, were a severe and serious indictment of them. There was also much superficiality and even hypocrisy in each of their ranks, and in their corporate conduct, and this continued and even grew worse as the Victorian era progressed. Even so, each of these Christian traditions certainly cannot be dismissed as effete, ineffectual, feeble and in decline in this period. Neither can such criticism be validly levelled at them for their record in the remaining part of the century and up to the end of Victoria's reign.

Revivals, evangelists, evangelical agencies and philanthropic work

Viewing the nineteenth century globally, the most prominent, well-attested and well-documented revivals again, as in the eighteenth century, occurred in North America and Britain. The most sensational of these, with the greatest long-term consequences, occurred in both countries between 1857 and 1860. In Britain, they were especially prominent in Ulster,[39] Scotland and Wales.[40]

Revivals did not last long and were quite confined geographically. The work of local churches throughout the land was variable in quality, and even when it was excellent it easily relapsed into lifelessness or stagnation without the appropriate leadership. It was therefore beneficial to the churches as a whole that both were complemented in an unprecedented way by the work of evangelists and evangelistic agencies, and also by a host of other societies, organizations and movements.

Three North American evangelists in particular made their mark in England between 1800 and 1860: Lorenzo Dow, James Caughey and Charles Grandison Finney. They received their greatest support from the Nonconformists, and in turn it was those co-operating denominations that reaped the greatest reward.

The climax of nineteenth-century evangelism through such special preachers came with the visits of Dwight L. Moody and Ira D. Sankey. Moody, more perhaps than anyone else, inaugurated the modern form of 'mass' evangelism. The campaigns he conducted in York, Newcastle, Edinburgh, Dundee, Glasgow, Belfast, Dublin, Manchester, Sheffield, Birmingham, Liverpool and London between 1873 and 1875 helped greatly in promoting late nineteenth-century evangelism and missionary enthusiasm.[41] Taken as a whole, they were the most remarkable example of large-scale evangelistic outreach in Victorian Britain.

At the conclusion of his meetings in Cambridge in 1881, a host of undergraduates responded to the appeal, which was customarily given at these events, and those converted included some of the finest Christian missionaries and Church leaders of the century.

One feature of the Moody gatherings was the use of secular buildings. Largely due to the efforts of Lord Shaftesbury, the passing of the 1855 Religious Worship Act permitted the holding of services in unconsecrated buildings, and this opened the gate to events in Exeter Hall, London, and elsewhere. A further innovation was the use of the naves of St Paul's and Westminster Abbey for evening services.

In contrast to the sweeping in and out of the evangelists, and the periodic holding of services, another indication of the fervency of Christianity in Victorian Britain was the creation of evangelistic agencies, many with philanthropic concerns as well. The Salvation Army and the Church Army were prime examples.[42]

For both of these organizations and their members the holiness movement was of immeasurable influence. It emerged on both sides of the Atlantic in the second half of the century, and found expression in England most notably in the annual Keswick convention in the Lake District, started in 1874. The teaching focused on the need for a post-conversion experience of total holiness or sanctification. The convention had untold reverberations throughout the world. It resulted in many men and women offering themselves for Christian service at home and abroad, and it generated extremely generous financial support for the overseas work of the Church just when such dual support was imperative. In fact, its foundation coincided with an astonishing missionary advance in Africa and Asia in particular. The Church Missionary Society was especially indebted to the challenge to Christian service that sounded forth every summer at Keswick. It was at Keswick, in 1893, that members of an already fruitful and energetic student movement met together a week before the convention and were incorporated under the title Inter-University Christian Union. The following year, again at Keswick, the American watchword 'the evangelization of the world in this generation' was adopted as a most evocative and effective rallying call to service.

The overwhelming number of Christian-inspired philanthropic societies that sprang up in the Victorian age were very much part of this incredibly profuse and multifaceted surge of Christian energy, creativity and activity. In fact, regardless of some academic opinion, the evangelicals 'are remembered for what they did rather than for their theology'.[43]

The single most inspirational and influential evangelical in this demonstration of 'religion in action' was undoubtedly Lord Shaftesbury[44] The volume and range of his endeavour was astounding. It embraced factory reform, the treatment of so-called lunatics, social reform in India, including work for the ending of such practices as suttee (the burning of widows on the death of their husbands), a variety of matters to do with public health, the founding of ragged schools, the provision of refuges and dormitories for destitute and deprived children, an emigration scheme for children and for placing them in employment, help for the blind, for cabmen, needlewomen and members of the merchant services, and much else.

The Roman Catholics

The Roman Catholics played their part in the vibrancy of Victorian Christianity. This was most notably the case during the 1840s to the 1850s.

The greatest public demonstration of a rejuvenated English Catholicism was the restoration of the Roman Catholic hierarchy in 1850. The Pope sanctioned thirteen new bishoprics, mostly in the densely populated industrial urban areas, which had expanded so dramatically during the previous century, such as Birmingham, Liverpool and Salford. Nicholas Wiseman was elevated as Archbishop of Westminster and created England's first cardinal since the reign of Mary Tudor. Under his inspirational leadership, there was an expansion in the number of Roman Catholics and a marked increase in their self-confidence.

Summary

In summary, it may be concluded that in Britain, despite some contrary indications, Christianity was, at least in parts, impressively animated and vibrant right through the nineteenth century and into the first part of the twentieth century. It was likewise with Continental Europe:

> In spite of the adverse factors, the Protestantism of Western Europe came to the year 1914 more vigorous and with a wider

impact on mankind as a whole than in 1815. Partly because of that vigour, the contrast between the convinced Christian and those who were being alienated from the faith was sharp, perhaps sharper than at the beginning of the century. But the abounding vitality was obvious. In some respects the nineteenth century was even more the Protestant century than the sixteenth or the seventeenth century. Clearly it was more so than the eighteenth century.[45]

North America – continuation of the Second Great Awakening

The period from 1790 to 1840 has been depicted as the great age of church expansion in the United States.[46] It was certainly an exceptional time for the establishment of the Christian faith in the country. Once more, as in the time of the First Great Awakening, it was revivalism that was at the very heart of this outstanding move forward. It, 'combined with an exploding quantity of voluntary organizations',[47] and provided what one historian has called an effective 'organizing process' for a thinly populated and widely fragmented society.[48] It played a vital part in making 'the thirteen colonies into a cohesive unit', and it gave them 'a sense of unique nationality'. The Second Great Awakening was of fundamental importance in defining 'what the manifest destiny of the new nation was.'[49]

Even by the 1820s, the camp meetings had moderated considerably, but after that the gatherings became further regularized and dampened down, with printed manuals that contained diagrams for seating and sketches of preachers' stands. In many southern counties the Methodists established camp meetings as annual, late-summer, events that were part of the accepted social and religious season. They were accommodated in specially designated camp-meeting grounds with tents and a covered preaching stand.

Important as the camp meetings were, however, the backbone of the southern church, and the powerhouses of its regular work, were the local churches and preachers. 'All the more aggressive frontier churches stressed the necessity of conversion, and all of them had their own way of helping to bring it about. All were intensely individualistic in their dealings with their members and exercised rigid disciplinary oversight over them.'[50] There was an overall zeal and dedication to pastoral work and evangelism that was most impressive.

Throughout the New World, and not just in the Southern Colonies, the 1820s also saw the appearance of a new form of evangelism. Again, as in Britain, it was pioneered by Lorenzo Dow, James Caughey and, most especially, Charles Grandison Finney. All three of them concentrated on larger towns and cities in the north as well as the south, which was a departure from the largely small town or rural setting for the camp meetings, and the evangelism in former times.

Numerical growth

In the early decades of the nineteenth century hundreds of thousands of new converts became full members of Protestant churches in the States. 'By mid-century evangelical Protestantism was the principal subculture in American society. Although the decade of the 1840s marks something of a fault line, the awakening's influence persisted in a variety of ways, including the renewed outcropping of revivals in 1857–58.'[51]

The Methodists in particular flourished as never before in the New World. 'Methodist theology, organization, and institutions meshed perfectly with the religious needs of the new American republic. The rise in membership proved startling.'[52] In 1800 it was 65,000 for the whole of the republic, but this had increased to 274,000 by 1820, and to over 1.25 million by 1850, when it became the largest Protestant church in the nation. The numerical growth was accompanied by a steady rise in the social standing of the membership.

In all the states of the South, the Baptists, Methodists and Presbyterians, together with the Disciples of Christ, were completely dominant from about the fourth decade of the century. 'For example, in 1850 there were in the twelve southern states 5,298 Baptist churches, 6,061 Methodist churches, 1,647 Presbyterian churches, and only 408 Episcopalian (315 of them were in the four seaboard states: Virginia, both Carolinas, and

Georgia), 179 Catholic, 166 Lutheran, 52 Quaker, 26 German Reformed, and two Congregational churches.'[53]
A yet further sign of new life and progress was the establishment of colleges. Again, the Methodists well illustrate this thrust forward. Before the Civil War, they founded about thirty colleges. These included Emory (1836), Indiana Asbury [Depauw] (1837), Trinity [Duke] (1838), Boston (1839), Ohio Wesleyan (1842), and Northwestern (1851). During the rest of the century after the Civil War there were added Syracuse (1870), Vanderbilt (1875), the University of Southern California (1880), and the American University (1893).

The evangelicals formed but a minority of the population, and a large proportion of them were disenfranchised women and children. Nonetheless, they exercised a huge cultural influence. The mid-century revivals were especially effective in adding to their ranks, and in providing North American Protestants with a much welcomed shot in the arm.

Several revivals occurred in the course of 1857 both in the North and the South, and they engaged the attention and enlisted the support of all the major denominations. The first was at Lawrence, Massachusetts, the second at Pittsfield in the same state, a third among Baptists in South Carolina, and a fourth among the Methodists in Columbia, South Carolina.[54]

A fifth took place outside the United States, in October 1857, in Hamilton, Ontario. There was what the New York weekly Methodist paper, the *Christian Advocate*, described as a 'Revival Extraordinary',[55] and it helped to generate a major revival in the States.

Conversions were frequent. Although figures quoted varied quite alarmingly, they were all stupendously large. One magazine recorded that there were 25,000 in the first three months of 1858.[56] The *Presbyterian Magazine* stated that by May 1858 the number of New Yorkers converted and in the care of the churches was 50,000.[57]

The influence of these events reverberated through the whole nation. The revivals continued unabated for many months, and it has been estimated that in the space of about two years while it lasted around one million converts were added to the American churches.[58] No other awakening or revival produced such astonishing numerical results.

The end of the century

City-wide or region-wide interdenominational evangelistic campaigns were characteristic of the later nineteenth century and the early twentieth century. Once more we encounter the greatest, most effective and renowned of the professional evangelists, Dwight L. Moody. The specialism of this son of a bricklayer was city campaigns, which he conducted in Brooklyn, New York, Chicago, Boston, St Louis and San Francisco. His ability to bring men, women and children to the point of conversion was truly astonishing. Ira D. Sankey sang movingly and was responsible for the musical side of each meeting. The two of them swept through the country with devastating effect.

Other evangelists at that time, including J. Wilbur Chapman, Sam P. Jones and Billy Sunday, also undertook similar city campaigns and, as with Moody and Sankey, they received support across the denominations.

In parallel with this new-style urban evangelism, there was, as in Britain, the massive influence of the holiness movement. Although there was a holiness strand that ran deep within the Wesleyan tradition, it came to prominence in a new and forceful way in the movement associated with Phoebe Palmer, in the 1858 revivals, in the ministry of Charles Finney, and with the perfectionism that emanated from the staff and students of his Oberlin College. New life was breathed into old bodies. The new holiness movement 'lifted supernaturalism to a higher plane', and 'both inward awareness of the divine Spirit and faithful service to humanity in need'[59] were elevated to new heights of importance.

The missionary impulse

As can be seen from the foregoing review, there was a prolonged and pronounced era of vibrant Christianity in Continental Europe, Britain and North America from as early as the last decades of the seventeenth century to the third quarter of the nineteenth century. In North America it had at first been most evident in the north, then more focused on the south, and it finally engulfed much of what was by then a single country of gigantic size. In Continental Europe, it was more patchy and periodic, while in Britain it was more continuous, but changed its character from one period to another.

The abundance of such vehement, vigorous, vital and energetic faith, which so characterized much of these territories over such an extended period of time, despite dips and depressions, provided a firm and solid basis for the European, British and North American participation in the global missionary outreach of the nineteenth and twentieth centuries. Traditions of dedicated Christian life and service had been inculcated. It is little wonder that Britain in particular witnessed the birth of the modern missionary movement, and that the other areas soon joined in. When the opportunity arose, the motivation for mission, the manpower and the money were readily at hand, even though there was initially much dragging of feet. Such a readiness to launch out in global mission was the product of a groundswell of vital Christianity that had been built up over many years. It was to prove of inestimable value as the opportunities for service in South America, sub-Saharan Africa and Asia in particular opened up. It is to that heroic saga that attention must now be focused.

2

World Mission in the Nineteenth Century

The world outside Europe at the beginning of the nineteenth century can conveniently and accurately be divided into two from a Christian point of view. First, there were those lands that have been called 'the larger Europe'.[1] These were territories that were sparsely populated by indigenous peoples, and Europeans poured into their relatively vacant spaces. This New World included North America, Australia and New Zealand. The newcomers set about establishing their own communities and 'new nations either came into being or, already in existence, grew with breath-taking rapidity'.[2] In the other division, the overwhelming majority of the population were indigenous, non-European, peoples. With the exception of South America, the native inhabitants were mostly, but by no means entirely, non-Christian. In Asia they were frequently Hindu, Muslim, Buddhist, Confucian or Shinto, while in Africa they largely held to a well-developed form of traditional religion, or were Muslim. The minority Europeans were to a great extent merchants, government officials, plantation owners, or missionaries. In considering the nineteenth-century missionary outreach, the focus in the present work is on the second category, as the concern is to demonstrate the remarkable way that Christians in the Old World helped to break new ground and provide the foundation for a new and universal Christendom.

A powerful missionary initiative in the early eighteenth century

Until the last dying months of the seventeenth century Protestants had made no organized, corporate effort to spread the gospel. Effective, co-ordinated Protestant missionary work awaited some visionary initiative, and into the breach stepped Dr Thomas Bray.

When he and three of his acquaintances met in the Lincoln's Inn rooms of one of their number, the barrister John Hooke, on 8 March 1699, and formed themselves into the Society for Promoting Christian Knowledge (SPCK), they were inaugurating the modern era of Protestant missionary enterprise at home and overseas.[3] The new society 'had one central concern: the implementation of a programme of evangelical philanthropy, which would reassert the spiritual and political primacy of the Church of England in the nation'.[4] The work was to be effected by two particular means. First, there was the distribution of Christian literature, and the society took advantage of such recently introduced literary devices as the tract, the newspaper and the pamphlet to attain this objective. The second channel for disseminating Christian knowledge was through the existing charity schools system, which attempted to reach out to the poor and underprivileged.

But Bray was not content to address this domestic task alone, important and significant though it was. He was also concerned about the work of the Church overseas, and he was instrumental in founding the Society for the Propagation of the Gospel in Foreign Parts (SPG) on 23 June 1701. He especially had in mind the promotion of Christianity in the plantations, with almost sole concentration on trying to meet the needs of the Anglicans in North America and the West Indies, who for two centuries had been left without immediate episcopal oversight. At the same time, however, high priority was given to missionary work among non-Christian peoples, and more specifically 'the conversion of the Negroes whom the colonists employed as slaves, and of the Indian tribes whose land they had entered'.[5]

The new society began its work enthusiastically and zealously but, as could be expected, the results were mostly somewhat paltry and disheartening. The difficulties of undertaking evangelism and pastoral care among the North American Indians were formidable. There was the hurdle of innumerable languages, all of which were difficult to learn, and there was the nomadic life that made continuity of contact a major problem. In addition, there was resentment concerning the white man's acquisition of land, the alarmingly degenerative consequences of the rum trade, which was associated in the perception of many with 'Christian' civilization and values, and the possible demise of the Indians as a race, partly as a consequence of the actions of the so-called Christians. The wonder is, not that so little progress was made initially, but that so much was accomplished. The same almost insurmountable hindrances to missionary work were not so evident when it came to the Negroes. But even with them, slavery and, as an expression of that inhuman system, the persistent cruelty and insensitivity of brutal or coarse masters, erected serious barriers in any attempt by white Christians to commend the gospel. It was far from helpful that the faith of the missionaries was clearly identified with such a callous regime.

In India the obstacles were hardly less formidable. The East India Company was hostile to all missionary efforts, largely because of its policy of non-interference in the affairs and customs of the country, and the fear that religious propaganda and proselytizing might provoke resentment and be detrimental to the development of commerce. The SPG also suffered from lack of personnel. It had to enlist the service of German missionaries in order to partially meet the pastoral needs of the troops and other British subjects who were increasing in number in all regions of the subcontinent. One of these, Christian Fredrich Schwartz (1724–98), who served in India for 48 years without a break, was especially effective in his ministry in the south, where the East India Company policy was more relaxed. There were many converts as a result of his work. In the Tanjore area he helped to lay the foundation for what was to be a thriving Christian centre at Tinnevelly, out of which in little more than a hundred years there was to come the first native Indian bishop of the Anglican Communion.

The outstanding discernment, vision, drive and achievement of Bray and his companions were in stark contrast to the overall phlegmatic insularity that characterized much of contemporary

Anglicanism. Sydney Smith probably displayed his mild eccentricity when he ridiculed missions and implied that Anglicanism was not for export; but such a view may well have been typical of mainstream clerical opinion for most of the eighteenth century. It may also help to explain why the SPG, which started with such a flourish in the early years of the century did not progress as many of its supporters hoped. During those pioneering years there was much scope for Christian service abroad. There was considerable colonization, and the British command of the seas facilitated a rapid growth in trade and wealth. But the counterbalancing lethargy of the Church may largely account for the fact that the work of the SPG first 'expanded while the vision lasted, then kept on a fairly steady level, and at the end began to decline'.[6] A new injection of energy was required, and a new generation of Christians who would dream dreams and have large, ambitious ideas for taking the gospel to far-flung corners of the earth. This came at the end of the century, in the main as one fruit of the evangelical revival.

The late eighteenth-century missionary surge

By the end of the eighteenth century the Protestant churches in Britain and the countries of mainland Europe were generally still very blinkered in their outlook. Notwithstanding over two hundred years of colonial penetration into North and South America and Asia, as well as parts of Africa and other regions of the world, Christianity remained a predominantly European religion. This had not always been so. Indigenous churches in many non-Western countries could look back hundreds of years, even to the early, formative, centuries of the Christian era itself, to discover their Christian roots. In former times, long ago, the faith had been stronger and more established in parts of the world outside Europe than in Europe itself. Europe was not the main and focal point of Christianity in the known world of the day. Although the calculations of David Barrett in Table 2.1 are clearly open to many qualifications, and are inevitably to a great extent speculative, they give a broad-brush picture of how the world Christian scene changed in the course of a thousand years.

Table 2.1 Distribution of Christians in the pre-sixteenth century period (in millions)

	AD 500	AD 1000	AD 1200	AD 1500
Africa	8.0	5.0	2.5	1.3
Asia	21.2	16.8	21.0	3.4
Europe/Russia	14.2	28.6	46.6	76.3
Global total	43.4	50.4	70.1	81.0

Source: Barrett, World Christian Encyclopedia, *1982, p. 796, quoted in Jenkins,* The Next Christendom, *p. 24.*

*

The trends this reveals seem to have been maintained throughout the next 300 years, so that few of the non-European churches were high in numbers or in a healthy state around 1800.

The churches of the non-Western regions received very little help from Western Christendom to put a check on their downwards numerical slither. From 1500, the Roman Catholic Church stretched out a hand in various areas, most notably South America and parts of Asia, but no European Protestant country or church had embarked on a systematic programme of overseas mission, or even made much effort to confront non-Christian peoples, lands and cultures with the Christian gospel up to the end of the eighteenth century. 'In 1800 it was still by no means certain that Christianity would be successful in turning itself into a universal religion.' Even where it had been exported as part and parcel of colonialization, the overseas Protestant church had remained almost wholly Eurocentric both in membership and in its language and general ethos. 'America, together with the West Indies, had become a white man's world. The dominance of his religion and his civilization in those areas provided no answer to the question whether Christianity could make itself permanently at home in the lands of the great and ancient non-Christian civilizations.'[7]

The 1790s saw a leap forward in the application of the churches in England to the global missionary task. It was the beginning of a period of two hundred years and more of universal Christian expansion. The progress made then proved to be the first stage in an amazing saga of world mission, the momentum of which had not been lost by the twenty-first century. Even by 1910 only a handful of countries, such as Afghanistan, Tibet and Nepal, remained obstinately closed to all missionary endeavour. Some remote regions were still to be reached, and a few, such as Northern Nigeria, were to all intents and purposes kept closed by the colonial powers. 'Otherwise, there were hardly any limits to the extent of the missionary enterprise. It stretched from China to Peru, and was at work both beyond the Arctic Circle and in the desolate and hostile wastes of Tierra del Fuego.'[8] Of course, much of the Christianity in these wide-flung regions of the world was superficial in that eventful century, with vast tracts of countries and continents merely touched by the gospel; but with each year that passed the totally unevangelized territories were becoming fewer, and the maturity and profundity of the native Christians was becoming ever greater.

It was in the 1780s, and more especially in the 1790s, that the energy and drive forward was first set in motion in a largely quiet and unostentatious, manner. In 1784, John Sutcliffe, the Baptist pastor of Olney, issued a 'Prayer Call', and at the Baptist Association meeting he proposed that churches should be encouraged to hold a special gathering on the first Monday evening of every month for united prayer. In an Association Circular Letter he urged its readers not to remain parochial in their praying, but 'let the whole interest of the Redeemer be affectionately remembered, and the spread of the gospel to the distant parts of the habitable globe be the object of your most fervent requests'.[9] The 'Prayer Call' was replicated in other lands. By 1814 there were similar monthly prayer meetings in Holland, Switzerland, Germany, America, India and Africa. A new and intense missionary concern was gradually spreading through the churches. Sutcliffe's call widened 'the geographical and spiritual horizons of Christians of all denominations in this land and beyond'.[10] In the meantime there was an astonishing outburst of innovative missionary activity.

It was the Baptists who once more took early and decisive action. In 1792 William Carey published a work entitled *An Enquiry into the Obligation of Christians to Use Means for the Conversion of the Heathen*. He argued that the Great Commission

of Christ to go and preach the gospel to all nations was still binding on Christians. Here was an expression of the activism that
was one of the salient features of the new breed of evangelicals.
And the challenge issued by Carey had prompt and far-reaching
results. The last decade of the eighteenth century was full of
Christian 'firsts'. In the same year, 1792, Carey was the catalyst in
establishing the Baptist Missionary Society, 'the first foreign mission to spring from the revival'.[11] By the following year he was
pioneering its operation in India. It was the 'first British missionary society designed exclusively to convert the heathen',[12] and as
such it was a major step forward in world mission. While Carey
was laying the foundations of his missionary work in India,
Samuel Marsden was spearheading another missionary thrust,
initially in the islands near New Zealand, and then in New
Zealand itself among the Maoris.

Meanwhile, back in England in 1795, a group of Congregationalists, Anglicans, Presbyterians and Wesleyans inaugurated
the London Missionary Society. It was 'the first interdenominational society and the first to make such a large-scale bid for
public support'.[13] It was launched amid scenes of unbounded joy
and great expectation. Financial support was immediate and
prolific.

But it was within the Church of England that the greatest
efforts were made, largely through the unstinting and tireless
work of the Clapham Sect. It was the determination and persistence of the members of that remarkable evangelical fraternity
that almost single-handedly was responsible for perhaps the
most auspicious initiative in this eventful decade. On Friday, 12
April 1799 a public meeting was held which established The
Society for Missions in Africa and the East, later to be renamed
the Church Missionary Society. It was to become the largest
Christian missionary organization in the world.

The spiritual vitality and verve generated in the eighteenth and
nineteenth centuries provided the logic, the logistics, the propul-
sion, but only later the personnel, for the first major phase of the
modern missionary movement. First, the cumulative effect of the
revivals and the newly released spiritual energy operated at a
cerebral level, giving good logical reasons for launching out in an
effort to reach the whole world with the gospel. The potential for

worldwide outreach was greatly increased by the evangelical belief that the gospel was for all people, irrespective of social status and standing, and it was incumbent on the believers to make known their saving message to all and sundry. 'The revival clarified the rationale for such activity by transmitting the understanding that there was no difference between the spiritual state of a pleasure-seeking duchess (though baptized and adhering to the prevailing religious system of the higher and middle classes) and that of a South Sea Islander.'

The recognition and acceptance of the spiritual parity of the unregenerate of Christendom and the heathen abroad was a quantum leap forward in thinking, and a break through emotionally. It gradually established new 'mindsets'. It had immensely important missionary consequences. 'Like the admonition to Lady Huntingdon's titled friend, who did not want to enter the kingdom of heaven in the same manner as her coachman, it took a hatchet to some axiomatic superiorities.'[14] In retrospect, it was perhaps almost inevitable that such a highly developed sense of evangelistic responsibility for all Christian members of society in Western countries would widen its scope and lead to a powerful global evangelistic concern, but the fact that such a shift of thought and action actually took place was of incalculable importance.

Secondly, the revivals and awakenings paved the way for global outreach by supplying the necessary networks. These were 'interregional, international, interdenominational', and they 'undergirded the movement'.[15] This is evident in the 'unending stream of correspondence, crisscrossing the Atlantic', which 'reveals just how important as a missionary factor were the African-Americans and the Afro-West Indians'.[16] It was also manifested in the extent to which magazines 'on two continents gathered and disseminated "missionary intelligence" without regard to denomination or country of origin'.[17]

Then thirdly, the evangelical awakenings and revivals fired converts with the motivation to engage in world mission. This was not just a matter of rational calculation and the formal establishment of organizational structures through which to offer sacrificial service. There had to be an inner drive in the case of each individual patron, and founding member, as well as for every missionary who 'felt a calling' to venture forth beyond the comforts and familiarities of their own society and culture. They went out with the certainty of discomfort, the high likelihood of suffering, and a reasonable possibility of death. These were pioneer days, and it took immense courage to undertake hazardous journeys and to face unknown perils in lands of which there was often little knowledge. It needed great inner resources and a huge and sustainable drive to overcome fear and trepidation, to take the first steps, and then to sustain the effort and enthusiasm amidst trying and frequently dangerous and depressing circumstances. It is a measure of the depth and profundity of the faith that had been received by the revival and other converts that gradually the volunteers came forth, first by ones and twos, then, as the nineteenth century progressed, in far larger numbers.

Before considering various aspects of 'the great missionary century', however, it needs to be reiterated that the picture often painted of totally non-Christian peoples throughout the world quite suddenly receiving the light of the gospel as Western missionaries went forth to lands that were in darkness is in many respects a travesty of the true situation. The missionaries often encountered an already existing church, or at least places where, as previously mentioned, the Church had once existed and even prospered. In a number of places the Church was 'in some ways returning to its roots'.[18] The whole post-eighteenth-century Western missionary movement was to a great extent 'the renewal of a non-Western religion'.[19] Certainly, the depiction of Christian history, as well as the present-day interpretation of its global state of health, has been and is now far too often excessively Eurocentric if not Anglocentric.[20] It is far from accurate to portray Christianity 'as a White or Western ideology that was foisted on the rest of an unwilling globe, under the auspices of Spanish galleons, British redcoats, and American televangelists'.[21]

The churches in many of the regions of the non-Western world to be covered, had indeed shrunk, and in some cases disappeared, by the early nineteenth century, and there was generally a desperate need for an injection of Christian life from without. But this should not engender an attitude of pride or paternalistic self-satisfaction. During the nineteenth century, and for much of the twentieth century, the churches of Europe and Britain played their role as 'sending countries'. In the latter part of the period vigorous independent, indigenous, churches continued the process of growth and development, in almost all cases at a much accelerated pace and in a far more dramatic and impressive manner. Indeed, many South American, sub-Saharan African and Asian countries have themselves started to send out 'missionaries' to other lands, including Continental Europe and Britain. Such a scenario is hardly compatible with any portrayal of a universal Church that has been undergoing terminal decline since the onset of modern urbanization and industrialization, or one that has been clinging to the raft as it has been tossed about by the alien winds of 'secularization'.

From tentative beginnings to almost worldwide coverage

After centuries of lethargy and slumber over their evangelistic responsibility for the non-Western world, it is perhaps understandable that it took some time for the new missionary impulse to infuse the Protestant churches. Although the twenty or so years from about 1790 witnessed a new and compelling sense of responsibility to go and make the gospel known unto the uttermost parts of the world, this burden of obligation and missionary responsibility was initially limited to a quite small number of visionaries with an adventurous spirit. There was no sudden wave of missionary enthusiasm that engulfed European, British or American Christendom. Such a great event as the departure of William Carey for India in 1793 was only seen to be epoch-making many years later. At the time the 'consecrated cobbler' was mostly the recipient of sneers and an object of indifference, ridicule or even hostility. The new missionary societies were ill supported: the glamour of their engagement in pioneer ventures was only recognized in retrospect, after what they had endeavoured to do and what they had achieved was appreciated because by then it had assumed a certain respectability and prestige. For many years no bishop joined the CMS and no home-grown missionaries could be found. The early years were tough for all concerned. When Simeon called for chaplains for India the response was good. Clergy were prepared to travel to the farthest ends of the earth in order to work among white people, but to serve among peoples of other cultures and different religions was an almost unheard-of thing. There was 'no missionary tradition; the whole scheme seemed vague and nebulous, and not a man would come forward.'[22]

The only suitable candidate who offered his services to the recently formed CMS, and who would have been joyfully accepted, was the brilliant Senior Wrangler Henry Martyn, and he had to go to India as an East India Company chaplain because of difficulties and restrictions to which a professed missionary would have been subjected. By the time that the Society was ten years old it had sent out only five missionaries, all Germans, of whom one was dead, one had been dismissed, and three were still at work.

There was much tragedy, hardship and loss, as in 1823 when, of seven new schoolmasters and five wives who landed at Sierra Leone, ten died within eighteen months, and there were also the deaths of three other missionaries and two chaplains and their wives.

Nonetheless, despite such trials, testings and tribulation, much apathy, opposition and trauma, the British societies set an example that others followed. As previously mentioned, North America entered the lists in 1810 with the mainly Congregational American Board of Commissioners for Foreign Missions, and in 1814 with the American Baptist Missionary Board. In Continental Europe, Switzerland gave the lead in 1815 when the Basel Mission was founded. Germany joined in with the Berlin Society in 1824. Denmark (1821), France (1822), Sweden (1835) and Norway (1842) added to the growing body of missionary societies. And then the list became rapidly longer, so that by the end of the century every nominally Christian country and almost every denomination had begun to share in the missionary cause.

The work accomplished by the combined efforts of the societies and churches, Protestant, Catholic and Orthodox, in the course of the century was phenomenal. Some measure of the stupendous growth of this global outreach is the way the CMS, as but one society, and despite innumerable setbacks, extended its areas of service. Throughout the nineteenth century the work progressed in India, Sierra Leone and New Zealand. But, in addition, new mission fields were opened up, including Ceylon (1818), Egypt (1826), British Guiana (1827), Abyssinia (1830), Ibadan (1851), Lagos (1852), Mauritius (1856), Hong Kong (1862), Madagascar (1863), Japan (1868), Persia (1875), the Seychelles (1875), Uganda (1875) and Mombasa (1887). Missionary work was also undertaken in Palestine and China, and among the Zulus.[23]

A brief look at the advance of Christianity in Asia, sub-Saharan Africa and South America will give a taste of what amounts to one of the greatest and most enduring legacies of the nineteenth century.

Asia

India

As with many of the areas to be surveyed, India had its own Christian history stretching back to the first century. It is possible that the apostle Thomas initiated Christian work in the subcontinent. Certainly, in the south-west the very ancient Church of the Thomas Christians still exists. In the modern era, it was perhaps the Jesuit Francis Xavier who, in the 1540s, had the distinction of first introducing Christianity to the subcontinent. Another Jesuit, the Italian Roberto de Nobili arrived in 1606 and henceforth made his distinctive and distinguished contribution to the establishment, or re-establishment, of Christianity in southern India.

The first non-Roman Catholic missionaries to reach the subcontinent from Europe were two young Pietists, Bartholomew Ziegenbalg and Henry Plutschau, sent by August Francke in 1705. They did a magnificent work at Tranquebar. They were succeeded by the massively important forty-eight-year labours of Christian Friedrich Schwartz in Tranquebar, Trichinopoly and Tanjore, which came to an end only with his death in 1798. Before this valiant church planter died, William Carey had arrived in Bengal, bent on a fanatical crusade to convert India, and fired by the slogan 'Expect great things from God, and attempt great things for God'. Soon after his arrival, and in circumstances that are very far from clear, the first Protestant mass movement in India broke out among the hardy and vigorous, but almost totally illiterate community in the neighbourhood of Cape Comorin. 'Between 1795 and 1805, the Tanjore missionaries and their Indian colleagues baptized upwards of 5,000 people.'[24]

In 1812, two years after they had helped in the establishment of the American Board of Commissioners for Foreign Missions, Adoniram Judson and Samuel Newell and their wives embarked for India. The age of international engagement and co-operation in mission was beginning to unfold.

In addition to his part in administering a kick-start to world mission, and himself being a pioneer missionary, William Carey's monumental work was that of translator and author. Whether by his effort, or that of others under his supervision, by the time of his death in 1834, translations of the Scriptures, in whole or in part, had been made in thirty-five Indian languages or dialects. 'In addition to these he compiled and published grammars in the Sanskrit, Bengali, Marathi, Telgu, and Sikh languages, and dictionaries in Bengali and Marathi, besides editing numerous works in both English and the native languages. The magnitude of his literary accomplishments was truly astonishing, and justifiably earned for him the title of "The Wycliffe of the East".'[25]

Carey, together with Joshua Marshman and William Ward established a stronghold for Christianity at Serampore. It was a seminal and fruitful ministry. In the following decades others followed who accomplished great things. They merit mention not only because of their outstanding work but for the policies and principles they helped to forge. By an arrangement with the Serampore missionaries, Henry Martyn undertook work on the Persian translation of the New Testament. The High Church scholar Thomas Fanshawe Middleton arrived in India in 1814 as the first bishop, and most notably founded Bishop's College, Calcutta, for the training of young men for the ministry of the Anglican Church. William Hodge Mill was appointed as the first principal, and served with distinction in that capacity from 1820 to 1838. The redoubtable Scotsman Alexander Duff served as an educator in India from 1830 to 1863 and was especially influential among gifted and highly literate men, a number of whom renounced Hinduism and became Christians. Reginald Heber became the second Bishop of Calcutta in 1823, and in his short episcopate he worked hard to propagate the gospel in his large diocese and beyond. He is best known for his hymns, which include 'Brightest and best of the sons of the morning', 'From Greenland's icy mountains', 'The Son of God goes forth to war', and 'Holy, holy, holy, Lord God almighty'. The greatest of the early bishops of Calcutta was Daniel Wilson, who from 1833 tirelessly ruled the see for twenty-five years. As the British dominion in India grew, he was one of the key figures who helped to inculcate a sense of Christian responsibility for the well-being of the native people of the subcontinent. In this process, the renewal of the East India Company's Charter in 1833 was pivotal as it opened the country without restriction to missionary activity. From then onwards missionary reinforcements from many nations began to enter the field.

John Scudder served as the first medical missionary to India from 1819 to 1855; and during this long time as a doctor, preacher, teacher and translator, there was not a town in the south-eastern region of the subcontinent in which he did not publicly declare his faith. Amazingly, Dr and Mrs Scudder's whole family followed their parents in devoting themselves to missionary work, as did their children's children after them, and then a fourth generation kept up this tradition. It was symptomatic of the patience and persistence of innumerable Christians, both from the Western world and from the indigenous population.

A host of societies provided missionaries for all parts of India in the course of the nineteenth century, and between them they supplied a vast range of medical, educational and social facilities. There was hardly an area of human activity and need that was not covered. By 1851 there were 339 ordained male missionaries in the land belonging to nineteen societies, and no single women, although this was just about to change, as a novelty in the middle of the century for all the missions, Protestant and Catholic alike, was the recruitment of single women for the first time. Together with the wives, and most of the men were married, this meant an active and dedicated force of approximately 600; a considerable advance in the course of half a century, but still a mere handful in a country with a population of 150 million. It was calculated that there were 91,092 Christians in total in the Indian subcontinent, of whom only 14,661 were communicants. Of these no less than 51,300 were in the Anglican missions in Tinnevelly and the LMS area of South Travancore, which meant that there were only 40,000 adherents scattered throughout the rest of India. A start had been made, but there was clearly a very long way to go.

It was fortunate that the devastating and destructive whirl-wind of the 1857 Indian Mutiny, which came unexpectedly and with unimaginable ferocity, was limited almost entirely to the Ganges valley. Even so, it appears that 38 missionaries, chaplains, and members of their families died in the course of the violence, together with about twenty native Indian Christians. But the fig-ures are uncertain, and many more than the number recorded may have perished.

The period from 1858 to 1914 was the heyday of colonialism when the life of the East India Company as a quasi-sovereign power came to an end, and the British government and people accepted their responsibility for good and humane rule and administration. During these critical years, the Christian Church in the land made great progress. The British administrators and officials as a whole recognized that Christianity should be central to everything undertaken by the mother country, and that Christian principles should guide and inform the new regime. Clearly, in practice the conduct of people at all levels fell far short of such an ideal, but at least there were openly declared Christian goals. The attainment of such well-intentioned objectives was made more feasible by an extended period of unexampled peace, and by a succession of unusually able and high-minded govern-ment servants.

Nevertheless, there was still much, and probably increased, resistance to Christianity from among thoughtful and highly lit-erate Hindus and Muslims. They became ever more concerned that the Christian gospel and teaching, and the penetration of Christian views and perspectives, even apart from the problem of conversions, posed a subtle threat to their whole way of life and to the age-long traditions of India. The ancient religions began to turn from defensiveness to the offensive. There continued to be conversions among the highest Hindu castes, and among the Muslims, but they were probably fewer than in former years.

Even so, between 1851 and 1901 the Protestant community in India increased tenfold. This was to a great extent due to further mass movements. These occurred in a substantial number of the

750,000 villages of the country. It was estimated in 1933 that half of the Roman Catholics in India and as many as 80 per cent of the Protestants were descendents of mass-movement converts or in some way a product of mass movements. This particular phenomenon provided convincing evidence of the reality of Christianity as a contemporary spiritual force in society. It was not a matter of people coming to faith en masse. But in every province and in many states, large numbers professed 'adherence to the Christian religion because of movements that developed within a group to which they, or one of their ancestors, belonged'.[26] The group concerned was ordinarily composed of one caste, and often included all the members of that caste in one, or more than one, village. The greatest number of mass movements occurred among the depressed, least privileged classes.

It appears that far from proving an obstacle to the conversion of the higher caste members, mass movements among the lower socio-economic groups increased the number of such converts. In areas where there were no mass movements there were generally not a large number from the higher castes converted. In areas where there were mass movements, large numbers of them were often converted. In several areas which did not experience mass movements a considerable proportion of those converted among the higher castes seem to have been influenced by mass-movement converts from other regions.

It is some measure of the progress in the establishment of Christianity in the country as an indigenous faith that by 1912 the Anglican Church dedicated Vedanayakam Samuel Azariah as the first native Indian bishop. He 'grew steadily in spiritual stature and in authority, and was widely acclaimed in both East and West as a missionary statesman. At last Indian leadership was coming into its own.'[27]

China

Prior to the sixteenth century there were occasional attempts to bring Christianity to China, as when John of Monte Corvino, who lived in Peking between 1293 and 1305, claimed to have baptized 6,000 people. He was later made the first *Archiepiscopus Cambalensis* of the Latin Church in the Far East, but after his death

in 1328 the mission gradually declined. In 1368 the rulers of the
new Ming dynasty took an aggressive stance against 'foreign religion'. They bitterly persecuted the Christians, and 'a blank of
nearly 200 years followed in the history of Christianity in
China'.[28]

But in 1557 the Portuguese managed to install themselves in
the tiny settlement of Macao at the mouth of the Canton river
and, more significantly, the Jesuit Matthew Ricci established a
Roman Catholic mission in the country that at the time of his
death in 1610 was prospering. Remarkably, in 1674, Lo Wen-Tsao
became the first Chinese bishop when he was appointed to the
See of Basilinopolis in Bithynia and made the Vicar Apostolic for
the northern part of China. Even so, the Roman Catholic mission
in China rather limped along, and was especially hampered by
clashes between the Chinese and papal authorities. In 1724
Christianity was proscribed by edict and missionaries were banished from the Empire.

Protestant missionary work in the country began in 1807 with
the arrival of Robert Morrison. He was sent out by the London
Missionary Society. He was a man of humble parentage and occupation – a shoe-last maker – but by dint of perseverance and
application he acquired a good education and mastered several
languages. In China his steely resolve was immediately tested, as
he was given a hostile reception alike by the Chinese, the East
India Company and the few remaining Jesuit missionaries at
Macao. His linguistic ability, however, proved to be invaluable. In
1809 he was appointed translator to the East India Company, and
thus received 'protection, a measure of security, and an income
on which to live'. It also gave him a 'little corner, the only
foothold the European had been able legally to secure in the
whole empire of China'.[29]

In 1813 he completed his translation of the New Testament into
Chinese, and six years later added the Old Testament. He ultimately published more than a score of works, including a
Chinese grammar and his monumental six-volume dictionary of
Chinese that went far to establishing the knowledge of that language on a scientific footing. A further great achievement was his
foundation in 1818 of the Anglo-Chinese College in Malacca, to
serve the many Chinese living outside China.

Others made their valuable contributions to the advance of Christianity in China in these difficult years. Most notable were Morrison's first associate, William Mile, the energetic and multi-talented Walter Medhurst, and the Revd E.C. Bridman, who strengthened Christianity in China with his literary works. To these should be added Dr S. Wells who distinguished himself as a printer, sinologue, historian and diplomat, and Dr Peter Parker, who was the first medical missionary to China.

It was somewhat ironic, and to an extent unfortunate, that the opening up of China to missionaries came largely on the back of the ethically dubious, if not downright immoral, commercial and political pressures of the Western powers. The Treaty of Nanking (1842) at the conclusion of the Opium War surrendered Hong Kong to the British, and five 'treaty ports' – Canton, Amoy, Foochow, Ningpo and Shanghai – were opened to receive foreigners. It was clear that missionaries no less than merchants could avail themselves of the privileges accorded to foreigners. A new era of missionary advance in China was about to begin.

'The response of Europe and America to these new opportunities was immediate. Almost every missionary society seemed ready to send workers to China, and almost all of them wished to be represented in all the six places which were open to residence.'[30] It was just one more sign that the revivals, awakenings and vibrant lives of many European, British and American churches during the preceding hundred years, had sown seeds that bore fruit in a lively missionary interest and vision, and in the willingness of Christians in the Old World in considerable numbers to serve in the far-flung corners of the world.

Another dishonourable war in 1856 over the wretched opium trade resulted in the Treaty of Tientsin in 1860. This stipulated that ten more cities should be opened to trade. It also threw open the whole of the Empire to missionaries and declared that Christian converts should be free from persecution. The reaction of the missionary societies was again prompt and decisive. There was at once an exodus of missionaries from the few centres already occupied to the new treaty ports. This was followed by efforts to penetrate the interior. Even so, by 1865 no Protestant missionary was to be found in eleven of the eighteen provinces; and in the seven that had a Christian presence, the advance was restricted to zones not far from the coast, except for a number of stations in the Yangtze valley. Also, despite the treaties signed and promises made, the opening up of China was tortuously achieved 'in the teeth of bitter opposition from the authorities and frequent anti-foreign uprisings of the people'. Christian work was a constant struggle. 'Missionary progress up to the very end of the nineteenth century was punctuated by insult, riot, and bloodshed.'[31]

In the midst of these hard, and in some respects depressing circumstances, there appeared on the scene one of those missionaries who stand out not only in their own day and generation but in the global history of Christianity. James Hudson Taylor played a 'role of unique importance in the task of evangelizing the millions of China'.[32] After a visit to the country in 1853, he became overwhelmed with concern for the spiritual needs of the people living in its vast interior. In 1865 he formed the China Inland Mission, and in the following year he sailed for China with a party of fifteen in order to begin its work.

From the outset Taylor adopted Chinese dress as the most obvious method of self-identification with the Chinese people; and such attire was required of all the CIM missionaries. The society he founded for a time became the largest mission in the world. It was also the first, and until 1950 the largest of what are called 'faith missions', because of their principle and practice of making no direct solicitation for funds either for the members' individual needs or for the society itself. The workers were guaranteed no fixed salary, but had to trust God to supply their wants through the voluntary, unasked-for offerings of fellow Christians. The mission was international and interdenominational. It included lay people as well as ordained, and it welcomed those with little formal education, as long as they could subscribe to its simple doctrinal declaration. It additionally introduced a new principle that the direction and administration of the mission would be in China, not in England. The primary aim of the mission was and remained evangelistic. The shepherding of churches, and pastoral and educational work were not ignored, but never were these or any other activities allowed to detract from the central and commanding purpose.

Almost from the start the success of the society was sensational. Offers to be CIM missionaries flooded in, and some had to be rejected. Some of those sent to China were failures, but the majority remained loyal and conscientious in their service, and a number of them were outstandingly successful pioneers. By 1882 all the provinces had been visited, and there were missionaries resident in all but three of them. A mere thirty years after its foundation the mission had 641 missionaries, work had begun among the aboriginal peoples in the far west of China, and missionaries were established in Sinkiang (Chinese Turkestan) and on the borders of Tibet.

China was plagued by serious anti-foreign riots and uprisings during the last three decades of the century. Serious outbreaks occurred in 1870 at Tientsin and Hankow, with over a score of foreigners being brutally killed and much property destroyed. Further militancy took place in the capital of Hunan province in 1890, with ensuing riots in the Yangtze valley and the murder of missionaries in Hupeh province in 1891 and 1893. Ten members of the Church Missionary Society were slaughtered in 1895 in the Kucheng massacre in Fukien province. In total twenty-eight Protestants were martyred before the climax was reached with the Boxer uprising of 1900, which will be considered in chapter 6, while many Roman Catholics, including members of the main Orders, and other foreigners suffered in a similar manner.

After all this Christian activity, accompanied by major setbacks, the numerical situation at the end of the century can be variously interpreted. There was a body of about 1,500 missionaries, including wives, and they were established in 500 stations, with almost all the provinces by then having their quota. Around them, and still to a great extent looking upon the foreigners as the leaders in every respect, were almost half a million Christian adherents, of whom slightly less than 80,000 were communicants. These believers were the core of a church, both Protestant and Catholic, that was to endure great agony in the twentieth and twenty-first centuries, but which finally underwent a most remarkable resurrection.

Japan

In the modern era, Europeans probably first made contact with Japan in 1542. It was in that year that a Portuguese navigator, Mendez Pinto, reached the islands after following in the track of

Vasco da Gama. Others followed soon after, including the Jesuits led by the intrepid Francis Xavier, who set foot on Japanese soil in 1549.

The conditions favoured the introduction of Christianity, as the political situation was chaotic, and the Shinto and Buddhist religions were decadent and degenerate. By 1581 there were reckoned to be 200 churches and 150,000 professed Christians. In these palmy days hopes were even cherished that the country would become wholly Christian. But the pendulum then swung violently in the opposite direction, and the Christians had to endure much hideous torture, pain, suffering and death, as Christianity was prohibited by edict, and a policy was adopted of totally eradicating the faith from the realm. By the mid seventeenth century the instruments of torment, the sword, fire and banishment had done their worse. Yet a remnant of believers remained, and when the country was reopened to Christianity in the early nineteenth century, 'whole villages of professed Christians were found who had retained the faith, albeit in a corrupt form'.[33]

In 1853 and 1854, the ports of Shimoda and Hakodate were made accessible to American trade. In 1858 the Americans and the British negotiated treaties that secured the right of their citizens to reside in certain Japanese ports. The long-closed door was thereby reopened to missionaries as well as to merchants. The response of Christian societies was immediate and enthusiastic. The Americans gave the lead, and within a few months seven missionaries from the USA and four societies had begun work in the country. In 1869 the Church Missionary Society and the American Board sent their first missionaries. But danger still lurked, and in the following year twelve foreigners were killed.

Nonetheless, the century ended on a high note for Christians. In 1873 the anti-Christian edicts were rescinded, and in response many more missionaries poured into the country. Religious toleration was further extended in 1884; and in 1889 all restrictions were removed. The missionaries were granted freedom to travel to all parts of the interior.

It was in the latter half of the nineteenth century that there were clear signs of Christian growth, even though at first the churches were like delicate plants needing careful nurturing.

Prior to that time the missionary effort had to be largely confined to educational or medical work, and mainly the former. With the removal of the straitjacket, and with the open preaching of the Christian faith, the second half of the nineteenth century saw an expansion of the Protestant church. The first convert in the new era of Christian advance was baptized in 1864, and the next two years later. The first open, public, Japanese church was established at Yokohama in 1872. It was in the Reformed tradition and initially had eleven members.

As the influence of the West was consolidated in the years from 1873 to 1888, so it became quite easy to attract people to Christian gatherings; Christian schools became crowded with pupils; and there were large accessions to the Church. Nevertheless, there was no mass movement towards Christianity of a type that promoted the rapid extension of the faith, as had taken place in some other countries. Perhaps the nearest approach to this was the sudden conversion of a number of students at an agricultural college in Sapporo in Hokkaido in 1876 and, even more sensationally, at Doshisha school in Kyoto eight years later, when no less than 200 students were baptized. 'On the whole, however, Japanese Christianity has remained intellectual and individual, and its history is largely that of the outstanding individuals who have influenced its course.'[34] In fact, Christians then and ever since 'have always been few in Japan; but their influence has been altogether out of proportion to their numbers'.[35]

Korea

Korea is included in this brief summary of Christian expansion in Asia in the nineteenth century because, as will be seen in chapter 6, it became one of the most astounding centres of late twentieth- and early twenty-first-century Christianity in the world.

Roman Catholics were the first Western Christians to bring the Christian faith to Korea in the modern era; and the story of how this came about is romantic and amazing. In about 1777, a group of Korean students became so interested in Christianity as a result of reading a number of the treatises of Matthew Ricci that in 1783 they sent one of their number to Peking to find out more about it. He was persuaded of the truth of what he was told, and of the need to embrace the faith for himself, and he was baptized under the name of Peter. On his return he was successful in proclaiming his new knowledge and belief, and he was able to baptize several converts. 'Having no priest, the Koreans organized their own Church, with a bishop and priests, the celebration of Mass, the hearing of confessions, and all the other practices of the Catholic world – an astonishing example of lay Christianity creating and maintaining itself in a remote and inaccessible area.'[36]

After closer contact with Peking these Christians became aware of their well-meant, but erroneous actions as conscientious Catholics, in trying to go their own way without clerical oversight or supervision, and in 1794 they gladly welcomed a Chinese priest to care for them. On his arrival, he found 4,000 believers prepared and enthusiastic to receive his ministrations. Seven years later he was put to death. It was the first of many martyrdoms. In 1836 and 1837 three European priests arrived, but they also were caught and executed after only three years of service.

Such persecution did not deter the Christians or prevent them winning additional converts; the Church continued to grow as believers met in secret, and a handful of non-Korean missionaries were able to enter the country and to maintain themselves. By 1886 it was calculated that there were 25,000 Christians. But the biggest trial then confronted them. In that year persecution broke out that was political rather than strictly religious in character. Nonetheless, two bishops, seven priests and at least 8,000 Korean Christians perished. The blow was devastating for the Roman Catholic Church, and it has never fully recovered from it, so that its adherents dwindled during the last quarter of the nineteenth century. Even so, the seeds had been sown for a blossoming that was to surface a hundred years later.

Although the Roman Catholic mission had largely been stamped out by the 1880s, that same decade provided new and unexpected opportunities for the Protestants. A treaty with the United States in 1882 opened the doors of the country to the West just as had happened with Japan. The first to take advantage of this relaxation of controls were the Presbyterians and the Methodist Episcopal Church, and others followed. Of great importance also was the visit of Dr John L. Nevius from Chefoo, China, in 1890. He was far ahead of his time in accepting the possibility and desirability of an independent, self-supporting and self-propagating national church. It was a vision that lingered with the Christians of the country until it became a reality.

Africa

In the early centuries of the Christian era North Africa was one of the main centres of Christianity, with Alexandria and Carthage being of particular importance.[37] By the third century the faith had probably penetrated to the native Coptic-speaking population of upper Egypt and the lands to the south of Egypt. In about 320 Pachomius (c.290–346) founded a Coptic-speaking monastery at Tabennisi in the Thebaid near the Nile, the first recognizable monastery in Christian history. Other foundations followed, and it is reckoned that at his death he was abbot-general of nine monasteries for men and two for women. Together with Antony, or Anthony, he was 'caught up in a wave of mass conversion in the African countryside' that 'was to prove one of the most truly decisive spiritual and institutional developments not only for the Egyptian Church, but for the world Church, and the Ethiopian Church too'.[38]

In about 340 Athanasius, the Patriarch of Alexandria, consecrated Frumentius as Bishop of Aksun, and thereby helped to lay the foundations of Ethiopian Christianity as an extension to that of Egypt. The church in Ethiopia can, therefore, rightly claim to be the oldest in sub-Saharan Africa by a thousand years and more, and it continued to be the one example in that region of a largely independent church, for much of the time within an independent country, right up to the present day.

Little is known of the Church in Africa south of the Sahara in medieval times. It was a period when many stateless regions were being slowly integrated into kingdoms of various sizes, with capitals and royal dynasties. A number of these were massive and long lasting, as with the extraordinary central African monarchy, Great Zimbabwe, which flourished in the fourteenth century in the plateau area between the Zambezi and Limpopo rivers.

By 1500 Islam had made huge strides in West Africa and up the Nile. Christianity had but a precarious and limited foothold. The Christian kingdom of Ethiopia survived, but its era of glory was well in the past, and the Church in Nubia to all appearances was on its last legs. 'Thus at times violently but more often quietly enough, did Islam advance while Christianity, like an ill-adapted dinosaur, declined and expired in place after place, crushed essentially by its own limitations, its fossilized traditions, and the lack of a truly viable, self-renewing structure.'[39]

The most notable development in the fifteenth and sixteenth centuries from the Christian point of view was the incursion of the Portuguese into the continent, and the initial evangelization by them of a kingdom known as Kongo. This particular Roman Catholic initiative became part of a more comprehensive and cohesive global policy with the establishment of the Sacred Congregation of Propaganda in the latter half of the sixteenth century by the Vatican to encourage missions to heathen countries and to provide for the ecclesiastical administration of territories where there was no properly established hierarchy. The Christianization of Africa in the modern era had begun.

There was no area outside Kongo where Christianity in that period was more than 'a mere appendage of colonial presence',[40] but the developments in Kongo had, by the beginning of the seventeenth century, given some, not entirely illusory, hope for the conversion of Africa as a whole. Even so, during the next 200 years virtually nothing happened to realize this potential. Christianity in Africa at the end of the eighteenth century was weak and ineffectual. Changes started to take place in the main as a result of the British anti-slavery campaign and the missionary impulse generated by the evangelical revival in Britain and North America.

There had been Protestant chaplains in the Dutch, English and Danish forts along the Slave Coast since the late seventeenth cent-ury, but even this Christian presence was disjointed and discontinuous. It was confined to small stretches of the coastland and largely to work among expatriates. The rate of white mortality was high, and volunteers for such hazardous, uncongenial and dangerous posts were, understandably, few and far between. The first Anglican missionary to Africa had been Thomas Thompson, who was sent out by the SPG in 1752 to live and work at Cape Coast Castle, but he was in favour of the African slave trade, and therefore not entirely suitable as an ambassador to the indigenous people.

The first real breakthrough came with the founding of Sierra Leone, as mentioned in the previous chapter. A large number of the Nova Scotians and others who constituted the population of Freetown were committed Christians, so the town became emphatically Christian from the time of its foundation. Not only were the English evangelical sponsors concerned that it should be so, but more importantly 'its African leaders were already boisterously Christian on arrival'.[41] The tone was reflected by the members of the Countess of Huntingdon's Connexion as they marched ashore and joined together in one of their favourite hymns, 'Awake and sing the song of Moses and the Lamb'.[42] A contemporary none-too-sympathetic observer wrote: 'I never met with, heard, or read of, any sort of people observing the same appearance of godliness'.[43] The Sierra Leone Company's aim of establishing a thriving settlement on the shores of Africa that would demonstrate the possibility of successful trading and viable commercial enterprises that were not based on slavery wholly failed, but a major step towards establishing an African church had been taken.

This was shown movingly and convincingly in the life and career of Adjai, a young Yoruba boy who had been released from slavery in 1822. Baptized and renamed Samuel Crowther, in 1864 he became the first native African bishop in the modern age. 'Others became Methodists. As Anglican or Methodist, they would carry the Afro-Christian confidence of the first Freetown settlers into a rather more structured, more educated, more mission-connected form of religion.'[44] Most importantly, Sierra Leone was a flagship. It was a land where black freedom was evident, and in which there were some signs of black prosperity. In co-operation with the white missionaries, albeit with considerable friction at times, by the 1820s it was beginning to look like a possible Christian bridgehead in Africa.

Of course there were blatant inconsistencies, and what later generations would regard as hypocrisy, in the motives and policies of the British who were associated with this experimental Christian community. There were attitudes that were an amalgam of unalloyed Christian concern and highly cultural and nationalistic interests and orientations, united with a large dose of ill-disguised snobbishness. The friends of the Sierra Leone

church often lauded it as a fine example of a black European civilization, 'Christian, literate, using the English language with
ease, differing from Europe only in being – potentially – more
religious, more moral, more literate.'[45] In what would later be
condemned as an unacceptably Eurocentric and patronizing
tone, some of the patrons and supporters of this Christian initiative praised it as a 'triumphant demonstration of the repeated
missionary assertion that given the same opportunities, Africans
were as capable of "improvements" as anyone else'.[46] The underlying assumption of all such observers and commentators that
European civilization was the only standard by which attainment
could be measured was subsequently criticized by many as reprehensible, but the whole enterprise was driven along by what
were fundamentally benevolent, compassionate and commend-
ably Christian objectives.

'When the large, grave figure of Samuel Crowther, clad in
immaculate clerical black, spoke convincingly on English public
platforms, had audience with Queen Victoria, and answered all
Prince Albert's intelligent questions about commerce in Africa,
the whole missionary enterprise seemed justified. The future
operations of missions in Africa must be directed to producing
more of the same.'[47] Of course the members of the British royal
family, the leading members of society, and those members of the
Church concerned were, understandably, children of their own
age, and rather proud Victorians as they showed such self-satisfaction and smugness. But they must surely be given credit for
having high aspirations for the native Africans, and the established church must be given respect as the foremost agency in
trying to ensure that these ideals were actualized.

In the meantime the Dutchman Johannes Van der Kemp was
having a major impact as the missionary responsible for the
Bethelsdorp settlement in the eastern Cape from 1803 until his
death in 1811. He was a truly charismatic, visionary man who lived
a life of absolute poverty, walked about bareheaded and bare-
footed, fed on the simplest of food, lived in the poorest of huts and,
despite his high intelligence and exceptional linguistic ability, lived
out his life on the principle of absolute human equality.

It was a group of Christians from Bethelsdorp who established
the mission of Kuruman among the Bechuana in 1816. The new

centre lay 600 miles inland from Cape Town, and it proved to be the first of many thoroughly successful and enduring missions established well beyond the colonial frontier. To this community in 1821 went Robert and Mary Moffat. They remained in Africa for fifty years and they provide the link with David Livingstone and the headline-catching, incredible and epochal exploratory, empire-building and church-founding enterprises of the latter part of the century. By 1835 the Moffats had built up Kuruman to a sizeable community with a canal, 500 acres of irrigated gardens, fences, fruit trees, wheat, barley, grapes and figs, and a population of 700 people. The Europeans were firmly but benevolently in control. Their authority was accepted by Africans 'because it worked, brought local peace, and produced such wonders as the printing-press'.[48]

Another great figure in the saga of South African missions was John Philip. He arrived in 1820 as superintendent of the LMS missions in South Africa. During his thirty years' tenure of that office he was 'an uncompromising supporter of the rights of the black man as against the white; he expressed plainly the conviction that, given the opportunities of education and training, the African would prove himself to be in every way the equal of the European'.[49]

Despite such impressive achievements in west and southern Africa, by the 1830s it was clear that Islam was the major successful missionary religion on the continent, and that Christianity paled by comparison. But the situation was about to change radically and permanently. The defining and decisive decade was the 1840s.

The pivotal 1840s

Up to the 1840s the progress of Christianity in Africa had to a large extent depended on the heroic efforts of a few dedicated and enthusiastic individuals and the bold, inevitably uninformed, ventures and experiments, and limited success of a small number of pioneer missionary societies. They made grievous mistakes, and there was tragic waste of life. Nonetheless, the societies and the redoubtable early missionaries had, above all else, given a lead and inaugurated an enterprise; and, considered in this way, despite all their failings it was a very impressive overall operation. For the most part, it was also a fine example of bridging denominational boundaries. The 'missionary movement was a singularly non-denominational function of international Protestantism of a rather lay and individualistic sort'.[50] It was quite simple, almost undifferentiated, and the Protestants were to a marked degree conscious of their oneness of purpose, even if the scene was somewhat anarchical at times. The whole missionary thrust was also on quite a small scale and it was confined almost entirely to Protestants. Unfortunately, although a start had been made, and impetus had been generated, it had all gone a little flat in the late 1820s and the 1830s. 'Consolidation rather than extension is the note of the period.'[51] But things were about to change in a sudden, pronounced and astounding way.

In 1841, there were three landmarks of considerable consequence. In that year, the Colonial Bishoprics Fund was launched and the Peninsular and Orient line was opened, thus facilitating access to India via the Red Sea. Both of these developments were symptomatic of widening mental and emotional as well as practical and operational horizons.

Then, likewise in 1841, there was the first major missionary endeavour of that decade with Sir Thomas Buxton's highly publicized, ill-fated Niger Expedition. It was a disastrous failure but it was successful in arousing awareness and concern for such issues as 'heathenism', and the evils of the still existing African slave trade. It also drew attention to the opportunities for both commercial growth and the propagation of the gospel awaiting those bold risk-takers who were prepared to take advantage of circumstances which, although dangerous and riddled with possible pitfalls, at the same time were full of potential for success, at least in the long term. The continent was standing on the verge of great and irreversible political, economic, social and religious changes.

Johann Krapt may justifiably be regarded as the first modern missionary in eastern Africa. He was the forerunner of a movement that was to alter the face and place of Christianity in the continent. For five years, starting on 7 January 1844, he worked in Ethiopia, and he then transferred to Mombasa. For the following thirty years he and his colleague Johann Redmann used that centre as a base from which they patiently explored the hinterland and came to grips with East Africa's coastal languages. They laid firm foundations for the remarkable establishment of Christianity in the region in the last quarter of the century.

Concurrently, a number of Bible translations were under way in various regions of Africa. Moffat's Sechuana New Testament appeared in 1840. The able CMS missionary linguist J.F. Schon, provided portions of the Bible for the Hausa and Igbo people, while Samuel Crowther worked on the Yoruba New Testament. Nearby, in Cameroon in 1847, the Jamaican Joseph Merrick, a member of the Jamaican Baptist Mission, produced a translation of Matthew's Gospel in Isubu, and an English missionary, Alfred Saker, provided the same service for the Duala-speaking people.

To add to the importance of the 1840s, David Livingstone settled at Kolobeng in 1847, several hundred miles to the north of Kuruman, at a point that was further forward than any of the existing network of southern African missions. The American Board of Missions was at the same time busy establishing a cluster of stations in Natal, as were Norwegian Lutherans in Zululand. To complete this astounding concentrated series of events and actions, in 1846 Henry Townsend and Samuel Crowther established the first inland mission in Africa north of the Equator at Abeokuta.

> The missionary movement was, then, by 1850, becoming more than it realized a truly creative force within African history, the provider of much that was genuinely new and revolutionary, both mental and material, things that neither African societies themselves, nor the old Catholic missionaries, nor European traders and consuls had, or could, provide. It was already a more important, and less easily labeled, force than modern secular historians mostly admit.[52]

Just as importantly, and in the long term far more importantly, in a gradual and little publicized way, the faith was being propagated by African Christians themselves. The Sierra Leone missionaries were clearly of great importance, but it was the

Africans, and the new settlers of African descent, who played the major part in establishing and widening the sphere of Christianity in the region. They were to the fore as Christian ambassadors, and the key element entailed in diffusing Christianity in West Africa in those pioneering days.

> As clerk, railwayman, mechanic, and above all as trader, the Sierra Leonean penetrated everywhere the British did, and often further. And wherever he went, he took his Bible, his hymn singing, and his family prayers. In area after area, well into the twentieth century, the first contact of African peoples with the Christian faith was through an itinerant or immigrant Sierra Leonean. And the mission to Yorubaland, which marked a turning point in bringing about a well-grounded church in inland Africa, came about because Sierra Leoneans had made their way back as traders over hundreds of miles to the places from whence they had once been taken as slaves.[53]

The Africanization of the churches not only in West Africa, but throughout sub-Saharan Africa, was to be the key feature in the modern history of Christianity in that territory.

Finally and very importantly, it was in the 1840s that the Catholic mission was revived. The impact of the French Revolution and the Napoleonic Wars proved to be the final and devastating blow to a Church that had already reached a low point, and it collapsed. All was not lost, however, for in the home-lands of European Catholic missions there was evidence of continuing vitality and of a rising tide of faith even before the final defeat of Napoleon in 1815. 'Again and again it became clear that among large numbers, probably a majority of the population of the Latin lands and the adjacent sections of Germany, the Low Countries, and Switzerland – the historic stronghold of the Roman Catholic Church – the faith had been too deeply rooted to be quickly killed.'[54] There were at least embers that could be fanned into life. 'In the face of the widespread antagonism to Christianity which was a feature of the revolution through which Western Europe was passing, the Roman Catholic Church was making an astounding recovery from what some observers hailed as its impending demise.'[55] This recovery was manifested in a new concern to win Africa and other regions of the world for Christianity.

The outstanding missionary commitment of Pope Gregory XVI (1831–46) was a turning point. In 1837 a vicariate-apostolic was established for the Cape of Good Hope, followed by one that was effectively for the whole west coast north of Angola in 1842, and a third for Egypt two years after that. There was yet another in 1846 for the Sudan or Central Africa. By 1850 the eastern Cape and Natal had been accorded the status of separate vicariates.

On the ground, this organizational surge was underpinned by the work of Catholic missionaries. Justin de Jacobis began work in Massawa in 1839, and Maximilian Ryllo headed up a bold and brave band of Jesuits who ascended the Upper Nile in 1847. Secular Irish priests were dispatched to the eastern Cape, and French Oblates of Mary Immaculate to Natal. A new Catholic attempt to reach out to Africa was 'well under way, but while the Protestant assault was centrally unplanned and largely under the management of a multitude of lay boards, the Catholic was far more centralized beneath the control of Propaganda Fide.'[56]

This highly co-ordinated Catholic missionary effort did not, however, place an embargo on individual dreams and initiatives. Such scope for talented and enterprising men with outstanding qualities of leadership to make their mark was made manifest in the life and activities of Cardinal Charles Lavigerie (1825–92). He 'had the most systematic vision of a concerted imperial campaign to convert the whole of Africa'. For him,

> Christianity was resuming its ancient dominance in Africa, in which the Muslim age had been merely an unhappy interval, a thousand-year night that was now ending. Reinforcing this claim to ancient continuity, the pope gave him the title of Archbishop of Carthage and primate of Africa. Lavigerie dreamed of a kind of modern-day crusading order, a well-armed *militia Christi*, which would wander Africa defending pilgrims and fighting slave traders.[57]

His founding of the White Fathers was but one method he adopted in an attempt to realize his dream.

Colonialism, commerce and Christianity

The second half of the nineteenth century was a time of intense Western political interest and activity in the continent. This culminated in the last three decades of the century in the so-called 'scramble for Africa' – with major European nations jockeying for advantage.[58] It was a period of unprecedented exploration, exploitation and commercial expansion by the West,[59] and an era of unparalleled propagation of Christianity. These various expansionist strands were clearly related. The basis and prerequisite for the political, economic and religious aspects was exploration – a story full of epic adventures, unimaginable feats of endurance, and countless examples of individual achievement of a high order. By the end of the century the great geographical puzzles of Africa had been solved. 'The hidden sources of the Nile, and also of the Niger, had been reached. Livingstone and Stanley had crossed and recrossed Africa.'[60] In the nineteenth century, Britain was first on the scene, extending its sway in a somewhat haphazard manner through a combination of government action and the genius of such leaders as Cecil Rhodes. France followed, and advanced in a more deliberate and purposeful way. Germany came into the act latter, after its unification in 1870, and picked up some of the remaining territories, and lastly Belgium took over the state of Congo. 'By 1900 all Africa south of the Sahara except Liberia had been occupied by one or another of the European powers.'[61]

The carving up of the continent by the Europeans as a result of negotiations in the smoke-filled rooms and corridors of the 1878 Berlin congress and elsewhere established the main colonial territories with little regard for the existing distribution of the native populations, or the rights of indigenous groupings. The partitioning exercise was conducted almost arbitrarily on the basis of European interests and European political and economic considerations. It is little wonder that by such a blatantly Eurocentric action, the 'great powers' were sowing a wind that they and others would reap as a whirlwind in the future. But in the midst of this political, economic and commercial manoeuvring for national and personal advantage, Christianity was making headway – even if this meant two steps forward and one back for much of the time, and one step forward and two back some of the time.

In exploration, pioneer Christian 'planting' and in alerting the home-based British public and church to its Christian responsibilities to take the gospel, and all the benefits that flowed from such action, to what was then regarded as the 'dark continent', the foremost actor and champion was David Livingstone.[62] He arrived in Africa in 1841 after a childhood within a doughty clan of Scotsmen, in which he was reared in poverty and godliness, and after having trained as a medical doctor. He spent ten years in ordinary, frequently rather routine and tedious, missionary tasks, but all the time he yearned to undertake ground-breaking, pioneer missionary work. He longed to break out of his mainly sedentary life and to realize his ambition to be an explorer. He was enthused by the accounts of the African scene, and he was keenly aware of the challenge to venture forth beyond the confines of the existing missionary compound and penetrate unevangelized territory with the gospel. The man most responsible for engendering this passion to take the message of Christ to those who had not heard it was Robert Moffat, whose daughter Livingstone was afterwards to marry.

> In 1840 Moffat had described to him how he had often seen the smoke of a thousand villages rising in the morning air, and the gospel had not been preached in one of them. This picture Livingstone never forgot, and the various expeditions which gave him a deathless name as an explorer were undertaken in order to open up ways along which the gospel might travel.[63]

And he used the fame he achieved as an explorer to good effect in order to promote the causes that consumed him. He accepted imperialism and commercial expansion as part of a general divinely ordered historical process. The flag did in many cases prepare the way for the Bible, but the advance of the gospel was supreme. He was noted for his unrelenting insistence on the overriding and basically spiritual responsibility of those who were privileged to possess the resources and wherewithal to open up and develop new, hitherto unexplored and technologically backward territories. There was an inescapable onus placed on the

Christians of the West to share the countless and precious spiritual and practical benefits they so richly enjoyed with innumerable benighted people. When, as a much honoured and respected figure of international renown, he addressed members of the University of Cambridge on 4 December 1857, he 'proceeded to his conclusion, in a shout which electrified his audience':

> I beg to direct your attention to Africa. I know that in a few years I shall be cut off in that country, which is now open. Do not let it be shut again! I go back to Africa to try to make an open path for commerce and Christianity. Do you carry on the work which I have begun. I leave it with you.[64]

In his more reflective moments he acknowledged the strictly limited value of commerce by itself. 'You will', he wrote, 'see I appreciate the effects of commerce much, but those of Christianity much more.'[65]

In the story of how the churches and missionary societies responded to the call from Livingstone and others, there are innumerable tales of valour and sacrifice, of persistence in the teeth of much opposition and discouragement, and of dogged determination when confronted by hardship, as well as patience and steady application in the routine work entailed. As the Christian gospel was declared with ever more resolve and energy, a growing number of Africans were converted; and as Islam increasingly felt challenged and threatened, so the opposition to Christian activity multiplied and intensified. This was understandable, as was the resistance to the Westerners by people who, often rightly, saw their traditional ways of life, including their distinctive traditional religion, threatened. These were titanic confrontations.

The Church in parts of Africa faced times of testing and tribulation. The advance of Christianity was achieved at huge human cost, with the African Christians bearing the brunt of the aggression and suffering. In Madagascar in the 1850s, as one example, perhaps 200 Christians were 'speared, smothered, starved or burned to death, poisoned, hurled from cliffs or boiled alive in rice pits'.[66] It is from Eastern and Central Equatorial Africa, however, that two further sagas will graphically illuminate what was involved as Christianity moved forward.

The Universities Mission to Central Africa[67] originated with Livingstone's Cambridge clarion call. The mission field was to be in the region of the upper waters of the Zambezi, and the mission was placed under the oversight and care of the Bishop of Cape Town and Metropolitan of South Africa.

The erudite Charles Frederick Mackenzie was chosen as the field leader, and consecrated bishop on 1 January 1861. He departed for Central Africa with six other helpers – the first missionary bishop to be sent out by the Church in England for a thousand years. On their journey inland, accompanied by Dr Livingstone, they encountered a party of armed Yaos, a local tribe, whom they disarmed. They released the train of eighty-four captive slaves, who then formed the nucleus of a new village, Magomero, which was made the headquarters of the Mission.

Within a short time the bishop had died as a consequence of a boating accident, and within the next year or so three of the missionaries had also died, and another was so desperately ill that he had to return to England. The depleted remnant had to withdraw from Magomero. It was a dark hour for the Mission.

A new location was found in Zanzibar. In 1867 a further attempt was made to enter the mainland around Lake Nyasa, and a base was established at Magela or, as it was later called, Msalabani. In 1872 a violent storm destroyed much of the Zambezi headquarters, and soon after that one of the most devoted of the gallant band of missionaries, and a particular friend of the new bishop, died. It was a terrible blow to the bishop on top of repeated troubles and a most testing time, and more than he could bear with his failing health, so he returned to England and resigned his bishopric.

It was another time of crisis, but in 1873 a treaty was signed between the British government and the Sultan of Zanzibar that entailed the closure of the slave market in Zanzibar. This changed the whole situation. The site was purchased by the Mission, a thatched mud hut was built, and at the place where the whipping post had stood, and where abominable cruelties had been perpetrated for countless years, the gospel was preached. A church was constructed, which later became the cathedral.

During the episcopate of Dr Edward Steere (1874–81) the mission made great strides forward. He called for volunteers who were to be paid a pittance and were asked to dedicate themselves to the work unreservedly, in a self-sacrificing way. The response was immediate and generous, and from that time onwards a stream of them carried the Christian message from the base at Zanzibar far and wide into East Africa. Gradually the mainland was evangelized. A missionary station was established at Magela, a freed-slave village was started at Masasi and, in 1879, John Swedi became the first African in the UMCA to be admitted to Holy Orders. In the same year the first sixteen freed slaves to be baptized were admitted to their first communions.

But with progress went further setbacks. In 1881 Bishop Steere died, and in 1882 the Angoni tribe made a terrible raid on Masasi, setting fire to the houses, looting, desecrating the church and killing seven people. Nonetheless, the missionaries carried on the work despite the tragedy and the threat of the Angoni to return again to slay all the Europeans they met and to take the heart of their leader as a charm to bring victory over the white men. Such courage and perseverance were to be rewarded, for the mission was ready for a great advance in the next few years.

Before he died, Bishop Steere had commissioned Dr W.P. Johnson to undertake an expedition into the Yao hills in order to begin work around Lake Nyasa itself. Johnson was faced with the warlike Angoni, in the midst of their period of slaying and plundering villages, but with astounding bravery he boldly went out alone to meet them, won their trust and friendship, and set up missionary work in the territory of chief Chityi in 1882.

Bishop Steere was succeeded by Charles Alan Smythies, during whose episcopate a theological department was established in the Kiungani school for the training of clergy, and a steamer was employed on the lake to reach lakeside villages.

As the mission reached the end of the nineteenth century and moved into the twentieth century, the process of consolidation went on. The hearts of the pioneers would have been gladdened by the consecration of the first Bishop of Nyasaland in 1892; and also, to stray a little into the following century, by the arrival of Bishop Hine as the first Bishop of Northern Rhodesia in 1910, and by the consecration of the first Bishop of Masasi in 1926.

To look forward even further, there would have been great rejoicing at the many African bishops, priests and lay people who were to play such a distinguished part in the life of their home-land churches and in the wider councils of the Church. It was the great missionary strategist Henry Venn (1796–1873) who con-stantly and persistently advocated the need for 'the euthanasia of missions'. He was concerned that the non-departure of European missionaries would result in native churches becoming mission-ary-dominated. The foreign missionary should always be first and foremost an evangelist. His target was to plant indigenous churches, which would be self-supporting, self-governing and self-extending. The European missionary presence should be interim only. Unfortunately, it was happening all too slowly in his day and generation, despite such examples of African witness and evangelization cited in this chapter, the appointment of Bishop Crowther, and the leadership provided by the famous African Christian chief Khama Boikano of the Bamangwato in Bechuanaland, but its day was to come, and foundations had been laid.

The second example of pioneering in East Africa comes from a territory further to the west of where the heroic acts of Christian service just considered took place.

As explorers thrust deeply into the interior of east-central Africa, there were reports of an inland kingdom called Buganda.[68] It was finally reached by John Speke in 1861 and by H.M. Stanley fourteen years later. In 1875, in a remarkable letter to the *Daily Telegraph*, Stanley, writing from Buganda, challenged Christ-endom to send a mission to the country. Two days later the CMS received an anonymous letter in which £5,000 was offered as an initial fund for such a project. The CMS made its plans with urgency and yet with great care and circumspection. Special con-tributions poured in, and soon £15,000 had been donated. In def-erence to the political situation in eastern Africa, the title Nyanza Mission was adopted, leaving its precise locale an open question.

The missionaries set sail in 1876, and journeyed inland. Two mechanics and one of the leaders, Alexander Mackay, had to return to England because of ill health; porters deserted, and Dr John Smith died of fever, thus creating the first missionary grave on the shores of the Nyanza. By then only three of the party were left. Soon after arrival in Buganda two of them were murdered. In 1878 the one survivor, the Revd C.T. Wilson, was joined by

Mackay. By 1882 the first Protestant baptism took place. In 1884 James Hannington sailed for Buganda as the first Bishop of Eastern Equatorial Africa. In the meantime, the young Bugandan church was facing persecution. Native Christians were banished and imprisoned. Three of them were put to death – cruelly cut about with long curved knives, and then thrown on a large fire. When Hannington and his group of fifty men arrived on the borders of the country they were held in a miserable hut, led out after eight days, surrounded, and all but four of them were slain. It was subsequently reported that the white man, before he fell, had given a message for the *kabaka* that he died for Buganda, and that he had purchased the road to Buganda with his life.

After this the church continued to suffer greatly. Some of the finest converts were burnt or tortured to death in horrific ways. A member of the church council was unmercifully clubbed and thrown into the flames. Another had his limbs cut off one by one and roasted before his eyes. Thirty-two others were burnt on one huge pyre. About 200 perished in all. The *kabaka*, Mwanga, was the instigator of much of this trial and slaughter. In England voices were raised counselling despair and the abandonment of the mission, but the CMS courageously continued on its course.

A period of quiet succeeded this onslaught. Mwanga was plotting the destruction of all the leading Christians, but he was deposed. Religious liberty was proclaimed and there was a rush of Ganda to receive Christian instruction. But the pendulum swung again. The Muslims expelled the CMS members and other missionaries in a determined effort to win the country for Islam, and once more voices counselling surrender were raised in England.

Ironically, Mwanga was reinstated on the throne, and he promptly evicted the Muslims and declared religious freedom for the Christians. By the end of the century there were thousands of Christians in Buganda, with their own churches, clergy and teachers; an eloquent testimony to twenty-five years of epic endeavour.

Many other tales of witness and endurance could be told, but these give some idea of the cost in terms of human effort, suffering and death that were entailed in planting Christianity in areas previously untouched by Christianity.

Of course there were innumerable failings and shortcomings not only as part of the process of Western colonialism and commercial activity, but by Christians as they went about their tasks. Also, regrettably, Christianity and the work of the Church became inseparable in some people's thinking from some of the less desirable aspects of the expansion of empire and trade, including the seemingly insatiable desire for profit. This has led to criticisms such as the complaint of the former Kenyan leader Jomo Kenyatta. 'When the missionaries came to Africa', he declared, 'they had the Bible and we had the land. They said "Let us pray". We closed our eyes. When we opened them we had the Bible and they had the land.'[69] Many Westerners rightly sympathize with such sentiments, for they contain a measure of uncomfortable truth.

There is likewise some ground for accusations that missionary Christianity entailed a kind of cultural leprosy, and unfortunate manifestations of ignorant paternalism. There were undeniably many individual and collective examples of unacceptable and reprehensible attitudes and actions, and there was a holding on to power and authority, combined with a failure to educate and train indigenous Christian leaders, that was highly injurious to the healthy development and expansion of Christianity.

Individual Christians, missionary societies and churches as official bodies, all undoubtedly erred often and seriously in many ways. But this most emphatically does not mean that the whole enterprise was wrongheaded. Despite countless and most regrettable inadequacies, it is clear that Christianity brought many benefits above and beyond the core message of salvation that it enshrined. Not only, from the Christian point of view, were numberless lives transformed by genuine conversion experiences, but Christian, or Christian-inspired schools, colleges, hospitals, and a multitude of churches and agencies for the relief of all forms of social need, testify to the spin-off gains from the Christian presence. Few would deny that the gains far outweighed the losses.

South America

It is astonishing how rapidly the Spanish and Portuguese conquered and established Christianity in South America in the sixteenth century. In the course of a hundred years after the first voyage of Columbus in 1492, virtually the whole of that massive

land had been entered, and priests and friars accompanied virtually every expedition for exploration or conquest. Initially the
major part of the Christianizing was accomplished by
Franciscans and Dominicans, but later the Jesuits were prominent. Bishoprics were established with incredible alacrity. The
first was Caracas, then Lima (1541), Asuncion (1547), San
Salvador de Bahia (1552), the metropolitan see of the enormous
province covering Ecuador, Bolivia, Peru and Chile (1575), and
then Buenos Aires (1582).

Perhaps the main obstacle to effective evangelization by these
outsiders from the Western world was the harsh way so many of
the colonists treated the native peoples. It readily appeared to the
native inhabitants as a denial and contradiction of the gospel being
proclaimed, and a transparent example of 'do as I say, and not as I
do'. Unfair, such a judgement may have been, but it was equally
inevitable. When Pizarro, the conqueror of Peru, was urged by a
cleric to put a stop to the spoliation of the Indians and to ensure
that they received Christian instruction, he reputedly replied: 'I
have not come for any such reasons; I have come to take away from
them their gold.' And this was the spirit that energized and animated a considerable number of what after all were hard-headed
adventurers seeking fortune and prosperity in a strange land.

The progress in establishing the faith in an alien environment
was also hampered by the lack of any serious attempt to build up
an indigenous ordained ministry. In places, there was an abundance of European priests, and the ministry of priests to the people
was facilitated by the widespread practice of drawing the inhabitants of an area into Christian villages. The Jesuits carried this to its
height in Paraguay, but it was not confined to that country, or to that
order. Administratively this made sense, but its main failing was
the spirit in which it was done. There seems to have been an overarching concern to maintain European mastery, and to keep the
native people in a servile and subordinate position; to keep them as
docile children dependent on the Westerners. The Jesuits and other
orders and the Catholic priests did very little to develop a sense of
independence, or to train adults for self-government.

'The nemesis of this policy came when the Jesuits were expelled; the
Indians had not the necessary self-discipline and power of leadership

to maintain themselves in a hostile world. Everything crumbled, and by the end of the eighteenth century hardly anything was left. The jungle had claimed its own.'[70]

This parlous condition came about in spite of attempts by the Roman Catholic Church to build on the foundations it had laid in the sixteenth century. During the seventeenth and eighteenth centuries, the region was, in fact, the scene of its largest-scale missionary effort. To it more Catholic missionaries went than to all the rest of the world put together. It was the field to which the Catholic Reformation directed its major energies for the geographical expansion of the faith, and the Catholic Church continued to give it priority, and to pour human and other resources into it in exceptional profusion. 'As a result the majority of the population professed allegiance to the Roman Catholic Church.'[71] But the roots of individual faith, and of the Church institutionally, do not seem to have penetrated very deeply into the native soil. Regrettably, by 1800 the Church had slithered into an anaemic condition, and much of the faith of the people that persisted was somewhat superficial and nominal. In addition, substantial non-Christian minorities remained. They consisted mostly of Indians, and in general were to be found in jungles, in the upper reaches of rivers, in mountain fastnesses, and in other zones on the frontiers of white occupation.

The earliest Protestant efforts to exercise a Christian influence in the modern era were piecemeal and sporadic. They started when James Thomson went to Argentina as an agent of the British and Foreign Bible Society to promote the Lancastrian method of education. And he was very effective in doing so. Until 1821 he was based in Buenos Aires and elsewhere in the River Plate region. With assistance from Roman Catholics, he organized a Lancastrian Society, which could soon report the founding of about a hundred schools with approximately five thousand children. He enlisted enthusiastic support as he went on to Chile, Peru and Columbia. In addition, he promoted the circulation of the Scriptures in Peru, and in 1825 he inaugurated the National Bible Society of Columbia. He and other agents of the British and Foreign Bible Society undertook the translation of the Bible into some of the Peruvian and Mexican languages. In parallel with this, in the 1830s the American Bible Society transported Bibles to South America and Mexico, and in 1833 it sent its own agent to Chile.

There were many in the United States who took a great interest in the emergence of independent South American republics, and there were attempts to begin Protestant missions in them. As early as 1823 the American Board of Commissioners for Foreign Missions sent two young men, Theophilus Parvin and John C. Brigham, to Buenos Aires, with a commission to explore the South American scene. After extensive travels Brigham reported to the American Board that the time did not appear propitious for the founding of Protestant missions. Somewhat later, he did, however, arrange for the American Seaman's Friend Society to place chaplains in several South American ports. All such actions now appear to have been somewhat tentative, hesitant, small-scale and inadequate. There was nothing remotely like a bold, co-ordinated approach commensurate and appropriate in some way to the size and challenge of the task.

The age of modern, continuous, Protestant missionary activity, and the establishment of official Protestant churches emerged, in fact, out of the ashes of what appeared to be a calamitous and a disastrous failure. It is one of the classic tales of modern pioneer Christian missionary work, and it led to the founding of the South American Missionary Society.[72]

The new society probably had 'the most tragic birth in the history of modern missions'.[73] Allen Gardiner reached the rank of Commander in the British Navy. He experienced an evangelical conversion during one of his voyages, and, in 1834, at the age of forty, he left the navy in order to devote himself to missionary work. His first efforts were in Natal. Arriving there in 1835 he visualized the possibility of a chain of mission stations stretching up the whole of the east coast of Africa as far as Zanzibar and beyond. But he was 'stronger in imagination than in execution'.[74] He had ideas of a mission to New Guinea, but then turned his attention to South America.

Having failed to undertake a work in Paraguay and Bolivia he went in 1850 with six companions to Tierra del Fuego, the desolate archipelago that forms the southernmost point of South America, one of the bleakest and most tempestuous regions in the world.

The ship with their provisions failed to arrive; the natives would not feed them; the drifting ice broke their nets so that they could not fish; and during the severe winter on that inhospitable shore the whole party died of starvation. In his diary Gardiner had written: 'Poor and weak as we are, our boat is a very Bethel to our souls, for we feel and know that God is here. Asleep or awake, I am, beyond the power of expression, happy.'[75]

After seventeen years of hard and demanding missionary work, without having seen a single convert or any fruit from all that he did, Gardiner's death was to achieve what his passionate appeals in life had failed to accomplish. When the bodies were found the words in his diary echoed around the world, and the churches in England were stirred to take an interest in South America. A schooner named after Gardiner landed a party of missionaries. But the seemingly calamitous saga continued. In 1859 the mission was almost wiped out when eight of its workers were murdered.

It only became evident many years later that the efforts of Gardiner and the other pioneers had not been in vain. Before the mission began, Charles Darwin had described the inhabitants of the area as the most degraded beings in the world. In 1870 he wrote to the South American Missionary Society saying that 'the success of the Tierra del Fuego Mission is most wonderful, and charms me, as I always prophesied utter failure. It is a grand success. I shall feel proud if your committee think fit to elect me an honorary member of your society.'[76] And he subscribed to the work from that day until his death. In 1872 the first group of Tierra del Fuegans was baptized.

The new society established its headquarters on the Falkland Islands, which had been British territory since the late eighteenth century. Gradually it expanded its work widely among Indian peoples never reached by the Roman Catholic Church. In Southern Chile the society laboured among the Araucanian Indians; in the Paraguayan Chaco the mission concentrated on the violent Legua people; in Argentina the mission was primarily to the aboriginal peoples; and in Brazil it was again the tribal Indians to whom the missionaries were sent. In 1869 the Secretary of the Society, and at the time the superintendent of its missions, Waite Hocking Stirling, was consecrated Bishop of the

Falklands with jurisdiction for the Church of England over all of South America except British Guiana. Such was the magnitude of his task that his efforts were confined largely to English sailors and businessmen to be found in most ports, and little or no attempt was made to reach out to the non-British population.

The challenge of trying to serve the native peoples of the South American republics, and of spreading the faith to those as yet unreached resulted in the establishment of new missions. Some of these were British, but the USA made the most extensive efforts. The Christians of that young and rapidly growing country were aware of their affinities with South American countries and of their responsibility for their less Christianized neighbours. Both regions shared in republican forms of government, and the two territories were associated in inter-American and Pan-American conferences and later in the Pan-American Union. There were marked cultural differences to overcome, and many South Americans distrusted, feared or disliked their northern benefactors, but the achievements of both Protestants and Roman Catholics from the USA ultimately proved to be considerable, long lasting and generally appreciated.

Among the many Protestant undertakings those of the Anglicans, the Methodists, the Baptists, and especially the Southern Baptists of the USA, the Presbyterians and the Seventh Day Adventists were most notable. Although the outreach to some degree impinged on Roman Catholic spheres of operation, the supply of Catholic priests had become alarmingly depleted, so that for a large number of the inhabitants there was little opportunity for instruction in the tenets of the faith, and the Protestants were to a great extent filling gaps. In any case, it was widely acknowledged that the faith embraced in the past by many of the aboriginal peoples had been nominal and lacking in depth. In a great number of cases it was superficial in the extreme.

Despite all the efforts made, however, the nineteenth century was still a time of quite small things for the Protestants. Although Protestant work had been established in all the republics of South America, by the end of the century there were probably no more than 500,000 Protestants in the region, including those in Central America, Mexico and the main islands of the Caribbean.

Otherwise the scene remained one of unbroken Roman Catholicism. Even so, the phenomenal growth that came in the twentieth and twenty-first centuries, very largely in the form of Pentecostalism and the charismatic movement, which to a quite marked extent bridged the divide between Protestantism and Roman Catholicism, probably showed that all the evangelistic efforts of Christians in the previous century were not in vain. These two new related but not identical forces transformed Christianity, not only in South America, but in the non-Western world as a whole. They, more than anything else, account for the worldwide Christian spiritual explosions that took place in the century from the early 1900s to the present day. What had been sown in the often traumatic and excessively hazardous earlier period bore fruit, in some cases thirtyfold, in others sixtyfold, and in many a hundredfold.

3

The Changing Face of Worldwide Christianity in the Twentieth Century

I: The Western world

The origins and spread of Pentecostalism in the Western world

It is unquestionable that in the twentieth century and the early twenty-first century Pentecostalism[1] 'has made more dramatic and rapid advance than any other branch of the Christian Church'.[2] 'It is the largest single group within what has been described as the Third Force in Christendom',[3] alongside the already existing Catholic–Orthodox and pan-Protestant types of world Christianity.[4] Such has been the combined success of Pentecostalism and the subsequent neo-Pentecostalism, or charismatic movement, which started in the 1960s, that they jointly have been widely acknowledged as a 'third mighty arm of Christian outreach'.[5]

It may be reckoned by most historians as somewhat of an exaggeration to claim, as has been done, that this Pentecostal and charismatic movement is comparable in importance to the establishment of the original Apostolic Church or the sixteenth-century Protestant Reformation,[6] although an expansion from zero to about 500 million in a century represents a growth 'which is unique in church history not excluding the early centuries of the church'.[7] No movement that started at the beginning of one century and by the end of the same century accounted for one out of every four Christians worldwide[8] can be regarded as anything but exceptional. The mammoth importance of Pentecostalism and neo-Pentecostalism is undeniable. They have each separately been key elements in the as yet largely unsung revolution that has made Christianity into a world religion as never before, and taken together may have constituted the most significant and important factor in that astonishing development.

Modern Western Pentecostalism may claim New Year's Day 1901 as its birthday. On that date, during a religious service at the independent Bible School in Topeka, Kansas, and in response to prayer and the laying on of hands, a certain Agnes Ozman spoke in tongues. The event was of little moment in itself, but from that date the school's leader, the itinerant evangelist Charles Fox Parham, publicly declared what he had probably concluded earlier, that speaking in tongues would always be evidence of the experience of baptism with the Holy Spirit.

Of course there were precursors for this one event. Among these must be included such phenomena in early Methodism, and in the holiness movement, and previous experiences of glossolalia, as with W. Jethro Waltthall, who spoke in tongues in 1879, was later ejected from the Baptist denomination, and subsequently founded the Holiness Baptist Association. But from 1901 onwards can be traced a continuous flow of what started as a small rivulet, then became a stream, broadened into a river and finally became a river in full spate.

In 1906 a black preacher, William J. Seymour, a student of Parham's second Bible School, at Houston, Texas, began to hold services in an abandoned warehouse at 312 Azusa Street in Los Angeles. 'Soon there were reports of tongues-speaking and walls covered with canes and crutches of those who had been miraculously healed.'[9] For the next three years the events that took place in that nondescript building helped to usher in 'the fledgling Pentecostal movement that was slowly disentangling itself from the various turn-of-the-century popular evangelical subcultures that had shaped much of its spirituality and practice'.[10]

The impact of the Pentecostal signs, of speaking in tongues and of healing in particular, was considerable. Most Christians and most of the mainline denominations understood that such gifts of the Holy Spirit had ceased at the end of the first century. Here was tangible, observable, and soon well-attested evidence that this was not so, and that the long gap between the Apostolic Age and the present time, in which there had been little similar teaching and experience, had not nullified the need for and value of the gifts. But there was also the form of worship associated with these new beliefs and experiences. Here was an anomaly for the American religious scene. To the astonishment of many observers at the time, blacks, whites and Hispanics were to be found worshipping together in harmony and with an unforced sense of unity, oneness and equality. The priesthood of all believers seemed to be taken seriously and literally. Leadership responsibilities in the church were shared by all, irrespective of colour or class, and equally between men and women. No status differences were recognized as a result of ordination or any form of 'setting apart'. Role differences between clergy and laity disappeared, since all the members of the church believed that the endowment of spiritual power for ministry was available to all.

The flame that had been lit in Topeka and Azusa Street quickly spread throughout much of North America and Canada. The spiritual stirrings in Los Angeles were given prominent press coverage, and by this means news of what was happening spread even to Europe and Britain. There then came into play the quite extraordinary 'untiring transatlantic journeyings of that pre-jet age'.[11] There was a constant two-way traffic of Christians across the Atlantic. As one consequence of this interchange of people, news and views, and also as a result of the Welsh Revival of 1904–05, which became influential in the formative years of Pentecostalism in the United States, some Christians in Britain were prepared to receive and embrace Pentecostalism.[12]

A key figure in transmitting the fire across the Atlantic was the 'Apostle of Pentecost' to Europe, Thomas Ball Barratt, a Norwegian Methodist. He strove successfully as the main advocate of Pentecostalism in Norway, Finland and Sweden. A visit to England in 1907, at the invitation of Alexander Boddy, the vicar of All Saints, Sunderland, led many people in the north-east to seek the baptism of the Spirit. Boddy's church 'became as important a centre for Pentecostalism in England as Azusa St. in America, and it was this spiritual awakening in the north-east as much as any that led to the inception of the Pentecostal Movement in Britain'.[13] By means of personal proclamation, and as a result of the ministry of and through his church, Boddy became an energetic ambassador of Pentecostal teaching. He also organized conventions in Sunderland from 1908 to 1914, which 'must occupy the supreme place in importance' in the early life of the movement in the British Isles.[14]

By then Pentecostalism was rapidly assuming the shape, coherence, form and organizational structure of a named denomination, separate from the existing mainline churches. In Continental Europe its progress was especially noteworthy in Scandinavia, and more particularly Norway and Sweden where, remarkably, it soon became stronger than any other Protestant denomination. In the USA, a Holiness body, The Church of God in Christ, adopted Pentecostal teaching in 1907. It was to become the largest Black Pentecostal Church in the country, although it was soon to be outdone by the even bigger Assemblies of God, which was an affiliation of Pentecostal churches formed in 1914.

In Britain three main Pentecostal denominations emerged before 1925. In 1915, in Monaghan, Northern Ireland, the first Elim Evangelistic Band was formed during a visit from George Jeffreys. It later changed its name to The Elim Foursquare Gospel Alliance of the British Isles, a title retained until 1966, when it changed once more to the Elim Pentecostal Churches. The Assemblies of God in Great Britain and Ireland was formed in 1924 as a fellowship of several Pentecostal groups with the aim of preserving 'the testimony of the full Gospel, to strengthen the bonds of fellowship between like minded believers, and to engage in aggressive evangelism at home and abroad'. The main distinction between the Elim Movement and the Assemblies of God was that the former had a somewhat Presbyterian form of organization, whereas the latter can be said to have been more in the Independent or Congregational tradition, with an insistence on the autonomy of the local church. The Apostolic Church of Wales was founded in 1917 at Penygroes, and the group of supporters, who were mostly products of the 1904–05 Revival, formed the nucleus from which the Apostolic Church emerged.

All of these Pentecostal denominations regarded missionary activity as a sine qua non of the Church. From the start they saw themselves as in the tradition of great evangelists like George Whitefield, John Wesley, Charles Finney, Charles Haddon

Spurgeon, Dwight L. Moody and R.A. Torrey.[15] In 1909, before Pentecostalism had assumed any central formal denominational structure or organization, a Pentecostal Missionary Union had been formed and missionaries took the Pentecostal message to Africa, China, India and elsewhere. The importance of this will become evident as their staggering influence and growth in parts of Asia, in sub-Saharan Africa and in South America in the twentieth century, and especially in the latter part of those eventful hundred years, is traced in the next three chapters. In order to give a firm academic and theological foundation to these early efforts, two training schools, one for men started in 1909 and re-established in 1913, and the other for women which opened its doors in 1910, were set up in London.

In the course of the twentieth century, Pentecostalism ceased to be a separate island of Christianity, complete unto itself, and deliberately engaged in ecumenical activities. This evolution can best be demonstrated in the life and career of David du Plessis. He was a key figure in that phase of Pentecostalism at a time when it had put its pioneer days behind it, and was establishing itself as a force to be reckoned with among the older denominational traditions of Christendom. He was a Pentecostal minister in South Africa, who in 1942 became General-Secretary of the Apostolic Faith Mission of South Africa. By 1949, he was Secretary-General of the World Conference of Pentecostal Fellowships. He became increasingly drawn into ecumenical circles, and in 1954 he accepted an invitation from Dr Visser't Hooft, the then Secretary of the World Council of Churches, to attend the Second Assembly of the World Council at Evanston. 'That morning', he later said,

> something happened to me. After a few introductory words I suddenly felt a warm glow come over me. I knew this was the Holy Spirit taking over. But what was He doing to me? Instead of the harsh spirit of criticism and condemnation in my heart, I now felt such love and compassion for those ecclesiastical leaders that I would rather have died for them than pass sentence upon them.[16]

As a consequence of this very public engagement of Pentecostalism in the ecumenical movement, world Pentecostalism 'became a term with meaning and specificity'.[17] The new pentecostalism was most definitely being placed on the world religious map, and its size in the mid 1960s warranted this. By 1955 it was reported that there were thirty-six Pentecostal bodies with a combined membership of approximately 1,500,000, with a further twenty-three organizations not reporting membership statistics.[18]

Before the century came to and end, the Pentecostalism-charismatic movement had one last major surprise to spring. From January 1994 onwards, the Toronto Airport Christian Fellowship (TACF), a church located near the Pearson International Airport, became the centre for such a distinctive expression of Pentecostalism that it was dubbed 'the Toronto Blessing'. What took place at the TACF was headline catching because of the behaviour of those participating in the services. It has been described as like getting drunk without the hangover, and also as ecstasy without the need of drugs.

The TACF soon attracted multitudes of the curious and the seeking. Over 300,000 different people had attended the church by June 1995, and by 1997 on average it hosted 800 people per night.[19]

What is clear is that the influence of the TACF was felt powerfully in many lands and places, and it gave a new impetus and sense of significance to the Pentecostal–charismatic movement as it entered the twenty-first century.

The charismatic movement

The charismatic movement that appeared on the scene in the Western world in the 1960s differed from early Pentecostalism in certain fundamental and specific ways. In its foundation stage at least, Pentecostalism had been associated with lower socio-economic groups; it was relegated to the fringe of evangelical Christianity; and it was found solely in separate denominations. The new movement found a home in the historic, often predominantly affluent middle class, mainline churches and, after much initial tension, it was gradually, although by no means fully, accepted and even later welcomed, by other evangelicals. After quite a short time it was even a highly potent force within Roman Catholicism, and to a much lesser degree within the Orthodox

Church. What its success vividly revealed was a strong and fairly widespread interest in spiritual gifts, including glossolalia and physical healing, and concern for individual and corporate Christian renewal.

News of what was happening began to surface in 1960 when considerable publicity was given to remarkable happenings in the ministry of Dennis Bennett, an Episcopal rector in Van Nuys, California. His fashionable congregation was stunned when he recounted in a sermon that he had been filled with the Holy Spirit and had spoken in tongues. Then there was the Full Gospel Businessmen's Fellowship International. This had been founded in 1951, and by 1960 was actively engaged in bringing together people committed to evangelism in the context of charismatic renewal. News of these developments soon reached England.

The charismatic movement in Anglicanism and other Protestant denominations

Between 1962 and 1964 members of the Church of England became vaguely aware that something new and extraordinary was taking place in parishes like St Mark's, Gillingham, St Mark's, Cheltenham and St Paul's, Beckenham. There were reports of exuberant forms of worship and of speaking in tongues. In 1964 Michael Harper resigned as curate of All Souls, Langham Place, London and founded the Fountain Trust to help Christians in all denominations who had been 'baptized in the Spirit' to be taught more about the individual and corporate experience of renewal. Perhaps the Trust did more than any other body or person to keep the new expression of Pentecostalism within the bounds of the established Church.

The new movement continued to grow among evangelicals. Between 1964 and 1970 leaders such as John Collins, David Watson, David McInnes and Tom Walker became deeply involved in it. Visits by David du Plessis and some of the foremost American charismatic personalities, including David Bennett, Larry Christensen and David Wilkerson, gave encouragement to the charismatics. Books by some of the British charismatic leaders began to be published. Journals appeared, and parishes received new vitality and sense of purpose and direction as they 'overflowed with the distinctive marks of Pentecostalism'.[20] The first international conference under the auspices of the Fountain Trust was held at Guildford in 1971. At this much-publicized event Roman Catholics, traditional Protestants and members of other designated Protestant churches shared the same platform for the first time ever. It was a milestone. 'After Guildford it was easier to talk about Pentecostal renewal in Anglican circles'.[21]

A mere recital, like this, of some of the landmarks in the history of the charismatic movement in the Church of England is in certain respects somewhat flat, prosaic and pedestrian; it does not capture the essence of countless life-transforming experiences for individuals, groups and churches. Any cool, detached, description or analysis of the movement can perhaps be likened to 'digging up the potatoes to see if they are growing'.[22] Behind the outward events that marked its progress there was all the vigour of what has been assessed as 'perhaps the most important single post-war movement to cut across every denominational boundary'.[23]

But it was not all calm and plain sailing. As well as, and partly because of, its ability to produce renewal and empowerment, the charismatic movement was controversial and divisive. Some non-charismatics found its distinctive teaching about a 'second blessing', when the Holy Spirit was said to be received by believers in power, in a post-conversion experience, the apparent emphasis upon experience rather than the authority of the Bible and, what appeared to its detractors as the disorderly conduct of public worship, questionable, disturbing and even abhorrent. This was so for members of the mainline churches in general, and not least of all for countless fellow evangelicals. Nevertheless, after much amicable discussion, there was far greater mutual understanding and respect by the 1970s. The wounds were in the process of being healed.

One by-product of this new or renewed Christian teaching and practice was the creation of the House Church Movement. By 1979, there were several hundred such 'churches' with over 50,000 members. Most of these were a result of charismatics deserting the historic churches in order to meet together in the enjoyment of their newly discovered experience of the Holy Spirit and the accompanying new forms of worship.

By the end of the twentieth century the charismatic movement represented the largest group of evangelicals in England.[24] For all its weaknesses and excesses, and the disruption it caused, it had great and beneficial effects, not only among the evangelicals but upon the whole Church of England and most other churches. It was also a powerful force in mainland Europe, the USA, Canada, Australia and New Zealand. Wherever charismatic renewal occurred there was almost invariably a deepening of faith, fellowship and prayer, an enhanced evangelistic concern, growth in the number of communicants and greater giving to the Church at home and overseas. The movement introduced forms of praying, praising, singing and sharing that were novel to most Anglicans and many Nonconformists, as well as Roman Catholics and Orthodox believers. The worship was, and still is, distinguished by the use of choruses, bodily gestures and dance, ministries of healing and deliverance, gifts of tongues and the interpretation of tongues, prophecies and singing in the Spirit. The general 'loosening' of public worship throughout the churches and the surge in hymnology was to a degree inspired and informed by the charismatic movement. Liturgical revision in many Christian traditions also helped to ensure that charismatic worship, with its awareness of the liberty, power, joy and the pulsating effect of the Spirit of God, did not become totally detached from the official services of mainstream denominations.

In the meantime, in the USA, the charismatic movement made great strides within the main Protestant denominations. In the mid 1970s there was a steady stream of official church reactions. Only a minority of denominations clearly, explicitly and formally opposed the movement. One denomination after another adopted positions of cautious openness, neither rejecting charismatic renewal as unauthentic, nor welcoming it with enthusiasm. Most of them accepted the Pentecostal experience in principle and acknowledged the availability of the charismata, but rejected the Pentecostal theology of a second blessing subsequent to conversion and the necessity of glossolalia.

In the 1980s the charismatic movement received a boost as a result of the ministry of John Wimber. By his teaching, example and relaxed, winsome but astonishingly powerful personality he exercised an amazing influence. He asserted that 'the words of

Jesus must be validated by the works of Jesus'.[25] When the Spirit is at work he confirms the authenticity of the gospel message being proclaimed by signs and wonders, such as healing of the sick and the casting out of demons. In the Wimber jargon this was what constituted 'power evangelism'. His church in California called the Vineyard became the nucleus for a network of centres in the USA and Britain, with regional supervisors and a hierarchy of senior and junior pastors. By 1997 this so-called Vineyard Ministry International had a worldwide membership somewhere in the region of 50,000 spread across 550 independent churches.[26] So comprehensive and innovative was all this that it has been designated the 'third wave'. Here was a call to release the entire laity into a full participation in the ministry of the Holy Spirit and his gifts, not just the anointed few.

In England, Holy Trinity, Brompton, in London, became particularly influential after the blessing was first experienced there in May 1994. The resulting massive impact of its reinvigorated ministry was facilitated by its central location in London; by the congregation of 2,000 and more each Sunday, who joining in its distinctively charismatic worship and, most importantly, because it gave birth in 1992 to the Alpha Course. This speedily became a means of sharing with the wider church something of the benefit that Holy Trinity itself had experienced as a consequence of its own renewal. From the beginning, the course was intended for use in almost any situation, including private homes, church halls, places of work, prisons and schools. It consisted of a series of very high quality, well-produced videos, with discussion notes, presenting basic Christianity in a thoughtful and stimulating way. The popularity of the course, and the impact it has had on people's lives has been staggering. From the time it was launched, it went from strength to strength. In 1992 five courses were held. The following year there were 200, with a cumulative attendance of 4,600. By 1997 this had risen to 6,500 courses with a total attendance of 800,000, and by 2003 there were 27,340 courses worldwide, with an attendance of 6 million. Because of the size of the operation involved, its international coverage, the highly professional publicity, and its familiarity to literally tens of millions of people in all continents, both within and outside the churches, it became a symbol of vibrant contemporary Christianity.

In the latter part of the century a yet further new element in the life of the churches as a whole, and in the ministry of Pentecostals in particular, came onto the scene, sometimes with quite devastating effects, both good and bad. This was the 'electronic church' – the world of the television evangelists. Oral Roberts and others had paved the way, but in the dying years of the century this means of communication assumed a much higher profile. Within quite a short span of time television ministries became multimillion-dollar industries, and the evangelists, including those with Pentecostal affiliations, attracted enormous followings. There was concern, however, about their lack of accountability, and the Pentecostals, together with all other church members, were rocked by scandals surrounding Jim Bakker and Jimmy Swaggart in the late 1980s. Nonetheless, there is no doubt that many heard the Christian gospel through the programmes of these specialist evangelists and, despite the question mark that remains over the permanence of their impact and the depth of spiritual life that may have been imparted, television and radio were obviously channels for communication that Christians in general, and not least of all Pentecostals, could and did use in a most powerful and persuasive manner.

The Roman Catholic Church

The decision of the Second Vatican Council (1962–65) that the Catholic Church should become a full and active participant in the ecumenical movement facilitated the subsequent penetration of that Church by the charismatic movement. While some individual Roman Catholics were touched by Pentecostalism and were baptized in the Spirit before 1967, it is to that year that we can trace the origin of charismatic renewal as a fully fledged, recognizable movement within the Catholic Church. The formation of a prayer group among faculty members and students at Duquesne University, Pittsburgh, in February 1967, which soon manifested gifts and fruit of the Spirit that are characteristic of Pentecostalism, sparked off what was to many observers an unexpected, surprising, and to some Catholics an alarming, movement that gained in pace with every year that passed.

Within a few months of the Duquesne group having been established, other similar college groups were started on other campuses. Annual conferences for Catholic charismatics were instituted, and the numbers they attracted are a measure of the growth of charismatic renewal among American Catholics. More than 450 attended the third gathering in 1969, and they came from most of the states and Canada; the number soared to more than 1,300 in the following year; and the fifth drew almost 5,000 people from as far away as Korea and Australia. In excess of 11,000 attended the 1972 conference from sixteen countries, and the number mounted to over 20,000 in 1973. After 1976, with the attendance reaching 30,000, it was decided to hold regional conferences, and to limit the central gathering to 12,000. As a result the numbers centrally dropped to about 8,000, but regional conferences reported ever more participants, with one such assembly at Atlantic City in 1977 attracting more than 37,000. In the United States these large gatherings were but the most impressive public face of the charismatic renewal movement within the Roman Catholic Church. Its typical corporate activity was the prayer group, of which there were reckoned to be over 6,000 by 1986.

A landmark in the advance of the renewal movement in the Roman Catholic Church was its appearance in 1971 at two of the most important Catholic universities in Europe: the American College in the University of Louvain in Belgium, and in Rome where some Americans and a Canadian began an English-speaking prayer group at the Pontifical Gregorian University. The latter had a particularly powerful symbolic importance, and it was significant that the group consisted largely of priests and sisters on study leave from all parts of the world. After their studies or other assignments, they carried the conviction of the need for renewal to wherever they returned or were sent on mission.

The USA

Regardless of what has been said about the centrality of Pentecostalism and the charismatic movement in helping to bring fullness of life and vitality to churches in the Western world, they have not totally monopolized the stage since the

1960s. The story of vibrant Christianity in the USA, Britain, Continental Europe, Australia, New Zealand and Canada during the post-1960 period is much more comprehensive than that.

Even though it is difficult to speak in general terms about such a vast country as the USA, with its many distinctive regions and a multiplicity of types and forms of the Christian faith, some sweeping comments are justified. First, it can be said that Christianity in some areas is still very prominent as a personal faith for a large proportion of the population, and as a determinant of social mores. This is most pronounced in the southern states. According to one computation in the early 1980s they contained about 45 per cent of America's evangelicals, and were 'more dominated by Bible-believing religion than any other part of the Western Hemisphere'.[27] The American 'Bible Belt' was a product of the eighteenth-century and subsequent revivals, camp meetings and intense evangelism, and finally the Pentecostal and charismatic movements.

It is a feature of the religion of the most fervent Christians of this and other regions of the country that it is not kept in a watertight compartment, but colours political and social attitudes. This was seen with prohibition, which was legally enacted in 1919 and lasted until 1933. Its imposition was but one demonstration of 'the power of a conservative, rigorist Protestant ethic in the American social system. And the country is prone to revert to this Christian-inspired cultural inheritance 'in times of stress'. Such a fall-back stance is in keeping with 'the tradition of the Great Awakenings that have occurred on that continent ever since the Puritans arrived, intent on founding the New Jerusalem'.[28]

Indeed, it is this aspect of American evangelicalism that has caught and held the attention of the media, especially since 1976, when the American people elected a Southern Baptist, Jimmy Carter, as president. 'By the late 1960s a social dimension was unblushingly restored to evangelical faith.'[29] The mobilization of conservative Protestants as a unitary, co-ordinated, body was most formally and forcefully achieved in the new Christian right movement under the inspiration and leadership of Jerry Falwell, which can be dated from the late 1970s and which peaked with the Regan Administration.[30] Of the various politico-religious organizations that surfaced in the late 1970s as part of this new emphasis by evangelicals, two of the most influential were Christian Voice and Religious Roundtable,[31] but Jerry Falwell's Moral Majority received the greatest publicity. All of these pressure groups were formed with the ultimate objective of influencing political decisions in order to re-Christianize America. Such a purpose was articulated most explicitly, and given political expression most obviously, in 1988 when the ebullient television evangelist Pat Robertson campaigned to win the Republican Party nomination for the presidency of the United States. He was viewed 'by both his supporters and his detractors as a standard-bearer for the new Christian right'.[32]

The story of the new Christian right makes it clear that American conservative Protestants in the last three decades of the twentieth century were sufficiently numerous that when organized they could bring their concerns into the public arena for discussion, but 'too weak to significantly change the socio-moral climate of America'.[33] They claimed 'credit for Reagan's success in both 1980 and 1984 and attributed the overwhelming victory of the Republican Party to the fact that they had for the first time been able to bring to the polls two to four million Evangelicals who had never taken much interest in politics',[34] and the voting statistics give support to this assertion.

This great leap forward in the successful electoral canvassing of the evangelicals is evidence of the growing influence of those who put their trust in 're-Christianization from above'. It was to an extent, a departure from the more typical approach the evangelicals had previously adopted of 'Christianization from below'. But it was only a phase in the socio-political approach of the evangelicals, and even during that time it is probably more accurate to say that 'Christianization from above' although it was to the fore, only supplemented 'Christianization from below', which remained the most characteristic, most familiar and most favoured policy.

Despite hindrances to political influence, evangelicals in the USA undoubtedly had a great impact on national life in the last quarter of the twentieth century, largely as a consequence of their sheer weight of numbers. A Gallup poll in 1976 revealed that 34 per cent of Americans were prepared to identify themselves as 'born again', and this figure had risen to 40 per cent by 1984. It is clear that evangelicalism was a considerable political and social, as well as religious, force in the land.

No other country in the Western world could either match this pervasive Christian influence, or compare with the USA in the spectacular growth of conservative Protestantism. It had actually begun in the 1950s, when the mainline churches as a whole experienced boom years. This was largely a result of the vigorous proselytizing of the members of various denominations. In the years of general expansion campaigns such as that of the Southern Baptists called 'A Million More in Fifty-Four', which resulted, for instance, in 29,000 baptisms in the denomination within the state of Alabama alone, were typical.[35] The Southern Baptists and others sustained this evangelistic thrust at a time when the mainline churches as a whole were finding it difficult to tread water, or were actually losing members. Other denominations also benefited from such continuous enlargement. For example, the Assemblies of God increased their membership by 71 per cent between 1973 and 1983. In the process of expansion some congregations grew massively, as with the independent First Baptist Church at Hammond, Indiana, which in 1982 claimed 67,267 members.[36] 'It was the United States that could boast the big battalions.'[37]

But the big battalions were not restricted to the Baptists and other such long- and well-established churches. The heavy artillery was, paradoxically, often to be found in the small sects and denominations. 'In 1967, for the first time in two centuries, this turning away from the mainline churches was reflected in the statistics. Ten of the largest denominations were affected, including Lutherans, Episcopalians, Methodists, Presbyterians and Congregationalists. In 1970 it was the turn of the Catholic Church in the United States to announce the first drop in membership since the beginning of the century.'[38] The sociologist Bryan Wilson has argued that the future for Christianity in the West probably lies with the sects and the more radically Protestant denominations,[39] and the sequence of events in America as well as other parts of the Western world in the last half of the twentieth century and the early years of the twenty-first century gives some support to his view. Another sociologist who observed this phenomenon, commented that 'while the mainline churches have tried to support the political and economic claims of our society's minorities and outcasts, it is the sectarian groups that have had most success in attracting new members from these very sectors of society.'[40]

Although the new breed of evangelicals did not focus entirely on personal salvation and the afterlife, they did not describe their social concern in the same terms as the liberal Protestants. The characteristic stance of evangelicals was to concentrate on the individual, and to move out from such personalized religion to more communal matters. They had a vision of a new society based on new communities of true believers.

> As the Evangelicals saw it, the way to check and deal with social ills was to unmask sin and redeem it. Their practice was to seek the cause of evil in separation from God; if this separation could be overcome, the evil would be banished and health restored. Sin was located in the individual, and it was individual salvation that would effect the salvation of the group.[41]

Another prominent aspect of American evangelicalism in the last three decades of the twentieth century was the improved access to education, and the consequent greater literacy and sophistication of the evangelicals.[42] There was a 47 per cent increase in the number of evangelical primary and secondary schools, and a 95 per cent increase in student enrolment between 1971 and 1978. By 1985 there were 18,000 such schools and colleges, with a total of 2.5 million children. This leap forward is made the more remarkable in view of the drop in the birth rate during the 1970s, which produced an overall 13.6 per cent fall in the number of American schoolchildren. The same story is repeated in higher education, where there was a jump from 7 per cent to 23 per cent from 1960 to the 1970s in the proportion of evangelicals who went to university. No other religious group experienced such a huge change in its relation to higher education at that time.[43]

Among the tertiary institutions was the Oral Roberts University, which by the late 1980s had 4,170 students, a teaching staff of 375, and a library of a million volumes. Perhaps the most politically impressive and dynamic of the new evangelical institutions, however, was the one established by Jerry Falwell in 1971 at Lynchburg, Virginia, first under the name of Liberty Baptist

College and then Liberty University. The complex was the key to understanding Falwell's 'plan for expanding his parachurch empire and his influence on American history'. His university sent out thousands of graduates who had 'been trained to think about the world in a manner highly consistent with his own religious beliefs and socio-economic philosophy'.[44] Evangelicalism in the USA was becoming big business.

Billy Graham

During the latter part of the twentieth century evangelicalism was unquestionably the mainstream of American Christianity; and the undoubted, if not totally unquestioned, figurehead and leader of the largest and most influential Christian bloc in the most powerful nation on earth was a former North Carolina farm boy, Billy Graham.[45] He was a product and part of Western Christianity, but he was at the same time a towering figure in world Christianity. In an astonishing way he was able to bridge cultural, ideological and national barriers, both as an evangelist and as a Christian strategist. In the course of a long career stretching from the 1930s to the early part of the twenty-first century, William Franklin Graham, Jr, went to most places in the world and was seen personally by more people than any other human who ever lived.[46] He preached in person to in excess of 70 million people in more than seventy countries, and to hundreds of millions through the medium of radio, television and film. He was quite possibly the most admired religious personality of the twentieth century, and he became by far the single most dominant figure in the burgeoning worldwide evangelical movement.

In keeping with his lifelong determination 'to do some great thing for God', he organized the mammoth international Lausanne, Amsterdam and other conferences which were crucial in cementing a coalition of worldwide evangelicals. And through these and other means he did untold good in the enhancement of religious freedom in Eastern Europe, China and elsewhere. He has additionally been a most effective ambassador for his particular brand of Christianity, helping as much as any Christian leader to promote understanding between evangelicals and those of other Christian traditions.

One of Graham's great contributions to a well-balanced evangelicalism was the encouragement he gave to evangelicals to engage in social action, and not to see any conflict between such involvement and evangelism. In this, as with other aspects of his ministry, he was in tune with the rapidly evolving thought and practice of evangelicalism throughout the world.

In Britain, for example, for twenty years after the Second World War, evangelicals in general did not engage in much serious thinking on social and ethical issues, nor did they become involved very extensively or intensively in the relief of human need. Then, as a result of two Church of England evangelical congresses, at Keele in 1967 and Nottingham in 1977, things began to change. They represented a watershed for British evangelicalism. In very broad terms, the evangelicals explicitly recognized the need to present the gospel to every citizen of the country in such a way that they could understand it, and the need for steps to be taken to help make the country 'more just, more righteous, more responsibly free, more compassionate, and so more pleasing to God'.[47] The resolutions agreed at both the congresses were not empty, vacuous and meaningless. They were taken seriously. From 1977 onwards, considerable progress was made in implementing them, and in turning them into concrete action. The Evangelical Race Relations Group was established, the Shaftesbury Project was started, the Nationwide Festival of Light was launched, *Third Way* was inaugurated, and the Grove booklets on ethics began to be published. In addition, evangelicals expressed their concern for human rights, and for such matters as government aid to developing countries. They founded and gave continuous and extremely generous financial support to The Evangelical Alliance Relief Fund (TEAR Fund), which developed into one of the main agencies for the relief of human need worldwide, and to other efficiently organized, effective bodies dedicated to social action of some sort.

The new, balanced evangelical agenda arising out of the two congresses did not mean that evangelism was neglected, or put on the back burner. It was in fact pursued with a new vigour and resolve. This was exemplified by the 1973 'Call to the North', the initiative of the evangelical Archbishop of York, Donald Coggan, with its emphasis on local action, and by the 1975 'Call to the Nation' issued jointly by Coggan, by then Archbishop of Canterbury, and the new Archbishop of York, the evangelical, Stuart Blanch.

It was while all this was going on that Billy Graham came into the picture in a new and powerful way. The Lausanne Congress on World Evangelization, held in July 1974, came about because of his vision and determination. It was a pivotal event. Half of those present, including 50 per cent of the planning committee and of the speakers, were from the less developed countries. The Congress put such nations on the map of evangelical Christianity in a new way. It was another acknowledgement that the Western domination of the Church was over. It gave a fresh impetus to what has just been described as taking place in Britain, and to similar moves in other countries. It once more encouraged Christians to link social responsibility with evangelism.[48] It articulated new insights into the nature of mission in the modern world, which was seen as including both evangelism and socio-political action, but with priority given to evangelism.[49] This was particularly appropriate in view of the worldwide consideration being given to liberation theology.

Continental European Catholicism

Battered and bruised as it was by the First World War, the Roman Catholic Church made extensive and commendable efforts to relieve the suffering entailed as a consequence of that and other wars of the period. It was much to its credit that in the decades that followed 1914 its worldwide missions were greatly enlarged. Despite the huge disruption of much of normal life brought about by wars, most of the Catholic missionaries were from Western Europe. The Catholic 'home base' remained secure and supportive of the Church, and in large areas of Europe the devotion of the residents to the faith of their fathers remained firm. These strongholds were mainly in a wide belt from Flanders to Venice, with other centres in Brittany, La Vende, parts of the south-west and south of France, and in north-western Spain.

'On the whole, the Roman Catholic Church moved into the mid-twentieth century stronger than in 1914. It had experienced grave losses in its traditional heartland, Western and especially Latin Europe. But even there it had a loyal body of faithful numbering millions whose devotion and spiritual life were at a higher level than a generation earlier and very much higher than in 1815.'[50] Unfortunately, from the Roman Catholic point of view, although anti-clericalism was not as rampant and vicious as in the nineteenth century, a large proportion of the masses in Europe were becoming more lukewarm towards the Roman Catholic Church, and were drifting away from what for generations had been a central institution in the life of almost every member of many European societies. The loyal core continued to be vigorous in their faith, but they had by then probably become a minority.

'In Catholic Europe, the last quarter of the twentieth century opened on a paradox: never before, it seemed, had society been so massively secularized and de-Christianized, and yet re-Christianization movements were springing up everywhere.'[51] In addition, Vatican II had opened up new possibilities of Catholic openness and adaptation in the face of a rapidly changing world. The pontificate of John Paul II, starting in 1978, with its reaffirmation of Catholic values and identity, and the charismatic movement, also helped to give a new lease of life to the Catholic Church.

Continental Europe – general

Because of the unique diversity of political, economic, social and religious situations within such a comparatively small geographical area, generalizations are made especially difficult and hazardous. This is especially true when it comes to pronouncements about the state of religion overall in the continent. Nevertheless, a few tentative comments are justified.

First, we 'should treat with caution statements about the secularisation process – in particular unqualified ones – either within Europe or anywhere else. For the data are complex, contradic-tory even, and clear-cut conclusions become increasingly difficult.'[52]

The European Values Study of 1981, designed by the European Values Systems Study Group (EVSSG), and later updated for 1990, provides material for some observations. The Study revealed an overall 29 per cent European average for church attendance at least once a week for 1990, with 10 per cent attending once a month, 8 per cent just at Chrismas, Easter and other such festivals, 5 per cent once a year, and 40 per cent never, except, presumably, for weddings and baptisms. This masks a wide variation from 81 per cent for the once-a-week category for Ireland, 40 per cent for Italy, 33 per cent each for Portugal and Spain, 23 per cent for Belgium, and 10 per cent for France. For the Netherlands and Germany, where there were substantial Catholic and Protestant communities, the average was 20 per cent for attendance at least once a week, with 13 per cent attending once a month or more, 16 per cent at Christmas, Easter and other such festivals, 7 per cent once a year, and 44 per cent never. For the Lutheran countries, Denmark, Iceland, Norway and Sweden, the only data available showed a once a month or more average figure of 10 per cent. As an aside, it can be noted that for Great Britain the figures were 13 per cent for at least once a week, 10 per cent for once a month, 12 per cent for Christmas, Easter and other special festivals, 8 per cent once a year and 56 per cent never; and that for Northern Ireland, the respective figures were 49 per cent, 18 per cent, 6 per cent, 7 per cent, and 18 per cent.

As a result of these findings, it seems reasonable 'to suggest that West Europeans remain, by and large, unchurched populations rather than simply secular'.[53] This does not mean that the people living in European countries were losing all traces of religious belief. Other data obtained from the EVSSG Study shows that this is far from the case. Taking the overall average responses of those questioned, 70 per cent professed a belief in God, 61 per cent belief in a soul, 43 per cent in life after death, 41 per cent in the existence of heaven, 25 per cent in the existence of the devil, 23 per cent in the existence of hell, 57 per cent in the concept of sin, and 53 per cent in the resurrection of the dead. Taking these statistics in conjunction with those on church attendance, it is clear that declining congregations did not inevitably mean that populations were ceasing to hold religious beliefs. 'For a marked falling-off in religious attendance (especially in the Protestant North)' did not result 'in a parallel abdication of religious belief.'

Europeans as a whole had up to that time 'not abandoned many of their deep-seated religious aspirations'.[54]

As a postscript to these comments on European Christianity, it is well to appreciate that some developments did not readily lend themselves to neat statistical measurement and analysis. Two examples will make the point: Lourdes and Taizé. Lourdes lost nothing of its attraction as a place of pilgrimage and healing. The Taizé Community, located in the rural village of that name between Lyons and Dijon, was a twentieth-century creation, having been started by Roger Schutz in 1940 with the idea of introducing some form of traditional monasticism into Protestantism, but being open to others than the brotherhood actually living on the site.[55] The first seven brothers took vows in 1947, and a written rule was introduced in 1952, which included celibacy, communal property, and obedience to the community. The members were drawn from various Protestant confessions. The public worship was designed to restore to Protestantism some elements of the pre-Reformation liturgical treasures of the Church, and to this end the Taizé brotherhood gladly learned from the Liturgical Movement in the Roman Catholic Church. 'Their rule stressed interior silence, meditation on the beatitudes, and prayer three times a day, accenting intercession for the church and the world.'[56] But worship was balanced by practical 'secular' work, so that the gospel was related to and spoke to men and women living in the world. Thus, each brother was to do what he believed was his Christian vocation. 'All the brothers engaged in some form of labour – several with their hands in Taizé, one as a physician for the village and its neighbourhood, a few as artists (in pottery and painting), others as pastors of parishes, one in youth work in Africa, and still others in a centre in the Ruhr where they did heavy industrial work.'[57]

The Taizé Community was ecumenical in composition and in its ideals. In 1959 it consisted of forty members from Calvinist and Lutheran backgrounds in France, Switzerland, the Netherlands and Germany. Close contact was maintained with the World Council of Churches and the World Student Christian Federation, and at the same time fellowship was sought with Roman Catholics. Among its many concerns, the Community strove to promote the renewal and unity of the Church, and to bring the gospel of reconciliation and peace to troubled situations. Brothers were living in such disturbed and tense regions as the Ivory Coast, among the Muslims in Algeria, and with the manual working classes in Marseilles.

Both Taizé and Lourdes have exercised an inspirational teaching and practical role, which has been out of all proportion to their size, and even disproportionately great in view of the albeit considerable numbers of people visiting them. They have stood for, and been symbolic of, the often little-expressed, quiet and largely hidden yearnings, sensitivities and hopes of countless people, many of whom have had meagre or no involvement with organized Christianity and would not be included in any religious membership figures. In this respect, they have remained a small but significant reminder of the shortcomings of statistics as a sole measure of spiritual health, and a corrective to any overdependence on church membership and attendance figures as an absolute gauge of corporate spirituality.

Australia, New Zealand and Canada

Australia, New Zealand and Canada can be reckoned as part of the 'Western' world, and for over two centuries all three have been massively influenced by the Christian faith emanating mainly from Britain and Continental Europe. The result is that each has been thoroughly imbued with Christian values and a sense of the veracity of Christian belief. Nevertheless, they have differed considerably in the extent to which they exhibited vibrant Christian life in the latter part of the twentieth century.

Ever since 1788 Christianity has been an integral part of Australia's history, political and social life, and identity.[58] By the late twentieth century 70 per cent of the population still claimed Christian affiliation, of whom 27 per cent were Roman Catholic and 22 per cent Anglican. Between 15 per cent and 20 per cent of the total population of the country attended Christian worship, a higher figure than for Continental Europe and the United Kingdom, but lower than for the USA. Nonetheless, apart from Pentecostalism, which was on the increase, active church membership seems to have been in decline over at least the last half century, rapidly among urban Roman Catholics, and less sensationally among Protestants.

For the whole of the twentieth century the country had a reputation as an important bastion of evangelical Christianity.[59] It has been computed that evangelicals account for about one in every six of Australians; a figure that may have been fairly constant throughout the last two centuries. It has to be acknowledged that all these statistics are guidelines only. They are admittedly rather arbitrary and are based on many assumptions that do not bear close examination. They include not only those professing conversion who have become formal members of a church, but also those affiliated with evangelical congregations. Nonetheless, however inaccurate they may be, they are broadly indicative of the situation. There is a general consensus that the church in the country, and in particular pockets, most notably Sydney, was and has remained strong and energetic. 'The evangelical proportion of the population may be about the same as New Zealand, two-thirds that of the United States, and double that of the United Kingdom.'[60]

This is not to say that Australia has experienced the same sort of revivals or awakenings so typical of eighteenth- and nineteenth-century America. It has not, and there has never been the kind of burned-over district as experienced in western New York State during the Second Great Awakening, nor any equivalent of the American frontier camp meetings. Even during the period from about 1870 to 1910, when the country underwent its greatest religious excitement, there was not the same basic transformation as in America. The nation had to wait until the Billy Graham crusades of 1959 to experience a national spiritual awakening. Then, during the three and a half months of the Southern Cross Crusade, which included New Zealand as well as Australia, almost three and a quarter million people attended the meetings. This represented a quarter of the entire population of the two countries, and of those attending 150,000 responded publicly; the figure being 130,000 for Australia alone, or 1.24 per cent of the population.

The Roman Catholic Church was especially prominent and vigorous in Canada. In 1901 it claimed 41.7 per cent of the population, and by 1951 this had risen to 44.7, of which 66.7 per cent were

French. A measure of the Catholic vitality was their active engagement in missionary work. In proportion to its numerical strength,
the Canadian Roman Catholic Church sent far more missionaries
to other lands than did the Catholic Church in the United States.
Because of its predominance in French-speaking areas, and in
places where French culture was dominant, and the close control it
exercised over individuals and communities in the parishes of
such areas, notably in Quebec, the Roman Catholic Church did
much to shape the morals, the religious practices and convictions,
the social structure and conventions, and the cultural outlook of a
large proportion of the population. Except for some small communities, and for certain minorities, the impact of Protestantism,
while it was diffused, was not as pronounced as that of Roman
Catholicism.

The Canadian Protestant scene was in fact strangely mixed and
somewhat enigmatic. On the one hand, it was the venue for the
'Toronto Blessing' and other Pentecostal or neo-Pentecostal 'out-
pourings of the Spirit'. But on the other hand there were signs of
Protestant inertia. Thus, as but one indication of this, in proportion to their numbers Canadian Protestants sent far fewer missionaries abroad than did the Roman Catholics. Their total was
between 25 and 35 per cent of that of the Catholics, despite the
fact that they were more numerous than the Catholics.

Of great concern to both Roman Catholics and Protestants was
the apparent growing strength of atheism and agnosticism.
According to the census data for 1981, 7.2 per cent of the Canadian
population defined themselves as having 'no religion'. In absolute
terms this was 1,752,380 Canadians out of a total population of
24,083,495.[61] That meant that the number of people in the country
who placed themselves in this category was greater than the combined total of all Canadian Baptists and Presbyterians. In British
Columbia, in the same year, the 'no religion' group was the largest
'religious' group in the province at 20.5 per cent of the population.[62] In the last decade of the twentieth century it appears that
the circumstances of the time, rather than strengthening
Christianity, were 'transforming thousands of nominal Canadian
Christians into nonbelievers'.[63] It is the kind of situation that will
be addressed in the final chapter of this book.

4

The Changing Face of Worldwide Christianity in the Twentieth Century

II: South America

Introduction

The global expansion of Christianity during the final century of the second millennium of the Christian era eclipsed anything that had previously taken place within the span of any single century. The increase in the number of believers worldwide, and the enhanced impact the faith had on political, economic and social, as well as religious affairs, in great tracts of the world was without precedence. The importance of the faith in the general life of Western nations, and as a determinant of social beliefs, attitudes and mores in such countries may have declined as the process of secularization took effect, but this was more than counterbalanced by the huge developments in many areas of Asia, sub-Saharan Africa and South America, and the sustained Christian vitality in the USA. And even in the zones where secularization was most pronounced, there were many signs of life and vigour, as shown in the previous chapter. In any case, the validity of the criteria applied by sociologists and others to measure spiritual decline and to gauge spiritual health is most questionable, as will be suggested and explained in chapter 7.

In order to tease out the complex situation in the non-Western world it is best, and most revealing, to take a regional approach, describing and commenting on the various pieces of the jigsaw, and a start will be made with South America.

The Roman Catholic Church

In the first half of the twentieth century the Roman Catholic Church was still enjoying the fruits of 400 years of almost total Christian monopoly in much of the continent, with little competition from Protestants of any type, and there was at least a veneer of Catholicism in many of the countries. 'The overwhelming majority of the population would, if questioned, protest that they were Catholics. Much of a cultural Roman Catholicism persisted. Thousands who had little other contact with the Church cherished a warm devotion to the Virgin Mary and prized locally popular saints.'[1] Yet it has been calculated that in the twentieth century, by the most generous estimate, only about 10 per cent of the supposedly Roman Catholic adherents were practising their faith.[2]

As in the nineteenth century, there were far too few Catholic clergy to give the religious instruction and pastoral care that was required in order to sustain a large body of believers. Despite the fact that by the mid 1940s possibly a third of the Roman Catholics of the world resided in South America, the Church was woefully short of priests for the continent. It seems that two-thirds of the Brazilians were without organized parish life, that more than half the people of Peru were almost bereft of clergy, and that comparable conditions prevailed in several other countries.[3]

Nonetheless, despite the handicap of an inadequate supply of priests, fresh Roman Catholic movements surfaced that invigorated the Church and gave it a new lease of life. Eucharistic congresses were late in appearing, but after the First World War they became increasingly prominent and gradually started to kindle the devotion of hundreds of thousands of people to the central rite of the Catholic Church. A high point in this movement was the 1934 International Eucharistic Congress convened in Buenos Aires, the first in South America that drew delegates from most of the Roman Catholic world. It was an immensely stimulating and uplifting occasion for the faithful, whose eyes were raised above the often grim circumstances of their own part of the world, and were opened to the vastness and the variety of the worldwide Roman Catholic Church.[4]

Other gatherings gave signs of renewed Catholic activity in the early twentieth century. These included a Marian congress, a congress of missions, a congress of Catholic youth and a congress of young Catholic workers. The company of Saint Paul, for the purpose of combating atheism and Communism through lay and clerical co-operation, was introduced into Argentina in 1927 and then spread to other nations.[5] There were limited and scattered, but sometimes strikingly successful missions to the pagan or semi-pagan Indians,[6] and Catholic labour unions were formed in order to offset the then most powerful influence of Communism.[7]

In the mid century these various separate initiatives were more effectively harnessed to a co-operative and unified Catholic thrust forward. New moves were made as a result of the establishment of the Latin American Bishops Conference, known by the initials CELAM. With its headquarters at Bogota, it tried to encourage inter-American co-operation.[8] It used the press, television, the radio, films and educational institutions in an attempt to reach the whole of Latin America with a programme of Catholic Action.[9] 'It resolved to promote an intensive campaign to spur the establishment of the Confraternity of Christian doctrine in all the 17,000 parishes in Latin America to improve the teaching personnel, materials, and projects for combating ignorance of the faith among professing Roman Catholics.'[10] In a variety of other ways CELAM built up a comprehensive list of achievements, including work for the improvement of the condition of the 30 million tribal Indians, and assistance to about 4,000 charitable institutions that cared for approximately a million members of the population. It additionally helped in the production of new translations of the Bible from original South American languages into Spanish.

The Liturgical Movement was not especially active, but nevertheless there were indications that some clergy and laity received inspiration and spiritual renewal through it.

In spite of all these signs of alertness to contemporary challenges, South American Roman Catholicism not only failed to produce enough clergy to supply its own need for pastoral care, but it played almost no part in spreading the faith. Every bit of research carried out by the Roman Catholic Church, and every report produced, put its finger on the same central weakness – the shortage of priests and the unsatisfactory level of education and spiritual life among those already serving in the continent.

John Considine quantified this in the title of his notable 1946 book, *Call for Forty Thousand*. The tragedy was that still, as in the nineteenth century and the first half of the twentieth century, after having had more than four centuries of Christian pre-eminence, there was such a sadly insufficient local supply of quality priests. It was somewhat unfortunate that by 1960, 37 per cent of the entire Roman Catholic clergy were foreigners. In Venezuela they were over 60 per cent, and in Guatemala almost 85 per cent. The importation of foreigners simply enabled the Church to stave off the real issue of reshaping its own ministry in order to incorporate a large and ever increasing number of local priests.

This meant that the Catholic Church was not able to pastor its own flock adequately, and that it made little effort to reach the non-Christian elements of the population. It made some valiant, but very belated, attempts to recruit and train indigenous clergy in the post-Second World War period, but by the late 1950s it was estimated that the numbers were 9 per cent short of what was required just to fill the annual vacancies. The Church in the continent relied on a flow of both ordained and lay missionaries from abroad.

The health of the Roman Catholic Church varied considerably from one country to another. A Roman Catholic survey declared that in 1955 'the Church was strong in Mexico, Costa Rica, Colombia, and Argentina; that it was standing still in Guatemala, Nicaragua, El Salvador, Cuba, Chile, Venezuela, Peru, and Uruguay, and that it was dying in Bolivia, Paraguay, rural Brazil, Panama, and the Dominican Republic, Honduras, and Haiti.'[11]

In such a situation, it was gratifying that after the Second World War there was a large influx of priests and other personnel, both under the impulse of the Vatican and largely because of the willing response from the United States. By 1960 more than a third of all the US Roman Catholic priests, brothers, sisters and lay workers serving overseas were located in South America, Central America and the West Indies, making Latin America the largest single mission field for the States. But this reliance upon the 'big brother' to the North was not very desirable, or promising for the future development of independent, self-governing and self-funding churches in each of the nations of the southern continent.

The second half of the century was in some ways paradoxical for the Roman Catholic Church in South America. During that period, it underwent a numerical decline, but at the same time it demonstrated greater in-depth commitment to mission, with one especially bold attempt to reach out to the poorer members of society. Brazil, the largest and most populous of South American countries, and the one that had for centuries been a flagship of Roman Catholicism, will serve as an example of these parallel trends.

The reduction in membership numbers in Brazil was quite alarming for the Catholic Church. In 1980, according to Brazil's census, Catholics accounted for 88.45 per cent of the population, whereas just ten years later a Gallup poll revealed a drop in this figure to 76.2 per cent.[12] Catholicism was still a diffused force that helped to shape the worldview of the people, but its hold on the minds and affection of many was waning. It continued as an ideological influence that was almost as much cultural, social, and even political and economic, as it was specifically religious, but its force in this respect was not as great as it had once been.

The true weakness of Roman Catholicism as a church per se, is revealed in data on attendance at Mass and on surveys of people who intended to follow religious careers. The figures are somewhat enigmatical. By 1989 only about 20 to 26 per cent of the Catholic population attended Mass weekly. Brazil additionally had a low and declining ratio of priests to inhabitants. In 1970 there was one priest for every 7,151 inhabitants, but this had shrunk to one for every 9,367 by 1980, and to every 10,136 in 1991. The influence of the Roman Catholic Church over the people during the last few decades of the twentieth century, in shorthand known as romanization, persisted, chiefly through Catholic schools and religious movements, which were most notably effective among urban middle-class people, but it was apparently diminishing, and the impact was slight on the lives of the poorest people, who remained on the periphery or completely outside any form of Catholic life or influence.

But remedial action was at last taken in an effort to counter these adverse trends. This took the form of one of the most dramatic and headline-grabbing Catholic developments of the century. The absence of the poor from the Church started to become a particular concern among some clergy and romanized laity in the 1960s, and out of this concern there emerged a distinctively progressive Catholic Church. 'Catholic activism received a kind of official charter in 1968, during the conference of the Latin American bishops at Medellin, Colombia, an event that has been described as a virtual declaration of independence. Borrowing extensively from Marxist terminology, the assembled bishops condemned neo-colonialism, exploitation, and the institution-alised violence of capitalist society, and demanded fundamental economic and social reforms.'[13]

Some members of the South American and Central American Catholic Church became deeply involved in both the theory and practice of liberation theology. It was a movement that reached new heights of hope and expectation in the 1970s, especially when the Sandinista revolution triumphed in Nicaragua in 1979. A number of former priests served in the ensuing radical govern-ment. Priests and bishops spoke out courageously against abuses of human rights, and some suffered death as a consequence. Finally, as a climax to such outspoken protests, the assassination of Archbishop Oscar Romero created a genuinely popular martyr, and Central America for a time became the focus for the Christian Left worldwide.

But these were the high water marks for the Roman Catholic radicals of South America. The new pope in 1978 was the con-servative John Paul II, whose experiences in Poland had given him a deep distrust of Marxism in any form. 'Through the 1980s, the new regime in the Vatican systematically silenced radical theologians, like Brazil's Leonardo Boff. Meanwhile, revolution-ary hopes in Central America were dashed by' the 'U.S. inter-vention and the collapse of the Soviet bloc. The Sandinista regime lost power in 1990.'[14] The status and standing of politi-cally, economically and theologically radical Catholicism was clearly being undermined. Even so, one particular invention of that era remained, and it continued to be a central platform in the life of the Catholic Church in the region for many years to come: the Christian Base Community (*Comunidade Eclesial de Base*, or CEB). It was the most important and lasting instrument devised by the radical wing of the Roman Catholic Church in its golden age.

Base communities were small groups of poor lay Catholics who met for prayer and reflection. The number of them is a matter of debate with estimates varying from 8,000 to 10,000 or even less, up to ten times that number. It appears that only a small minority of Catholics were engaged in the groups, but they have attracted much attention and inspired a great deal of theological and sociological literature as well as much comment in the media. This is mainly because they advocated a revolutionary democratization within the Catholic Church and in society as a whole. 'Because of their socialist political proposals and their support of the Sandinistas in the Nicaraguan Revolution, CEBs in Latin America acquired a reputation that was almost mythical.'[15]

Nonetheless, most of the base communities had more modest aims. In practice, they proved to be not as politically aware or radical as many expected. There were manifold types of group in terms of their purposes and in what they attempted.[16] Some took leading roles in organizing the urban and rural poor, especially around land conflicts and land invasions. Some offered support to the poor in a region where the welfare state, political parties and trade unions were weak and gave little help to low-income sectors of the population. Some were valuable in giving special encouragement to the disadvantaged members of society to endure their poverty. In many cases the local base community was mainly engaged in Bible study and prayer; and in fact most of the discussion in the groups concerned matters of personal belief and morality rather than political questions. In a few instances, as in the Brazilian coastal city of Vitoria, the groups were integrated into the parochial and diocesan decision-making structures, whereas in other places the members and leaders looked upon the group as the nucleus of a 'People's Church' that would ultimately displace and dispense with the hierarchy's authority itself.

With all their shortcomings, a well-informed commentator in 1992 could affirm that the base church communities were 'one of the most important factors in the shaping of a new vision of the Church.' They played 'a key part in realizing the goal of creating a Church of the poor'.[17] They were channels for expressing the preferential love of the Church for the common people, and they also helped to discover the evangelizing potential of the poor.

They were effective locally as a result of their concentration on giving a role in the Church to some of the downtrodden members of society. Their strength lay in their members being always from the same area, always having the open Bible as their frame of reference and source of authority, always cherishing and enjoying regular participatory worship as a means of corporate exaltation and fellowship, and always finding individual and collective strength in their commitment to each other and to the group to which they belonged. They provided an energizing link between faith and 'secular' life.

In the 1970s and early 1980s the base communities found a new status and sense of purpose despite the decline of radical Roman Catholicism in general, and even its virtual demise in some areas. They became increasingly involved in pastoral decisions, and it became more common for members of local groups to assume the role and function of active neighbourhood associations, trade unions, political parties and other popular movements. It was a period of rapid growth for the communities, and it was at that time that the Inter-Ecclesial Meetings began, as a means of encouraging greater contact between the communities, and of welding them together in a self-conscious entity.

And it was well for the Roman Catholic Church in South America in the last few decades of the twentieth century that it had the Christian base communities to bolster its impact and enhance its relevance, for there is no doubt that its hegemony and that of traditional folk Catholicism in Brazil and other South American countries was deeply shaken and eroded as the second millennium drew to a close. The Catholic Church suffered from the corrosive effects of 'modernity', and changes in the international Roman Catholic Church may inadvertently have contributed to the undermining of traditional Catholicism in Brazil, as elsewhere on the continent.

> The innovations brought by Vatican II have had a direct impact on Brazilian religion. The *aggiornamento* of the Catholic church proposed by the Vatican II, as a process of rationalization and modernization of the Catholic church, included a lessening of emphasis on rituals, saints, and magic practices. These changes intensified the marginalization of the Brazilian poor in the Brazilian Catholic

Church, and Afro-Brazilian spiritism and Pentecostalism became attractive alternatives for Catholics who missed the enchantment and magic in their religion.[18]

In the midst of this strange mix, the Catholic charismatic movement appeared on the scene as a reinvigorating force. Some scholars are of the opinion that it came just in time, as it superseded the Christian base communities when they were losing much of their sense of purpose and empowerment. Whether this is so or not, the new injection of life was of paramount importance. It was not on anything like the scale of evangelical Protestantism and the burgeoning Pentecostal movement, but it was a significant new ingredient in Catholic life, and it remained so. It embraced perhaps up to four or five million Catholics, and was seen, as it still is, as a means of enjoying the benefits of Pentecostalism while retaining the advantages of abiding in the Roman Catholic tradition. 'It offers communal warmth and solidarity, it brings the family together in strong affective bonds, and it establishes a moral density. Catholic charismatics are often aligned with the renewals proposed by Vatican 2', and they 'offer a focus of loyalty which can supplement or even supplant a fideistic reliance on the magisterium. Though they are, on occasion, influenced by liberation theology, and by liberal attitudes to moral issues, they also revive some aspects of traditional doctrine. They resemble Protestant Pentecostals in their avoidance of head-on political confrontations.'[19]

In summary, it is well to appreciate that despite all its shortcomings and failures, of which it is only too conscious, the South American Roman Catholic Church remains a power in the land. The blossoming of Protestantism, and more especially Pentecostalism, is about to be considered, and it will be seen as one of the wonders of twentieth-century global Christianity. Nonetheless, Roman Catholicism was first on the scene, and 500 years of effort paid dividends. 'After decades of Protestant growth in Latin America, the Roman Catholic Church is still overwhelmingly the largest single religious presence on that continent, and the great majority of people still define their religious life in Catholic terms. If 50 million Latin Americans are Protestant (a fair estimate), then 420 million are not: most are, at least nominally, Catholic.'[20]

Protestantism goes from strength to strength

'When David Stoll placed a summary of his findings on Latin American Protestantism before the readers of the *Christian Century*, many religiously interested people in North America became aware for the first time of the massive transformation occurring in Latin America.'[21] The year was 1990, and changes had been taking place for some time, but consciousness of them had not yet percolated through to other parts of the world. What he presented was indeed astounding, and it set in motion a new academic and general interest in that region of the world. In recent years 'evangelicals have', he wrote, 'doubled their share of the population in Chile, Paraguay, Venezuela, Panama and Haiti; tripled their share in Argentina, Nicaragua and the Dominican Republic; quadrupled in Brazil and Puert Rico, quintupled in El Salvador, Costa Rica, Peru and Bolivia; and sextupled in Guatemala, Honduras, Ecuador and Colombia.'[22] News of what had been taking place had been made known before,[23] but this particular pronouncement, given greater substance by Stoll's book, *Is Latin America Turning Protestant?*, published in the same year, proved to be especially newsworthy, perhaps in part because the author called himself an unbeliever and had no promotional interest at heart.

The evangelicals arrived at this point of astounding growth as a result of much labour and dedicated service over many years. The few, and in many cases what seemed to be pathetically insufficient and insignificant, seeds sown in the nineteenth century by Protestants produced undreamt-of fruit in the twentieth century. 'The advance of evangelical Protestantism over the whole of Latin America from Mexico to the Argentine began in small stirrings in the mid nineteenth century, which sharply accelerated in the 1930s and reached hurricane force in the 1960s.'[24]

At the time of the First World War, Latin American Protestants were a tiny minority of the population, mostly in enclaves of British, German or North American citizens. The missionaries were mainly Baptists and Presbyterians directed from North America. But from as early as the second decade of the century there was the beginning of what was to prove a prolonged and spectacular growth. Some of this was due to immigration but most of it was by conversions, mainly it must be said of nominal Roman Catholics. By 1940 the religious map was evidently being redrawn, albeit to start with in a not particularly startling and evident way. Even so, the membership of the Protestant churches had grown to about a million, most of whom were Latins. 'At the same time their buildings remained small and at least in some countries the believers came for the most part from the marginal and the poor. Brazil was something of an exception in having a staid Protestant middle class; and in countries like Argentina and Chile the effects of social mobility, particularly among pastors, had taken Protestants into the lower middle class.'[25]

Protestantism in the first half of the twentieth century was being changed in a number of ways, although not as yet as dramatically as it was in the latter part of the century. There was the multiplication of denominations, and the more direct missionary involvement of North American missionaries, especially from the Bible Belt. There was also the establishment of Councils of Churches, as in Mexico and Puerto Rico in the 1920s, in Brazil and Argentina in the 1930s, Peru, Chile and Ecuador in the 1940s, and in Colombia and Guatemala in the 1950s. The first Latin American Evangelical Conference was held in Buenos Aires in 1949.

By the 1950s the expansion, and the widening of the social mix of church membership were becoming somewhat more sensational. The statistics available are admittedly imperfect, but those that are obtainable show 1,193,715 Protestant communicants in 1952, but 1,840,762, or an increase of over 50 per cent, just five years later, in 1957. For the total Protestant Christian constituency the respective figures are 2,866,000 and 4,534,000, which represents a still larger percentage growth. The real totals were unquestionably greater.[26] There was a pronounced advance in every country, and the estimates in Table 4.1 show that this growth continued into the following decades.

In the period up to the 1950s there were also attempts to evangelize those native South Americans beyond the confines of 'civilization'. These were tentative forays, and they were piecemeal, uncoordinated and on a small scale, but they did take place. As early as the second decade of the century, Pentecostals undertook evangelistic work in the region near the mouth of the Amazon

**Table 4.1 Evangelicals as a percentage of the total population
in South American countries for 1960 and 1985**

Country	Evangelical percentage of total population 1960	1985	Growth factor from 1960 to 1985 (in number of times)
Argentina	1.63	4.69	2.9
Bolivia	1.27	6.51	5.1
Brazil	4.40	15.95	3.6
Chile	11.71	21.57	1.8
Colombia	0.39	2.43	6.2
Costa Rica	1.30	6.48	5.0
Cuba	2.41	2.11	0.9
Dominican Republic	1.73	5.17	3.0
Ecuador	0.48	2.75	5.7
El Salvador	2.45	12.78	5.2
Guatemala	2.81	18.92	6.7
Haiti	6.09	14.18	2.3
Honduras	1.51	8.75	5.8
Mexico	2.21	3.08	1.4
Nicaragua	2.26	6.32	2.8
Panama	4.40	9.72	2.2
Paraguay	1.05	2.47	2.4
Peru	0.63	2.98	4.7
Puerto Rico	5.87	20.85	3.6
Uruguay	1.19	1.91	1.6
Venezuela	0.82	1.95	2.4[27]

*Note: The membership totals for each denomination were multiplied by
a factor, generally between two and three of the figures received depend-
ing on the social composition of the group, to account for children, neophytes, and other unbaptized persons participating in church life.
'Evangelical' refers to theologically conservative Protestants, not all
Protestants.*

*

and won a group of zealous converts. Other Pentecostal missionaries spread the Christian faith along the coast, and a large number of Brazilians extended the work into the interior.

In 1919 the Inland South American Missionary Union began work among the Brazilian Indians. Two decades later the name was changed to the South American Indian Mission, but the same spirit prevailed as pioneers penetrated the jungle to minister to the indigenous population. Undaunted by perilous journeys in hostile country, long periods of separation from spouse and family, with frequent exposure to pestilence and disease, and with a serious lack of food and medical care, these intrepid Christians stuck to their task. Despite the death in 1930 of two of their number, killed by the Nhambiquara Indians, and various setbacks, the mission continued with its outreach to the Indian tribes of eastern Bolivia, central Brazil, northern Colombia and eastern Peru.

The same resolve, determination and dedication was to be found among the members of the Unevangelized Fields Mission, founded in 1931, the Baptist Mid-Missions, which began work in the early 1930s, the New Tribes Mission, which commenced work in Brazil in 1946, and the Missionary Aviation Fellowship, which inaugurated its Brazilian air service in 1956. Other missions in Brazil included the Mennonite Brethren Church of North America (1946), the Free Methodists (1946), the Independent Board for Presbyterian Foreign Missions (1948), the Brazil Christian Mission (1948), the Inter-American Missionary Society (1950), the Wycliffe Bible Translators (1956), the Worldwide Evangelization Crusade (1957), the West Indies Mission (1957) and the Church of the Nazarene (1958).[28]

In the 1960s the Roman Catholic Church itself spoke of 1,000 people a day leaving its membership in order to join one or other of the evangelical bodies. And it was said that the number of evangelical Christians in the continent was not less than 7 million, with possibly twice that number if those seriously interested in what the evangelicals proclaimed are included.

Since 1960 the average annual rate of Protestant growth in South America has been about 6 per cent, so that today Protestants make up around a tenth of the whole population. Brazil stands out as the front-runner, with nearly half the total number of Latin American Protestant communicants, and it offers a set of figures that help to bring into sharper relief the picture of Protestant growth in the twentieth century. According to the data available from official sources, which make a distinction between Protestants in general and Pentecostals in particular only from 1980 onwards, the Protestant expansion in this the largest and most populous of the countries of Latin America has taken place throughout the century, but with an upward curve in the graph in the later years. It should be noted that the figures stated are well below those in table 4.1, but this is probably because they are for members only, and do not include a multiplier to allow for children, neophytes and other unbaptized persons participating in church life. The trend is still made very clear in both sets of figures. The percentages of Protestants (including Pentecostals) are as follows: 1900, 1.07; 1940, 2.61; 1950, 3.35; 1960, 4.02; 1980, 6.62 (Pentecostals 3.30); 1991, 8.56 (Pentecostals 5.57). The annual rate of growth for the last period was 7 per cent. In absolute figures, 12,567,992 Protestants were enumerated in 1991, of which 8,179,708 were Pentecostals.[29]

One remarkable feature of the Protestant scene in the mid-century period was the high number of nationals who were engaged in some form of paid Christian work. Incomplete figures of missionaries for 1957 include about 2,300 ordained men, approximately 1,100 laymen, and in the order of 2,800 women, giving a total of about 6,400 foreigners. To set against these, there were around 2,400 ordained men, 7,000 laymen, and approximately 1,400 women, making a total of 10,800, who were native South Americans. The number of such nationals both absolutely and in proportion to overseas workers has increased substantially between then and now. It has been an impressive move forward towards an indigenous church, and a sure sign that Protestantism was becoming firmly rooted in local cultures and societies.[30] 'Existing data indicate quite clearly that the groups that have experienced the largest, most impressive growth are those that have received the least assistance from the North American sending agencies.'[31] Most of the evangelical work in South America in the twentieth century only depended to a small extent on foreign missionary societies, church aid, or overseas budgets. As early as 1969 the *Latin American Church Growth* study attributed two-thirds of the total communicant evangelical membership in the region to the efforts of indigenous groups.[32]

Indeed, throughout the twentieth century there was almost invariably a stress on self-sufficiency, and the need for the local, indigenous, church to be the dominant factor in the evangelization of its immediate region, and of the continent as a whole. The quest by South Americans for control over their own destiny, with particular emphasis on the need to be free of dependence on North American patronage, is well encapsulated in the sardonic lament, 'Poor Mexico, so far from God and so close to the United States.' Increasingly, the churches generally, and the evangelicals more specifically, saw themselves as initiators in the spiritual reconstruction of their own nations, with minimal reliance on foreign help. This did not preclude a most impressive international assistance within South America itself. 'Brazilian missionaries, for example, have long been at work in Uruguay, Paraguay, and Bolivia in substantial numbers, and Puerto Rican evangelists are found virtually everywhere in Latin America.'[33] Some South American evangelicals have gone as far as suggesting, not altogether with a glint of delight, ironically, or with their tongues in their cheeks, that perhaps they should help their North American counterparts to evangelize the United States.

The independent spirit of the evangelical Christians in the mid-twentieth-century period, is clearly demonstrated by their self-identification. As one well-informed commentator at the time remarked: 'They do not like to be called Protestants, rightly claiming that differences of opinion in Europe in the sixteenth century are no concern of theirs. They live, as they understand it, in a rediscovery of the original Evangel; hence the name by which they prefer to be known, *Evangelicos*.'[34]

The evangelicals have not only shown highly impressive increases in numbers. Quantity has been matched by quality. There is ample evidence that the evangelicals in general were, and have remained 'spiritually alert, theologically sound, and morally vigorous'. They 'have often paid a high personal price for their faith and are enthusiastic and committed'. They 'tend to be self-renewing because of the form of their organization. Members are required to participate actively in a variety of demanding responsibilities.'[35] They were and still are imbued with a sense of their own obligation to be evangelists. It was an every member onus to make the faith known to others. There were constant energetic and imaginative efforts to reach out to the non-believers in society. Lay leaders for much of the twentieth century were often encouraged to establish their own congregations. This resulted in a multiplication of churches and cells, which were typically small but structurally strong.

In fact, most if not all these evangelical groups seem to have been effective to the extent that they communicated the gospel in the idiom of the people. They appear to have done this in most cases not just by the proclamation of the 'good news' to the outsiders, but by the role they fulfilled in the communities in which they were located. The evangelical churches established themselves in their communities, not only as lively Christian fellowships, and as centres of evangelism, but as 'a means of stabilizing existence for large numbers of Latin Americans who' were 'caught in various stages of transition from a traditional to a modern world'.[36]

The denominational distribution of these Protestants around the middle of the twentieth century is revealing and a pointer to later astounding developments. The Lutherans, Reformed churches and Seventh Day Adventists were to the fore, but the Pentecostals were already more prominent. And, what is more, it was the Pentecostals who from the beginning penetrated the lower socio-economic strata of society. Before the spread of Pentecostalism, it seems that only the Baptist Church had been able to gain members among low-income groups, and there were thus great sections of the population in all the countries that were unevangelized. Other churches than the Baptists had won few converts, and most of their rather small number of members were overwhelmingly from the middle classes.

The Pentecostals in South America originated in Brazil. Shortly after the turn of the century, two Swedish laymen, Gunnar Vingren and Daniel Berg, were expelled from their small Baptist church in Belem for speaking in tongues. They moved to Rio de Janeiro, where they established Brazil's first Pentecostal congregation, which was the nucleus of the Christian Congregation, *Congregacao Crista*, founded 1910, and which affiliated in 1911 with the newly organized Assembly of God, *Assembleia de Deus*. The latter grew with considerable rapidity, and in some years at an astonishing rate, as from 1942 to 1947, when membership went up from 1,700 to 3,529. By the end of the century it probably had between 11 and 15 million Brazilian members. It was to become the most important of all Pentecostal churches in Brazil and probably throughout the world. But there were several hundred Pentecostal groupings in the country in addition to the *Assembleia de Deus*. As with other churches in other countries, these were local, almost entirely home-grown. The 'founding experiences of Latin American and North American Pentecostalism were occurring more or less simultaneously in a number of countries. Latin American Pentecostalism, then, is not simply another foreign invasion of religious imperialism; it must not be studied as a derivative of something else or dependent on outside explanation. Latin American Pentecostals developed their character with virtually no North American influence.'[37] The North American birth of Pentecostalism did not directly lead on by personal contact to the Latin American movement. 'Missionary presence at the inception of Latin American Pentecostalism was infinitesimal. And to a great extent this has remained so. Not only leadership but by far the majority of the financial support of "classical" Pentecostals comes from Latin Americans.'[38] The predominantly indigenous nature of Latin American Pentecostalism from its inception and ever since may well go a long way towards explaining its staggering achievement.

New churches emerged in what has been called a second wave of Pentecostalism in Brazil in the 1950s and 1960s. The greatest expansion was experienced by the Foursquare Gospel Church (*Igreja do Evangelho Quadrangular*) from 1951; Brazil for Christ (*A Igreja Evangelica Pentecostal O Brasil para Cristo*), from 1955, and the first church to have been founded by a Brazilian; and God is Love (*A Igreja Pentecostal Deus e Amor*) from 1962. It is important to note that the first two of these pre-date the renewal linked with Dennis Bennett in California in 1960. It is a serious twisting of historical fact to claim that the second wave of Pentecostalism, not only in South America, but globally, was inaugurated in the United States. It was the same, for instance, with Africa, where there was 'renewal among black Anglicans in South Africa in the 1940s, usually ignored because preserved in oral history',[39] and because of the American publicity given to the phenomenon in their own country.

Some scholars identify a third wave that began at the end of the 1970s and corresponded with the development of televangelism.

The foremost of the churches associated with that injection of new life was the Universal Church of the Kingdom of God (*Igreja Universal do Reino de Deus*), founded in 1977, and 'made up more than the other Churches of recent converts'.[40] Since 1990, its growth seems to have been exceptional, even for the Pentecostals. Before the end of the century it appears that its number of places of worship went up from 500 to 3,000, and its membership apparently soared from 500,000 to 3.5 million, with places of worship in sixty-five countries, mostly in Latin America and Southern and Western Africa, as well as the United States.[41] The churches of this third wave made full use of television as a means of successful proselytizing. As a result of these latter two waves, the expansion of Pentecostalism was stupendous and seemingly inexorable in the second half of the century.

Even by 1957 it formed between a third and a half of the Protestants of Brazil and the large majority of the Protestants of Chile; and it was to be found in several other countries of Latin America. As elsewhere, and at other times, the Pentecostals stressed the need for conversion and baptism in the Spirit, had a profound belief in the inspiration and inerrancy of the Bible, appreciated warm, largely unstructured, and often quite emotional worship, and insisted on high standards of honesty, frugality, industry, cleanliness and freedom from sexual irregularities.

In the last quarter of the twentieth century the greatest shift in the character of Latin American Protestantism was the accelerating way the balance of numerical power 'passed unequivocally from the older denominations to the conservative evangelicals and, above all, to the Pentecostals. The older denominations were themselves quite conservative theologically, but they were fairly sedate in style. The newer denominations' were, 'if anything, more conservative and for the most part they' were 'charismatic, rather after the manner of John Wimber's "Vineyard Christian Fellowship".'[42] In the Rio de Janeiro area in the 1990s, of the fifty-two largest Pentecostal denominations, thirty-seven were of local origin. Their successes were striking. A research centre affiliated with the World Council of Churches revealed in 1992 that in the previous three years no less than 700 new Pentecostal churches had been opened in Rio. According to a recent estimate, one new church per workday was opened in the early 1990s;[43] and another puts this figure as high as approximately forty every week in the opening years of the twenty-first century.[44]

In Central America there was a swing to Pentecostalism that was as dramatic as in South America. In that region the Pentecostals accounted for only 2.3 per cent of the Protestants in 1936, but by the 1960s this had risen to over a third, and in the 1980s to well over half.

The multiplication of Pentecostals also had notable political repercussions. Pentecostalism 'emerged as a distinctive force in mass politics across Latin America, and has destabilized long-familiar social arrangements. Protestant and Pentecostal voting blocs have emerged in several nations, with the churches serving as efficient electoral machines and propaganda outlets.'[45] In 1986, and largely arising out of a *Newsweek* report and the subsequent comments in newspapers, a large number and wide range of people became aware that Protestants, especially Pentecostals, were entering party politics in Latin America, especially in Guatemala, El Salvador, Colombia, Peru and Brazil. 'Political activity brought Pentecostals a notoriety that they had until then escaped.' Up to that time they had largely been ignored. 'Now journalists, the general public, and other churches found themselves faced with mysterious groups with sufficient numbers to have strong national influence.'[46]

Just as significantly, the faith of the Pentecostals often led to substantial local and even national social service involvement, which itself could, but by no means always did, have political implications. The Pentecostals were among the most vocal in decrying and protesting peacefully about polluted drinking water, dangerous buses and roads, unstable and insecure tenure of house plots and the absence of electricity. Indignation was quite often turned into action to improve educational facilities, to provide assistance for the needy, or to help with some form of rehabilitation. Most of these activities were small-scale and local, but some were extensive. In El Salvador, there was the Liceo Cristiano, a Pentecostal school system that was started in the early 1970s, and expanded to include thirty-four campuses and over 24,000 students. It was affiliated to the international Program Integral Educational de las Asambleas de Dios, which

itself had affiliated schools throughout Latin America and provided schooling and many social services for 125,000 students. It
was the largest private, non-Roman Catholic network of educational facilities in the region. The majority of its schools were
located in the most economically distressed areas, and the majority of them provided meals, uniforms, and medical and dental
assistance if required.[47]

But all was not light and unalloyed purity and progress in the
evangelical, and more especially Pentecostal, camps. One most
unfortunate and regrettable aspect of this incredibly impressive
expansion of indigenous, self-governing Pentecostalism, both in
South America and elsewhere, was the frequency of schism. The
story is repeated time and time again with monotonous and
painful regularity. Fragmentation was a disastrous by-product of
a completely free market in competing versions of evangelical
Christianity. 'Of course, most of the "market"' was 'served by
about a dozen major organizations, in particular the Assemblies
of God, but the number of alternatives on offer' went 'into hundreds.'[48] Repeated inability to avoid schism was most regrettable.
Nowhere was 'the ambiguity of the Pentecostal-charismatic phenomenon more evident than in the issue of unity and division.
The glory' was 'manifested in the powerful reconciling and uni-
tive thrust of baptism in the Spirit, while shame' attached 'to the
pettiness of the quarrels and the scandals of constant division'.[49]

The breath-taking growth of Pentecostalism was matched by
only one other religious tradition in the late twentieth century:
forms of spiritism such as the Africa-based Umbanda religion.
Indeed, this distinctive religious tradition, which had much in
common with Pentecostalism, may have grown at an even
greater rate than Pentecostalism. It certainly held its own in the
battle for the hearts, minds and souls of Brazilians, and to an
extent of South Americans as a whole.

At the end of the twentieth century, the mass appeal of
Pentecostalism was still very much to the poor and marginalized
members of the community in all the countries of South America.
But it had greatly extended its reach. It had attracted many of the
middle classes. Whether this was the result of economic, demographic and social changes that had produced widespread
anomie, with Pentecostal churches supplying their members

with a new, compensating, sense of coherence and a strict set of rules to live by, as well as a life-transforming spiritual experience as a counter to other losses in their lives; whether the Pentecostal lifestyle meant that members had gained good reputations, which had helped them to promotion and a new social status; or whether it was a consequence of a mixture of these factors, the enhanced social standing of Pentecostals was seemingly undeniable.

This was made extremely obvious and public by the large and often somewhat plush auditoriums and places of worship that were constructed. The Jotabeche Cathedral in Santiago had seating for 18,000 people and the Temple of Brasil para Cristo took even more. Some of the structures were multipurpose community churches, with amenities, air-conditioning and other kinds of expensive appointments of a size and quality to compare with any that were to be found in any North American city. And they were not rarities. They could be found all the way from Mexico City to Lima and to Rio.

The modern South American Pentecostals, like their North American brothers and sisters, increasingly made full use of modern means of communication, and especially television, radio, cassette and film. At the local level they frequently and avidly seized opportunities to utilize modern technology, and particularly local radio, for evangelism and pastoral work. When it came to more large-scale enterprises, however, their willingness, and often eagerness, to avail themselves of the opportunities provided by the most recent technology was facilitated by the wealth, expertise and generous support of their fellow believers in the United States. Indeed, this was the sphere of activity that demonstrated most clearly the remaining influence, and in some cases control, of the United States. Vast resources were required for the extensive use of television, as they also were for large-scale evangelistic campaigns using arenas holding 100,000 people or more, and United States Christians often stepped in to supply much-needed assistance.

The widening of the social base of South American Pentecostalism also had some significant knock-on effects. One of the most notable of these was the tendency for the Pentecostal believers to be politically conservative. Although in its earlier phases Latin American Pentecostalism had been closely linked to some revolutionary political movements, in the latter part of the twentieth century it was far more typically associated with the status quo.

This was seen, for example, in the general late twentieth-century hostility of evangelicals as a whole, and Pentecostals in particular, to liberation theology. Not only did Pentecostals over-all start to react against politically radical interpretations of the Bible, and especially the Old Testament, and to oppose the refor-mulation of the doctrine of the just war concept to encompass rev-olutionary violence, they also began to regard liberation theology as a major rival in providing a theological and practical approach to the poor, dispossessed and deprived members of society. In this, however, they may have been mistaken. The status and effec-tiveness of liberation theology as a competitor was probably more apparent than real. To whatever degree it may have offered an option for the poor, and to whatever extent it may have been embraced as a philosophy and theology by hundreds of thou-sands of the poor themselves, it largely remained a concept and theory eloquently formulated by radical intellectuals in the quiet and retreat of their studies and ivory towers, but with minimal repercussions in the actual social and economic situations of indi-viduals and communities. As one contemporary sociologist and historian observed at the time: 'However idealistic and decently concerned and shocked the leaders of "liberationism" may be, they are not usually "of the People". Liberation theology has a decided middle class and radical intellectual accent alien to the localized needs of "the poor".' It has 'spokesmen – yes, spokes*men* – who are part of the international circuit of theological lecturers'. The 'language of liberationism can easily remain remote. Beyond all that, it promises to pull poor people struggling mainly for sur-vival into much larger and bloodier struggles of which they have often had more than enough.'[50]

In contrast, despite the fact that several of the larger Pentecostal denominations, after many years of ceaseless prose-lytization, had won a considerable number of middle-class con-verts, the bulk of the Pentecostal believers continued to reside on the margins of society. In research carried out at the ISER (*Instituto Superior de Estudos da Religiao*) in Rio de Janeiro in 1988, it was discovered 'that the proportion of evangelicals living on the impoverished west side of the city' was 'three times greater than on the affluent south side, famous for its chic districts of Leblon, Ipanema, and Copacabana'. In fact, the more prosperous part of that city had 'one of the lowest ratios of crente [believers] temples in the greater metropolitan area, with only 1.3 per 10,000 inhabitants'.[51] It is clear from all the data available that the poor of Brazil and much of the rest of Latin America continued to provide the nucleus of Pentecostal membership, and it is to the great credit of that Christian tradition that this was so.

It may partly have been a result of this social composition of the Pentecostals that few of them, or of the evangelicals in general, engaged very fully or deeply in the political, economic and social life of their respective countries, at least to the extent of exercising an influence in situations of manifest corruption and unacceptable individual as well as corporate behaviour. They had not yet learnt to play a part in influencing the secular life of nations that their numbers, and the vigour and profundity of their faith seemed to demand. There were examples of political experiments by Pentecostal and other evangelical leaders that came to nothing. This was so in Peru in 1980, when evangelical and Pentecostal leaders attempted to form El Frente Evangelico, a political movement that was intended to incorporate Protestants of various tendencies, but it was a failure.[52]

On the other hand, Protestants in South America struggled to know how best to make their undoubted vibrant faith a source of secular influence. The danger was that they would either withhold completely from such potentially fruitful engagement, or plunge into politics without experience, and become political activists without a firm enough theological basis.[53]

Nevertheless, Pentecostals, and Protestants in general, in South America were learning quickly. In a sense, they had 'irretrievably lost their ability to remain out of view'.[54] They represented such a significant sector of society that politicians had to take note of, and even seek, their views on divorce, public education, sexual questions, AIDS and similar issues. 'Apart from participation in party politics, Pentecostals' were 'being thrust willy-nilly onto the public stage by the mass media.'[55] This was but one more indicator of the astonishing surge of South American Protestantism in the twentieth century.

The number of non-Catholic Christians in many countries of South America were found in the 1990s to be growing at five or six times the rate of the general population; and this expansion apparently continued in the twenty-first century. In five or six countries, if the rate of increase persists, there could soon be non-Catholic majorities, and most of these would be Pentecostals. In several other nations the non-Catholics could well have reached 30 to 40 per cent of the total population in the very near future, again with a preponderance of Pentecostals.

By the end of the twentieth century, a spiritual revolution was 'transforming the socioreligious landscape of Latin America. From the *ciudades perdidas* (shantytowns) of Tijuana to the *favelas* (slums) of Rio de Janeiro, evangelical Protestantism, particularly Pentecostalism,' had 'replaced Catholicism as the leading form of popular religion in thousands of barrios on the urban periphery.'[56] Brazil was in the van of this remarkable transformation, although other countries were beginning to show a similar pattern of change. Brazil was home to some 60 per cent of Ibero-America's Protestants. Its Protestant population almost quadrupled between 1960 and 1985.[57]

Adrian Hastings neatly summarized the situation in 1999:

> The Latin American may need no reminding, but the outsider does have to beware of homogenizing Brazil and Peru, Argentina and Colombia, Chile and Mexico. Each has had its own religious history, clear enough in the nineteenth century and still more clear in the twentieth. What is certain is that, hitherto, nowhere else in the world did the Catholic Church have so huge a field almost to itself, that this is no longer the case, and that the religious development of the next 30 years from Mexico City to Buenos Aires may quite strikingly determine the entire balance of the Christian world.[58]

5

The Changing Face of Worldwide Christianity in the Twentieth Century

III: Africa

The number of Christians in Africa rose phenomenally in the course of the twentieth century. No sources allow for reliable figures, largely because of the 'ambiguity and incompleteness of the raw data on which they are based', the difficulty of defining a Christian for computing purposes, and because 'Africa is full of small, independent churches that have never filed a statistical return'.[1] Nonetheless, the broad picture is clear. According to a much-quoted, and not seriously disputed, reckoning, in 1900 there were about 10 million Christians, including the Copts, representing about 9 per cent of the total continental population. By 1950 this has been said by some commentators to have risen to 34 million, and approximately 15 per cent of the entire population, and in 1965 to 75 million, equal to a quarter of the population,[2] although another source says 143 million in 1970.[3] At the dawn of the twenty-first century the number of Christians had soared to between 360 and 393 million.[4] At each of these stages, this was well beyond the rate of growth for the population as a whole. One observer in 1984, calculated that, while 'every day in the West, roughly 7,500 people in effect stopped being Christians, every day in Africa roughly double that number became Christians'.[5] However accurate or inaccurate these figures may be they point to a quite staggering expansion.

In seeking to discern and understand the Christian growth points and areas of outstanding vitality in Africa during the twentieth century, a fourfold thematic, rather than geographical or chronological, division is analytically useful. It helps to identify the essential elements in a most complex situation of unprecedented change, and to make sense of a welter of facts, events, trends, movements and new developments.

First of all, there was the fascinating, and to Western eyes sometimes somewhat exotic and even peculiar, story of African Christian prophets and the astounding emergence of independent churches. Secondly, there were the frequently denigrated, or at least underrated, mainline, traditional churches and missionary societies that had undertaken pioneer work, and helped to establish Christianity in many regions in the nineteenth-century colonial era of the mainly British, French and Belgian empires, who had retained a valuable role even after the more flamboyant movements, groups and churches had taken centre stage. Thirdly, there was once again the amazing impact of Pentecostalism and the charismatic movement. And, finally, there was the continuing influence of the Roman Catholic Church.

A strand running through all four of these components making up the story of Christianity in Africa in the twentieth century was the transition from mission to church. Always an issue that aroused passion and perturbation, it was given a novel twist and new practical significance as a result of the highly emotive transfer of power on the gaining of political independence.

Prophets and independent churches

By the end of the twentieth century, more people in many parts of Africa were members of churches that had originated as a result of native African initiatives than of those churches that owed their foundation to European or North American missions.[6] The starting-point for the modern independent church movement may perhaps be traced back to 1892, when the Wesleyan minister Mangena M. Mokone seceded from the church of his ordination, and set up 'the Ethiopian Church' in Johannesburg. It has multiplied in size and membership ever since.

Across Africa, a common prophetic pattern has recurred frequently since the nineteenth century. An individual is enthusiastically converted through one of the mission churches, from which he or, commonly, she, is gradually estranged. The division might arise over issues of church practice, usually the integration of native practices. The individual receives what is taken as a special revelation from God, commonly in a trance or vision.[7]

The prophet begins to preach independently, and not infrequently this soon results in a new independent church. This nascent creation then has all the attraction to the local people of being rooted and grounded in native soil, and of being founded, inspired and led by a son or daughter of the African motherland. The new church and its leader have the additional appeal of exhibiting a profound understanding and empathy with the mindsets and traditions of fellow Africans. From the point of view of the present work, such churches

> are significant because they suggest the real fervour that Christianity inspired outside the West. They confound the standard modern mythology about just how Christianity was, and is, exported to a passive or reluctant Third World. Over the past two centuries, at least, it might have been the European empires that first kindled Christianity around the world, but the movement soon enough turned into an uncontrollable brushfire.[8]

A few examples will illustrate some of the main characteristics of these prophet movements and independent churches that loomed so large and were so prominent in promoting Christianity in twentieth-century sub-Saharan Africa.

In the first half of the century William Wade Harris set in motion one 'of the most remarkable movements in the whole history of Christianity in Africa'.[9] He was an Episcopal Christian from Liberia. In a vision, early in the century, he was instructed by the angel Gabriel to abandon his much prized European clothing. This was no mere matter of sartorial preference. Such change of dress was a most powerful and highly visible symbol of the fact that he rejected the privileged status of the white colonialists, and that he cast aside any pretensions to membership of the

Americanized black elite that monopolized power in his homeland. He started out in 1913 on what proved to be a series of
spectacular and highly successful preaching journeys across West
Africa. His appearance inspired awe and wonder, and he con-
veyed the aura of prophetic authority and dynamism. A contemporary observer graphically portrayed him as 'an impressive
figure, adorned with a white beard, of tall stature, clothed in
white, his head enturbaned with a cloth of the same colour, wear-
ing a black stole; in his hand a high cross and on his belt a cal-
abash, containing dried seeds, which he shakes to keep rhythm
for his hymns'.[10] He was reputedly responsible for 100,000
conversions during the following two years. 'The heart of his
simple gospel concerned belief in one God, the abandoning and
destruction of fetishes, the observance of Sunday as a day of rest,
and the prohibition of adultery'.[11]

In addition to being a black African clad in a distinctive way,
three things set Harris apart from European missionaries. First,
he took the people's ancient cult-figures or fetishes seriously,
whereas the missionaries scorned or ignored them. He was at one
with his fellow Africans in believing that they contained vast,
unfathomable spiritual force. To him they were evil, and he com-
bated their malignant power by burning them. Secondly, he
appreciated the power of witchcraft and did not dismiss it as a
delusion, as did the white missionaries. He called on his hearers
to spurn and abandon all occult practices. Lastly, and again in
accord with traditional African belief and practice, he did not
condemn polygamy, and indeed he was accompanied by several
wives in his travels.

Almost ten years after his sensational itinerant ministry, missionaries of the English Methodist Society followed up his work.
They found that although a great number of those baptized by
Harris had fallen away, something like 45,000 simple folk had
remained faithful to what they understood his teaching to be.
'They were eager to receive the missionaries and to learn the
teaching of the Book, which they possessed but could not understand, since in many cases it was in English. What followed was
the more normal history of the building up of a mission, with all
its lights and shadows; but the romance of its beginnings can
never be entirely forgotten.'[12]

Of equal if not more prominence and noteworthiness was Simon Kimbangu and the church he founded. He lived in what was then the Belgian Congo. In 1918 he received a vision calling him to be a prophet and healer. He had been a catechist in the English Baptist mission, and when he went out on his solo preaching and healing tours there appears 'to have been nothing in his teaching to which the Protestant missions would have taken exception'.[13] Up to this point Kimbangu can be compared to Harris, who preceded him by a few years. As with Harris, Kimbangu gave great importance to the abolition of fetishes, and there was a wholesale, most dramatic, discarding and destruction of them throughout wide areas where his influence was most strongly felt.

The main difference was the emphasis Kimbangu gave to healing. Although there were many unsuccessful cures, his reputation mounted, and Africans in their hundreds made their way to his house at Nkamba, where he built an enclosure in which services were held. After a while the hospitals were deserted, and multitudes flocked to the new centre. His healing ministry was greatly enlarged when he began to send out assistants to lay hands on people, and when others began similar practices in imitation of him.[14] For a time a far greater number of people than usual were drawn to the Protestant missions in the area on the crest of the wave created by Kimbangu's activities. But there followed a period in which such people, as well as more regular mission church members left both Protestant and Catholic missions in order to become his disciples. The seeds were being sown for the conflict he was soon to have with the authorities.

Although he was not originally either anti-mission or anti-white, his followers seem to have conferred on him the title 'messiah', which he did not reject. Gradually the movement was infiltrated by anti-white elements, and the authorities became alarmed. In June 1921 he was arrested, but he escaped. The idea of an Adventist movement with a distinctly revolutionary orientation now came to the fore. Kimbangu came to be viewed as a champion of the Africans, and as the ruler of Africa. His followers were arrested, and eventually Kimbangu, following closely the example set by Christ, returned to his own village and allowed himself to be apprehended.[15] After what appears to have been a travesty of a trial, he was sentenced to death, but this was subsequently commuted to life imprisonment, and he lived out the rest of his life in jail in Elizabethville, where he died in 1950.

It was a strange turn of fortune that not very long after his death, with the coming of political independence to African states, what 'had once been a despised prophet movement' readily and rapidly emerged in its homeland, Zaire, and in other countries 'as an honoured community'.[16] Perhaps it is equally amazing that this same discredited church was soon accepted into the international community of churches. 'The election of the Kimbanguist Church to the World Council of Churches in 1979 was an appreciated badge of acceptability, accentuating an incipient bureaucratisation of a vast prophet movement.'[17]

In May 1920, just before Kimbangu began his spectacular ministry, something not dissimilar was happening in western Nigeria that was to result in a church of even greater proportions and lasting significance than the ones associated with Harris and Kimbangu.[18] Prophets were multiplying among the Yoruba, as elsewhere. One of these charismatic leaders was Joseph Sadare, a prominent Anglican at Ijebu-Ode, forty miles south of Ibadan, who in response to a dream formed a prayer fellowship, which he called the Precious Stone Society. By 1922, the group of members had deserted the Anglican Church and temporarily joined themselves to a small faith-healing church called Faith Tabernacle. Similar groups sprang up in other nearby places, so that by the mid 1920s there was a small network of Faith Tabernacle communities in Yorubaland led by Sadare, Isaac Akinyele, a compatriot lay member of the diocesan synod, and others. They were collectively given the name 'Aladura', or praying people.

They continued as 'no more than a number of small praying groups of committed Christians functioning on the edge of, or just outside, the main Churches, especially the Anglican, strong on faith-healing, on the value of dreams and visions, and very much opposed to traditional religion'.[19] Aladura added little to the rapid expansion of the mission churches that was taking place in the 1920s. But, in 1930, and largely as a result of the preaching of a certain Joseph Babalola, there was a mass movement. Great numbers of people burnt their idols and juju, were converted, and swelled the ranks of the Aladura, so that it became one of the major religious groupings of the Yoruba, while others joined the Anglicans and Methodists. From the 1920s and 1930s onwards the Aladura movement spawned many offshoots, most of which were under the leadership of some much respected and honoured African charismatic leader or prophet. The multitude of constituent groups included the Cherubim and Seraphim Society, which itself was to show a staggering fissiparous capacity, and the Christ Apostolic Church (CAC), which became easily the largest of the Aladura bodies.[20] The CAC in particular was active in establishing a comprehensive educational network of primary schools and grammar schools, as well as its own training college.

As with the Kimbanguists, with political independence came a much greater measure of public and official recognition and approval. 'In Nigeria the Aladura, once controversial and marginalized, now became of central importance in society.'[21]

Moving from West to Southern Africa, we encounter a plethora of similar prophets and independent churches. Among their early native religious leaders, Isaiah Shembe was outstanding. In fact, he probably exercised a wider and more powerful and pervasive influence than any other Zulu of modern times. As a result of the special revelations he received, he gave up the four wives he had married as a young man, and in 1906 he was baptized as a member of the African Native Baptist Church. But he soon set out on his own, attracted by the so-called Zionist tradition which can be traced back to North American sects noted for their practice of faith-healing and their tradition of speaking in tongues. Shembe was the most famous of the Zionist prophets, and in 1911 he established the Church of the Nazarites, with its headquarters and focal point at Ekuphakameni, just north of Durban. It was especially distinguished for the quality of the liturgical cycle that Shembe devised. As one contemporary observer commented: 'By a transition perfectly natural to the African mind, the rejoicings over the splendour of Ekuphakameni "are, without warning, transported into a higher key and suddenly you find yourself, not eighteen miles north of Durban, but in heaven and Eden and Paradise".'[22]

In Southern Africa in the latter half of the twentieth century the Zionist churches as a whole were phenomenally successful, above all in the poorest urban areas.[23] By the 1990s there were 4,000 independent churches in South Africa, claiming a total of 5 million adherents; and there were 900 congregations in Soweto alone. The Zion Christian Church (ZCC) was the largest such body, and it wielded very considerable religious and political force in the country. Its popularity and magnetism was demonstrated regularly in its huge seasonal pilgrimages. The typical Easter gathering of more than a million ZCC devotees exceeded the number of pilgrims who greeted the Pope in St Peter's Square on Easter morning.[24]

Examples of African prophets, and of secessionist or independent churches might be multiplied. There was the Nigerian Garrick Braide, 'one of Africa's great prophetic figures',[25] and the remarkable response he attracted in the second, third and fourth decades of the twentieth century; there was the Blackman's Church of the 1930s, and the Lumpa Church of Alice Lenshina Mulenga among the Bemba of Northern Rhodesia (Zambia) in the 1950s, as well as a host of others. The ones cited in the foregoing paragraphs are but samples to indicate the vibrancy of African Christian spirituality in that incredible century for Christianity south of the Sahara.

The proliferation of independent churches is a sign of life, vitality and a healthy Africanization of Christianity. But it has also had its dangers and disadvantages. By the end of the twentieth century the number of such new fellowships was so great as to be beyond computation, and they were a source of constant potential if not actual instability. On the other hand, they were in many cases understandable expressions of dissatisfaction with the rigidity of alien traditional Western churches, especially as these were often firmly under white control until well into the century. They often originated because of the failure of white-dominated churches to make the native Africans feel at home and at ease. It is of little wonder that Africans responded when one of their own race had the courage to take action to provide a church that was more congenial to them, that was able to encapsulate the essential spirit and nuances of particular native African modes of thought, and that resonated in its worship, teaching and general ethos with what they felt at a deep level. It was an additional and huge bonus that such churches provided opportunities for African leadership at various levels and in a variety of roles.

Mainline denominations and missionary societies

Perhaps it is best to start a consideration of the contribution of the mainline Western missionary churches and societies to twentieth-century African Christianity, by focusing on one outstanding example of where a powerful revival movement, which could easily have resulted in a breakaway new independent sect, denomination or church, was contained within the existing organized churches. This was one of the most notable features of the East African revival – the movement of the Balokole, 'the saved ones'.

It all began in a simple way in the late 1920s when white European members of staff of the evangelical Rwanda Mission found their relationships with the Africans at the Gahini hospital were transformed as a result of openness, confession of sins and a sharing of their faith, including especially the experience of the saving 'blood' of Christ.[26] Among the most crucial interactions was that between Dr Joe E. Church and some of the assistants and helpers at the hospital, including Kosiya Shalita, a Tutsi from Ankole, who was later consecrated as the Anglican Bishop of Ankole. The medical staff was soon supplemented by the arrival of the Revd H.E. Guillebaud and his wife and daughter who were Bible translators, and they greatly contributed to the new influx of spiritual life. Church was also very friendly with Simeoni Nsibambi, a wealthy Muganda landowner, and his brother Blasio Kigozi, and they lent their support to the new developments. Church, other mainly British members of the staff, and their African fellow believers were primarily concerned that the Ganda Church should be renewed fifty years after it had experienced a mass conversion movement because, in their eyes, it had become dead.

The revival that was beginning so gently and yet decisively in Rwanda spread to Uganda, Kenya and Tanganyika. It was largely thanks to Bishop C.E. Stuart of Uganda, who remained calm, temperate and patient, and exercised judicious judgement at a time when roughness or insensitivity would have been disastrous, that the unity of the church was maintained, and the revival persisted for many decades.

By the 1950s the revival had become an integral part of the life of the Church of Uganda, and it continued to exercise great influence. Among the great Ugandan Anglican churchmen it helped to produce and foster have been Christians of the calibre of Archbishop Janani Luwum, killed during the Amin regime, Bishop Festo Kivengere, the evangelist, and John Sentamu, the current Archbishop of York.

Whatever their detractors might say about the Balokole, there was and has remained a quality of sanctity and conduct of life that is impressive and enduring. And this was demonstrated in a heroic and extreme form when times of trial came upon Rwanda. The most intense and traumatic of these took the form of venomous and deadly antagonism between the Hutu and Tutsi people. At various times in the 1960s and 1970s there were horrific raids and massacres of the one against the other tribe, followed by horrendous reprisals. And in the midst of this, Christians suffered along with others, but often amazed observers by the way they faced tension, fear, onslaught and death. One example will stand for the many that might be cited.

Yona Kanamuzeyi was pastor at the Anglican Centre near Nyamata.[27] Despite several warnings that his life was in danger, he remained at his post, spending his days visiting and encouraging his people. There were a number of occasions when bands of Tutsi, known as *inyenzi*, or 'cockroaches', crossed the border from Burundi to try to regain a foothold in their homeland from which they had fled or been banished. This provoked unrest and retaliations. In common with many in Rwanda, Yona was of mixed descent, but he looked like a Tutsi, he helped displaced Tutsi at Nyamata, and he was regarded as a Tutsi sympathizer.

On 23 January 1964 a jeep full of Hutu soldiers came by night and took him and Andrew, the headmaster of the primary school, away for questioning. It was known that very few returned from such interrogation. Yona went with what witnesses said was calm resignation until they came to the local river. He told his friend and fellow prisoner that they were going to heaven, he prayed, and they sang a hymn. Andrew and another captive were left by the jeep with their hands tied, while Yona was marched off to the river. There was a single shot, and then silence. As Andrew wrote later, the soldiers were amazed. 'They had never seen anyone go singing to his death or walking, as he did, like a man just taking a stroll.'[28] It was a testimony by word, action and example that was reminiscent of the Ugandan martyrs a century before, and it was typical of much that was to follow in the next twenty-five years.

The Sudan is another arena where the mainline churches and missionary societies initiated, or were at the very centre of new and refreshing waves of spiritual life, that were experienced amid much hardship and suffering. The country has had to endure the agonies of prolonged civil war, brutality on a massive scale and the consequences of natural disasters. It was, and has remained, in many ways a traumatized region, and the Christians have not been immune from the suffering of the people as a whole. 'Largely hidden in one of the earth's most brutalized war zones, the Episcopal Church of the Sudan (ECS) continues to survive. Indeed, it not only survives but flourishes, often revealing a remarkable spiritual dynamism.'[29] The young church in Sudan had to wrestle with death and upheaval, and yet it held firm, retained its vital spiritual vision and persisted in its witness. This conquering spirit is well expressed in a song composed in the early, most ruinous, phase of the civil war:

> Death has come to reveal the faith.
> It has begun with us, and it will end with us.
> O you who fear death, do not fear death.
> It only means that one will disappear from the earth.
> Who is there who can save his life and leave death aside?
> We who live in the world, we are mere sojourners upon the earth,
> As the Lord has said: 'Let us serve the truth.'
> Upon the earth there is no man we can call our 'father'.
> We abide together equally in unity as brothers.[30]

In 1964 all foreign missionaries were expelled by the Islamic regime. 'Two Sudanese bishops and forty-four ordained pastors were left to care for beleaguered Episcopal communities, many scattered through the forests of Southern Sudan and in exile in neighbouring countries.'[31] Yet, it was this very isolation, this reliance on indigenous manpower and other native resources, that gave rise to distinctive and confident new insights, evangelistic initiatives, and profound pastoral care, in the face of extreme adversity. Out of obscurity, and a most unpromising situation, there emerged during the 1980s and 1990s, what has often been described as the fastest growing church in the Anglican Communion. It is an illuminating saga of life, light, faith, hope and love, amidst death, darkness, doubt, disbelief, uncertainty and hatred. 'Whether on the battle front, or in desolate displacement camps, believers' experienced 'the numinous, healing, recreating presence of God. An impoverished, often ill-administered Church continually' revealed 'its capacity to hold onto life, to build and rebuild through waves of devastation. Far from being acquiescent and depressive, it' was, 'in many contexts, celebratory, evangelistic, and charismatic.'[32]

The revival in post-1960 Mozambique was a further outstanding example of a strong church arising out of the ashes of a seemingly hopeless situation. In the face of civil war and chaos caused by the breakdown of the economy, by much social unrest, and the trauma caused by drought, floods and famine; and despite much and severe persecution; the church not only survived, but grew and increased fortyfold to 140,000 members in twenty-five years. This came about not as a result of any eye-catching campaign or movement, but largely as a consequence of the unostentatious witness and work of ordinary people going about their daily lives, but with a message of hope burning in their hearts.[33]

A yet further, but very different, example of a mainline church standing foursquare for Christian values is South Africa. This was the arena for the noble, courageous, memorable and deeply influential work of Geoffrey Clayton, Ambrose Reeves, Trevor Huddleston and Michael Scott. They and other vocal white European critics of racialism and of the policies of the Nationalist government remained as loyal Anglicans, and stood their ground despite much bitter opposition, even from within their own church. They certainly did not represent most, or even many, white Christians within South Africa. 'Nevertheless, in terms of moral passion, gospel conviction, and even sheer political longsightedness, they won the debate hands down.'[34]

Geoffrey Clayton was described as the 'most consistent and powerful witness to the rights of man, regardless of colour, to be found within the leadership of the church'.[35] As Bishop of Johannesburg from 1934 to 1948, he witnessed at first hand the devastating effects, and the insidious pervasiveness of racial prejudice, and the complications, as well as the subtle nuances of the South African political, economic, social and religious scene. Then, as Archbishop of Cape Town, he occupied what 'was, at least potentially, the most influential ecclesiastical position on the whole continent'.[36]

He was a highly sophisticated, intelligent, man, with great clarity of assessment and judgement, and a sure touch in handling difficult and complex matters. He possessed the finesse, acumen, shrewdness and discernment of a statesman, although he was somewhat insensitive, lacked originality, and was inflexible in his rigid and unquestioning Anglo-Catholicism. He had little tolerance for priests who differed from him in his assumptions, and he was highly suspicious of anyone whose concern for the things of the world apparently outweighed their concern for the Church, which for Clayton was to the fore in all his thinking and planning. It was for this reason that in spite of his deep concern for justice across racial divides, he found Ambrose Reeves and Trevor Huddleston intensely irritating. His view of them and their way of conducting their campaigns was very much tied to his temperament.

> Dry, unemotional, distrustful of populism of any sort – Pentecostal or political – an English upper-middle-class type who was constitutionally as incapable of identifying with blacks as with women, or with the poor anywhere in his own life style, he was yet able to assess the general situation with courage and a very clear judgement, and he did not for one moment question that the church's task – secondary but still immensely important – was to speak up for the poor and the weak.[37]

Richard Ambrose Reeves was different in both temperament and tactics. He was enthroned in June 1949 as Bishop of Johannesburg. Throughout his time in South Africa he was 'a disturbing prophetic presence' and 'an evangelist looking for ways to build up the church into a real loving, caring, worshipping community'.[38] He achieved a worldwide reputation as a consequence of his forthright, sustained and heroic struggle for justice and civil rights. He abhorred apartheid, and everything directly or indirectly connected with it. He regarded it, and the treatment of non-whites that it entailed, as unjust and un-Christian. He believed that the Church had a duty to speak out against the system, the philosophy that underlay it, and the actions it provoked. He was a realist, and he appreciated the difficulty of ordering the life of a complex, multiracial society. He was not a fanatical agitator or demonical antagonist, but a peacemaker and reconciler. Nonetheless, he could not see common ground between what he regarded as a true Christian understanding of how to think and behave in such a situation, and the policy being adopted by Dr Malan and his government.

In too many ways to be enumerated, he actively and very publicly campaigned to oppose what he saw as oppressive legislation, and in doing so he was fiercely and bitterly resisted. He headed up 'probably the most important and potentially effective instrument of opposition to the Nationalist Government of his time', and he became 'possibly the one man in South Africa capable of uniting all opposing factions to the Government's policies'.[39] He became the recognized leading white radical figure and champion of the non-white cause in South Africa. As a consequence of his activities, he also became the friend and trusted adviser of African leaders like Chief Albert Luthuli and Oliver Tambo. He counselled and assisted a multitude of individuals, and he encouraged African writers, artists and musicians. He was a force in the land.

Trevor Huddleston was a member of the Community of the Resurrection who, in 1943, was sent by his Order to South Africa to be priest-in-charge of the Community's mission in Sophiatown. In 1949 he was appointed Provincial of the Community in South Africa, and Superintendent of St Peter's School, which has been called the Black Eton of South Africa.

He became a legend in South Africa, loved by the black people and feared and hated by many whites, especially those in authority. The black people called him 'Makhalipile', the dauntless one, after a bold warrior who had been adopted by another people when their leaders had been lost or captured. What seems to have especially appealed to the Africans was his great sense of humour and joyous nature, which had such affinity with the African character. Through his writings, most notably his book *Naught for Your Comfort*, and his frequent media communications, he became a household name in Britain and other parts of the Western world. He used all the opportunities he could to enlist support for those engaged in the struggle against apartheid in South Africa and to help in the establishment of a just and equitable society. Underpinning his extended struggle was his theological view of man:

> I believe that, because God became Man, therefore human nature in itself has a dignity and a value which is infinite. I believe that this conception necessarily carries with it the idea that the State exists for the individual, not the individual for the State. Any doctrine based on racial or colour prejudice and enforced by the State is therefore an affront to human dignity and 'ipso facto' an insult to God himself. It is for this reason that I feel bound to oppose not only the policy of the present Government of the Union of South Africa but the legislation which flows from this policy.[40]

It was not in books that he learned to hate apartheid, but in his encounters with people. His was not an armchair, merely theoretical, ideological or philosophical opposition in principle. He found by experience that the entrenchment of racism was totally destructive of people, denying them the exercise of their latent gifts, and demeaning them in every way as human beings. Two incidents will highlight his attitude and his conduct in the midst of such a degrading national policy of race discrimination. On one occasion, in Sophiatown, he raised his hat to a black washer-woman. The gesture was observed by her son, Desmond Tutu, who happened to be watching. He had never before seen a white man do such a thing, and he there and then decided on his vocation. On a second occasion, and in keeping with his personal motto, 'Act on impulse', he provided the fourteen-year-old Hugh Masekela with his first trumpet, and thereby set the young man on his path to becoming a jazz musician of world renown.

Michael Scott arrived in South Africa in the same year, 1943, as Trevor Huddleston, but their careers in the country were very dissimilar. Huddleston exercised a priestly ministry in one place, and within a clearly recognised, institutional setting; Scott undertook an itinerant, very personal, type of ministry. But both became national, and indeed international, figures of stature for the same reason – their fearless stance against apartheid. Huddleston was a clearly defined, easily identifiable, member of a religious order, a High Churchman with well-thought-out and well-articulated beliefs and practices; Scott was something of a maverick.

> A curate in Johannesburg with an unsettled background, no university degree, no clear vision of what he either sought or believed in, no great capacity as a public speaker, an Anglican priest who had previously drifted about Asia and Britain on the fringe of the Communist Party, he was within a few months of arrival helping to organise, and then chairman of, a national non-party organisation called the Campaign for Right and Justice.[41]

In his desperate concern for justice, and in his passionate determination to fight in defence of the poor, he went in 1946 to Durban, where he sided with the Indians who were nightly assaulted by white thugs on account of their involvement in the founding and work of a Passive Resistance Movement in opposition to the new Asiatic Land Tenure Bill. He was arrested under the law of trespass. After three months in goal, he returned to Johannesburg, where he lost his curacy because Clayton would not allow him to keep it without promising to refrain from unauthorized further action of the type he had indulged in at Durban.

But he would not be silenced. He took up various matters to do with social justice, such as opposition to the notorious slave-driving farms of the eastern Transvaal. He wrote articles for newspapers and even went to the United Nations year after year to plead the cause of the Herero people of South West Africa. He suffered further imprisonment, and in 1950 he became a prohibited immigrant. He was by then immensely well known throughout Africa and the Western world, and he used his reputation to good effect by promoting the causes closest to his heart. He even managed to persuade the International Court of Justice at The Hague to take up the question of the status of South West Africa and the condition of the Herero people. He was a man of remarkable authority and sway not only in South Africa, but in the councils and courts of the world. It was an astounding achievement.

A generation later, and the baton of these bold champions for justice and the rights of all people regardless of the colour of their skins was taken up by others within the Church, but by then it was largely Africans themselves who were in the forefront. Prominent among them was Desmond Tutu,[42] the boy who witnessed Trevor Huddleston's act of respect towards his mother. His story need not be told in full to appreciate the outstanding ability and standing of this remarkable Christian man. Grit, determination and innate ability, together with opportunities to progress in his education led to good academic training in South Africa and England, and helped him to a distinguished career as Associate Director of the Theological Education Fund, then Dean of Johannesburg Cathedral, Bishop of Lesotho, General Secretary of the South Africa Council of Churches, and finally Archbishop of Johannesburg. Throughout his tenure of these posts, he consistently showed concern to act as a peacemaker, and to serve all his people, but especially those who were underprivileged, repressed, and wounded daily by the political, economic, social and educational system that was designed to relegate them to a thoroughly subordinate, harsh and demanding life. He received the recognition and acclaim that such dedication to being the 'voice of the voiceless' and the upholder of high standards of justice and reconciliation deserved, when he was awarded the Nobel Peace Prize in October 1984.

It is of little wonder that even after his 'retirement', he was called upon to chair the Truth and Reconciliation Commission, which was a noble expression of the spirit that animated both Nelson Mandela and Tutu, and, it must be said, ex-President P.W. Botha as well, as a new order of government was established with the ending of the rule of the Nationalist party. It was one further expression and demonstration of the role the Church could play in political life if the person of the right calibre was available to be a channel of grace and good works. It was also one of many marks of the slow but effective Africanization of the Church in the territories south of the Sahara.

These examples of the mainline churches acting as salt and light, and providing a much needed evangelistic and pastoral ministry in East-Central Africa, the Sudan, Mozambique and South Africa were to an extent replicated in other parts of the continent. In parallel with such exemplary Christian witness, there emerged the kind of Pentecostal and charismatic movements that have already been encountered in the Western world and South America.

Pentecostal churches and the charismatic movement

Of course, many of the independent churches already considered, owed their foundation and continued life to what they described in Pentecostal-like terms as the work of the Spirit. But the influence of Pentecostalism and the charismatic movement went well beyond them and their congregations. Sometimes this was made more evident than usual, as with the already described East African Revival movement.

Pentecostal phenomena have been very explicitly manifested all over Africa, within the mainline Western religious traditions as, for example, in the Iviyo loFakazi bakaKristu of Bishop Alpheus Zulu,[43] and in the charismatic renewal movement that so profoundly affected Anglicanism in South Africa in the later years of the century.

As already mentioned in this present study, not enough acknowledgement has been given to the indigenous nature of much of African Pentecostalism. It 'is essentially of African origin with roots in a marginalized and underprivileged society struggling to find dignity and identity. It expanded initially among oppressed African people who were neglected, misunderstood, and deprived of anything but token leadership by their white ecclesiastical "masters". But fundamentally, it was the ability of African Pentecostalism to adapt to and fulfil African *religious* aspirations that was its main strength.'[44]

The pneumatological emphasis of these types of churches accorded well with the felt needs of many Africans, especially at a time of newly acquired independence, when there was a seeking after personal and corporate empowerment, and the opportunity to exercise and give expression to personal gifts. These Pentecostal churches and those most fully affected by the charismatic movement, to a greater degree than was true of most of the mainline Western churches, provided both the ambience and the opportunity for individuals to use their talents, to realize some of their aspirations, and to release some of their pent-up emotions. It is these churches that 'help us to see the overriding African concern for spiritual power from a mighty God to overcome all enemies and evils that threaten human life and vitality, hence their extensive ministry of mental and physical healing. This is rather different from the Western preoccupation with atonement for sin and forgiveness of guilt.'[45]

The distinctive forms of worship, and the beliefs, practices and lifestyles of the Pentecostals as a whole, seem to have had an appeal that the more circumspect, less congregational, more restrained and cerebral forms of corporate and individual devotion, and the daily conduct associated with the main old-established Western churches and denominations, lacked. The foremost features of the new spirituality have persistently and consistently been, 'an oral liturgy, a narrative theology and witness, the maximum participation of the whole community in worship and service, the inclusion of visions and dreams into public worship, and an understanding of the relationship between the body and the mind manifested by healing through prayer'.[46] Repeatedly, Africans have found in Pentecostalism a system of beliefs and behaviour, and a total, all-embracing ethos, in which they have felt comfortable.[47] Here, naturally, without any inhibitions, and without any planning and strategy emanating from Western churches or missionary societies, has been an indigenization of Christianity, and a transfer from colonial tutelage to a genuine and heartfelt African way of doing things.

> African Pentecostalism has Africanized Christian liturgy in a free and spontaneous way that does not betray its essential Christian character, and has liberated it from the foreignness of European forms. This sympathetic approach to African life and culture, with its fears and uncertainties and world of spirits and magic, has been a major reason for the attraction of these Churches for people still oriented to the traditional thought world.[48]

In view of its resonance with Africans who are closely attuned to their ancestral traditions and thought processes, it may be deduced that urban development would detract from the Pentecostal appeal. This is not so. Indeed, the attraction of the spirituality just depicted seems to be accentuated in African towns and cities,

> where rapid urbanization and industrialization have thrown many people into a strange, impersonal, and insecure world, where they are left groping for a sense of belonging. African Pentecostals, with their firm commitment to a cohesive community and their offer of full participation to all, provide substantially for this universal human need. For this reason, among others, they grow even faster in an urban environment than they do in a rural one.[49]

By the 1990s, the Pentecostals were investing huge financial and human resources to achieve the greater evangelization of the African continent. This included considerable support from outside the continent. For example, in 1991, the Assemblies of God had about 318 missionaries scattered across Africa, but it was the common practice for each missionary to raise support for their own work, often by visiting North American churches. The same denomination also invested heavily in establishing fifty-three Bible schools in Africa, with a total student enrolment of over 4,250 students.

There is no doubt that the energy and zeal of the Pentecostals, and the appeal that Pentecostalism had to many Africans, resulted in a host of defections from the traditional Western churches and denominations. In South Africa, according to official government statistics, the proportion of the total population belonging to the older 'mission churches' more than halved between 1960 and 1991, from 70 per cent to 33 per cent. In South Africa, Zimbabwe, Ghana, Nigeria and many other places African Pentecostals rapidly became the most numerous, vocal and influential Christians.

Nonetheless, as found in other continents and countries, much of this Pentecostal emphasis was contained within existing non-Pentecostal churches in the form of the charismatic movement. In 1985, in an essay in *African Concord*, it was noted that the charismatic movement was the fastest growing endeavour in West

Africa, and it was to the fore in Kenya, Tanzania, Zambia and Zimbabwe. By the 1990s there were probably 8 million charismatics in Africa, with between two-and-a-half and three million in Nigeria alone. Although this overall figure is small compared with the total for all Christians in the continent, they were among the most committed, dedicated and vigorous members of their various churches, so that 'charismatic churches' packed a punch that far exceeded what might be expected given their numerical strength.

The leadership and a substantial proportion of the membership of the charismatic movement was consistently drawn from the educated elites – the brighter school leavers and the university and college graduates. A pronounced and identifiable charismatic movement can in fact be traced back to the University of Ibadan in 1970, when a few undergraduates claimed to have experienced a baptism in the Holy Spirit and to have spoken in tongues. From the fire kindled at Ibadan sparks helped to ignite other such corporate experiences, initially at the University of Ife, then elsewhere within Nigeria and in other areas, notably East Africa. During the 1980s it started to make a major impact on students and others in French-speaking Africa. By as early as 1972, it was reinforced from abroad for the most part by masses of books, tracts and magazines from North American Pentecostal ministers, and by crusades conducted by North American evangelists.

Charismatic organizations were founded in many countries. In the period up to about the early 1980s these concentrated on personal evangelism through the witness of individuals and the distribution of tracts. At that stage, however, there was a marked change in the character of the movement, and for the rest of the century, there was a clear tendency for individual charismatics to operate more definitely within their own denominational boundaries. Retreats, which had been popular, were almost completely phased out, while distinctly charismatic Sunday services were introduced in addition to weekday meetings. Books and pamphlets replaced tracts. Many of the organizations began to publish newsletters or periodical magazines as a means of giving greater unity and a sense of coherence and common purpose to their members. As a supplement to personal evangelism, crusades or mass evangelistic meetings became common.

In 1996, one well-informed observer, Matthews A. Ojo, usefully gave expression to the belief of many knowledgeable commentators concerning the significance and potential of the charismatic movement in Africa, and his remarks will serve as a suitable appraisal of its status and standing as the century neared its end. 'It is', he wrote,

> a movement unified by common origin, language, doctrinal approach and social basis. The movement is incorporating African religious elements into contemporary political and socio-economic situations, thereby causing the transformation of religious and social structures. It creates new values based on the needs of the present time. The movement has been an important precursor of social awakening. The progressive and modern orientation of the movement can play a significant role in the process of development.[50]

These are big claims, but he adds to them brief thoughts about the future that were not contradicted by the subsequent course of events, and in fact still hold true. The charismatic movement in Africa 'is not', he asserted,

> merely the spirituality of the educated elite, but the entire membership is being led into a deeper analysis of their faith and their contemporary situation. Charismatics have read the Bible extensively and have appropriated its inexhaustible store of symbols to meet their various needs. Certainly, the implications for the future are clear. The structures of the organizations will continue to be adapted to reflect socio-economic changes. The readiness to incorporate new forms and structures will therefore give more strength to the movement. The charismatic movement will continue to dominate the religious scene in Africa throughout this decade. This is what the omens indicate.[51]

The Roman Catholics

In 1914 there were 7 million baptized Roman Catholics and a further million catechumens in Africa, but by 1938 these figures had doubled.[52] The numbers then levelled out, so that by 1955 there were only 16 million; but since then they have multiplied incredibly. Between 1977 and 1987 the Catholic population of ten African countries doubled.[53] By the year 2000 there were 120 million. Despite the amazing growth of independent churches, there were by the end of the century three times as many Catholics as independents, and this number was growing daily. Tanzania is not untypical. In the four decades after 1961 there was a 419 per cent growth, and the country developed a strong ecclesiastical structure, with four provinces incorporating twenty-nine dioceses, in eight of which Catholics were a majority of the population.[54]

The Roman Catholic Church has always placed great emphasis on the work of missionaries, and more particularly on the need for priests, and they have remained less squeamish than non-Catholics about the continued employment of non-African priests in the midst of ever-greater indigenization in all other spheres of life. It is therefore highly pertinent to Africa that Roman Catholic missionary organizations continued to expand, and missionaries to increase at least until the 1960s, at which time there were in excess of 60,000 worldwide – which was more than all the non-Roman Catholic missionaries put together. The scale of the operation involved is indicated by the fact that in 1957, one single missionary body, the White Fathers of Cardinal Lavigerie, had more than 2,000 ordained missionaries in Africa, together with 1,200 White Sisters from the parallel organization for women.[55] This most impressive mobilization of human and associated resources from outside Africa was made possible to a large degree by the emergence in 1908 of the United States as a sending country after a prolonged period when, peculiar as it may seem, it was itself regarded by the Roman Catholic Church as a mission field. In Africa, as elsewhere, the ever-increasing availability of air travel permitted missionary access to great tracts of land that had hitherto been beyond reach, and this allowed Catholic missionaries to be more effectively deployed.

Such external Catholic targeting of the continent was complemented by the Africanization of the Catholic ordained ministry. In Tanzania, for instance, whereas in 1965 fewer than a quarter of the bishops were native Africans, by 1996 local men were at the helm in all the dioceses.[56] Taking Africa as a whole, from the 1960s onwards, Catholic archbishops and bishops of African stock started to emerge. Of the 488 Catholic archbishops and bishops in Africa in 1996, which included twelve cardinals, the vast majority were African nationals.[57] Considerably more than half of the 20,500 Catholic priests were native Africans, and the number of African vocations to the priesthood was continuing to rise.[58] Seminaries and theological centres were filled to capacity, and Bigard Memorial Seminary in Nigeria, with its 821 students on two campuses, could probably qualify as the largest theological college in the world.[59] The continent could also boast of 50,000 Roman Catholic religious, who were mostly African women, and a formidable army of lay catechists.

As the Roman Catholic Church in Africa entered the twenty-first century, it must have found some satisfaction in the statistics with which it was confronted.[60] Of the 18 million Catholic baptisms recorded in 1999, 3 million took place in Africa. In 1996, even the huge growth in the number of Catholic priests could not keep pace with the yearly increment of baptisms, and there was a growing problem of how to minister to Catholics in dispersed rural settlements, as well as in densely populated urban slums.[61] At the turn of the century, the annual baptismal totals for Nigeria and for the Democratic Republic of the Congo were each higher than for such bastions of traditional Roman Catholicism as Italy, France, Spain and Portugal, the leading centres of European Catholicism. It is also significant, and to some people somewhat astonishing, that, by the early years of the third millennium, 37 per cent of all baptisms in Africa were of adults. This can reasonably be interpreted as an important gauge of the successful evangelistic efforts made by the Roman Catholic Church.[62] Finally, taking the total number of Catholics at 2000, and applying a growth percentage in line with the rate of increase at that time, it is calculated that by 2025 the Catholic population of Africa will be 228 million, almost twice the total for the year 2000.[63] All these statistics lead to the inevitable conclusion that the Roman Catholic Church in Africa progressed outstandingly during the twentieth century, and is in a healthy condition as it enters the twenty-first century.

It is a telling commentary on the changing Christian scene in the world that in its missionary outreach in Africa, the Roman

Catholic Church in the early part of the twenty-first century recruited help not so much from Europe and America, as from South India, South America and the Philippines, as well as from Africa itself, with Africans serving in sub-Saharan countries other than their own. The whole operation had been internationalized to encompass mobile Africans and a host of Christians from non-Western countries. By the 1990s better-staffed African dioceses were increasingly prepared to help those that were less well provided for, and African missionary societies, such as the Congregation of the Apostles of Jesus in East Africa, or the Society of St Paul in Nigeria, were supplying personnel to other dioceses and countries. The whole Roman Catholic system had become flexible and fluid as never before, in a situation that demanded adaptability.[64] The main shortcoming in the use of external resources was that the Catholic Church in Africa was not financially self-supporting. And it still can only survive as a result of regular and generous injections of foreign funds.

This is far more serious than a mere monetary matter. The Zairean theologian Oscar Bimwenyi, has pointed out that Roman Catholics in Africa were receiving their Christianity at second hand.[65] 'They pray to a God with a liturgy that is not theirs. They live according to a morality bequeathed to them by foreigners. They are ruled by a Canon Law which does not derive from their own juridical realities; and they reflect on their faith using alien philosophical and theological systems.'[66] The Catholic Church may well put at risk its growth and African rootedness if it does not abandon its preference for Western cultural forms, and create what has been called 'a culturally polycentric Church'.[67]

6

The Changing Face of Worldwide Christianity in the Twentieth Century

IV: Asia

The churches in Asia in the twentieth century operated within a very different context and milieu than was the case with South America or sub-Saharan Africa, or indeed anywhere else in the world. The big distinguishing and defining factor was the long-established, almost monopolistic, position of non-Christian world religions that were, and remain, so embedded in most of the countries that they determined not only the religious affiliation of the vast majority of the inhabitants, but the character of the political and social life of the territories as well. In almost all of the Asian countries Christianity, even if it originally established a foothold as long ago as the first few centuries of the Christian era, had remained a small, and often very small or even miniscule presence for the whole of the modern era since the sixteenth century. So, we are talking about progress, where this is apparent, from a very low base, minority, position, and there is not generally the same spectacular story to tell for the twentieth century as with South America and sub-Saharan Africa. Nonetheless, this does not mean that the region is an exception to the advance of Christianity in the last 300 years, and in the last 100 years in particular, that is the major theme of the present work. This is far from so, for there is once more an interesting, and in some cases staggering and dramatic, tale to tell.

Closely connected with what has just been said, and making the situation for Christianity even more complex, is the vastness of the countries concerned, their massive populations, and the diversity of their histories and recent political, social and religious situations. There is, after all, China, the most populous country in the world, where Confucianism and Buddhism have reigned supreme from before the time of Christ; the India-Pakistan subcontinent, with a population in excess of 1,000 million, second only in the world to China in the number of inhabitants, and likely to overhaul that country in this respect by 2050, where Hinduism has dominated life from time immemorial, and Islam has been a powerful force for 1,500 years; Japan, one of the economic miracles of the post-Second World War period, where Shinto, Buddhism and Confucianism have held sway for so long that they have become an integral part of the life of the people; and the many lands where Buddhism or Islam is firmly, extensively and comprehensively entrenched. Such variety means that generalizations are more difficult than for any other part of the world. The only credible and comprehensible approach is to take sample countries, and to attempt some broad, but restricted, analytical comments on them. Facile, sweeping statements will be avoided, but an overall pattern will, nonetheless, be sought, even if the description of it is inevitably hedged about with reservations and qualifications.

China

It is appropriate to start a survey of individual countries with China – the leading Asian contender to become a superpower in the first half of the twenty-first century. The twentieth century started with few Christians in the country, and seemingly little prospect of the situation being improved. Around 1890, there were probably about 37,000 Protestants, the result of arduous efforts by foreign missionaries and some national Chinese. In such a vast land, with poor means of transport and communication, the prospects for spreading the faith in any but a very limited way, were bleak. There was then the discouragement of the vicious Boxer uprising of 1900, 'which had as one of its goals the extirpation of Christianity and Christians from China'.[1]

But, strangely, the events of 1900 worked to the advantage of Christianity in the country, and things began to look up for the faith. After the tragic violence of the rebellion, the nation was subjected to a humiliating foreign occupation and heavy reparations, and there ensued an unprecedented opening up to the West.[2] 'And for the first time, there was a quantum jump in interest in Christianity.'[3] The provision of Christian mission schools greatly expanded, and the number of baptized Christians surged from fewer than 100,000 in the late 1890s, to 178,000 in 1906.[4] News of Christian events in other parts of the world, including the Welsh revival of 1904, Pentecostalism in the United States, and the revival in Korea, helped to raise expectations. What took place in the next few years in China probably consisted of a large number of local events rather than a co-ordinated and flamboyant nationwide movement, but it nevertheless resulted in a very definite stride forward. This fruitful period saw the emergence into greater prominence of native Chinese evangelists and pastors, such as Ding Limei. 'The years 1911 to 1919, bracketed by the political watersheds of the Republican Revolution and the May Fourth Movement respectively, were probably the high point of joint Sino-foreign mass evangelism and revivalism in modern China.'[5]

From about 1920 onwards fewer foreign evangelists visited or served in the country. But, to more than compensate for this, amid what was a pronounced increase in hostility to imperialism and Christianity both among the political leadership and in various quarters of society, a new generation of Chinese Christian leaders was coming of age. The best known of these to people outside China, and a thorn in the flesh of the authorities for his outspoken witness, was Wang Mingdao (1900–91). Because of his forthrightness, he was imprisoned in the 1950s and not released until 1979. Another of this new breed of able, bold and courageous leaders was Ni Duosheng (1903–72), famed around the world as 'Watchman Nee'.

Little is known of Christianity during the time of the Second World War, and the ensuing period of civil war from 1946 to 1949. But then came the radical restrictions imposed on the faith and its practitioners by the new Communist government after 1949.[6] The establishment on 1 October 1949 of the People's Republic of China by Mao Tse-Tung, heralded a progressively severe and repressive policy towards Christianity. In 1950 the Three Self Patriotic Movement was inaugurated in order to control the church, and all foreign missionaries were expelled by 1952. Although, at the beginning of this period there were an estimated 700,000 Christians, by 1966 all the churches had been closed, and pastors and other church leaders had to a great extent been banished to labour camps. The church was largely driven underground, and anyone meeting with other Christians for whatever purpose was in great danger. Up to the mid 1970s no religious activity of any kind was permitted. This was the era of the little red book, enthusiastically waved about by the Chinese Communists as enshrining the only acceptable philosophy of life for individuals and for society, and of the Red Guards as an instrument of venomous oppression and repression. The philosophy of Mao reigned supreme, and there was general adulation of him, when in reality the monstrosities he perpetrated place him alongside Hitler and Stalin in their enormity and horror. It was a testing time for Christians, and to some it seemed to spell the death of Christianity in the land. By the 1970s the faith appeared to have been completely annihilated.

Then, in 1976 Mao died, and within a short time Madam Mao and the leftist 'Gang of Four' had taken over the reigns of government. But within the same calendar year they had been swept from power. Deng Xiaoping and a more moderate Communist policy designated the 'Four Modernizations' soon surfaced, accompanied by the rehabilitation of intellectuals and greater religious freedom. And the same more tolerant attitude persisted for the next twenty-five years, into the twenty-first century. In 1979 the first churches under this more enlightened regime were opened and, to the astonishment of many, Christians emerged into the open in their tens of thousands. It was the beginning of one of the most astounding Christian awakenings of the twentieth century.

The statistics do not have to be sensationalized or exaggerated; they tell their own story. According to 'official' figures published in 2000, there were approximately 15 million Protestant believers in China.[7] Indeed, a careful calculation based on many local estimates puts the figure substantially higher. According to Hong Kong sources in 2000, the estimate of internal Chinese government departments was 25-35 million Protestant believers. To this, or whatever census figure is used, must be added an unnumbered and incalculable membership for the house churches that proliferated throughout the land. It is reasonable to conclude that the total for all Protestants in China in 2000 was around 50 million, with about 10 million to 12 million Roman Catholics. Between 1979 and 2000 the number of officially recognized church buildings went from nil to over 48,000. What is more, by the turn of the century an average of 6.5 churches were either being newly built or reopened every day. And Chinese-provided theological training was not being neglected. At the end of the twentieth century there were nineteen seminaries and Bible schools with a total of 1,200 theological students. There was a shortage of Christian literature of all types, but an ample supply of Bibles.

Behind these bald figures there was a reborn, lively, outward-looking and generally deeply committed body of believers. They were and have remained for the most part eager for teaching, with Sunday service sermons commonly one hour or up to one and three quarters of an hour in length, and seldom less than forty-five minutes even in the state registered churches. Persecution was not entirely a thing of the past by 2000, and believers in remote rural areas were still liable to brutal and ruthless treatment from officials, but it was not so hazardous to be a believer as under the former regime. Dedication and enthusiasm were evident to any person attending packed 7.00 a.m. weekday services before the participants went to work. And the number of converts, measured in hundreds each year in some churches, attests to evangelistic zeal of a high order. Many educated young people showed interest in the Christian faith. Neither were the churches in general tempted by the thousands of enquiries to slacken their demand for real evidence of true conversion before offering baptism. They provided careful and thorough teaching to ensure as far as possible that any commitment to the faith was based on a full understanding of what was entailed.

Here indeed was a church that had risen out of the ashes. Firm foundations had been laid so that the Christians could take advantage of favourable circumstances or be prepared for adverse situations if those were to be encountered by the believers in the future.

India

The Roman Catholics in India in the twentieth century continued the growth that had been evident in the preceding century.[8] The improving differential between births and deaths accounted in part for the mounting numbers, but there were also noticeable additions as a result of conversions. In 1912 the total number of Catholics, including the Portuguese and French possessions, was about 1,750,000.[9] By 1918 this was not far short of 2,500,000,[10] and by 1936 it was approximately 3,500,000,[11] thus almost exactly doubling in twenty-four years. These figures exclude Catholics not under Propaganda, and the Uniates, which are those churches of Eastern Christendom that were in communion with Rome, but in certain respects separate. When these two groups are added for the 1959 calculations, the total of Roman Catholics in India and Pakistan was shown to be about 5,744,000, a figure that had risen to roughly 6,000,000 two years later.[12]

A further good sign of the vigour and health of the Indian Catholic Church in the first part of the century up to the 1960s was the indigenization of its leadership. Between 1912 and 1959 the increased number of Catholic priests as a whole did not quite maintain its proportional ratio to that of the total number of the faithful, although it did so for brothers and sisters. What was of particular note, however, both immediately and as a signal of what was to come, was the steady growth in the number and proportion of Indian priests, so that by 1958 they accounted for more than 75 per cent of the Indian Catholic priesthood. This was almost exactly matched by the change in the composition of the brothers and sisters, so that by 1958 70 per cent of the former and 88 per cent of the latter were Indians.[13] The first Catholic Latin rite bishop, as contrasted with the Uniates, was consecrated in 1921. It was the beginning of a trend, for by 1958, out of a total of seventy-seven bishops, including auxiliaries, thirty-seven of the Latin rite and eight of the Oriental, Uniate, rite, were Indians. By the year 2000, all the 156 bishops were Indian.

Although these are impressive figures, there was not a massive accession of believers from among the non-Christian population. There was not the kind of staggering growth that has been encountered in South America and sub-Saharan Africa and can be cited for other countries of Asia, but still the increased membership and rapid advance of indigenization was noteworthy.

The Catholic Church also served the people in many and immensely valuable ways, not least of all by the provision of hospitals, dispensaries and homes for the aged, especially after the independence of the country, so that by 1960 there were said to be well in excess of 500 such institutions. A striking example of service to the destitute, and also a pointer to what was going on in a less publicized way in other places, was the work of the Albanian nun, Agnes Gouxha Bojaxha, known to the world as Mother Teresa.[14] She founded the Missionaries of Charity, who added to the customary vows of poverty, chastity and obedience, a fourth which explicitly expressed their dedication to work among the poor, initially those in the slums of Calcutta. It was an ambitious project. By 1960 the sisters were running primary day-schools for about 3,000 children, two commercial schools to teach girls shorthand and typing, seven clinics, and a home for fallen girls. This was appropriate service to be rendered by a church of which 60 per cent of its 16 million members in India at the end of the century were from among the poor, many of whom belonged to the lowest castes, or Dalits.

The Indian Protestants were not as numerous as the Roman Catholics, either on the eve of the First World War or in 1960, but the numerical gap between the two had narrowed in the intervening years. By 1956 there were said to be about 5,000,000 of them.[15] Although calculations are not entirely accurate, this probably means that the number of Protestants was less than three-quarters of a million short of the Catholic total.

This is an appropriate point at which to comment briefly again on mass movements, for they undoubtedly played a major role in boosting Protestant, as well as Roman Catholic, numbers. Indeed, as previously noted, it has been estimated that by the 1930s not less than 80 per cent of the Indian Protestants were the product of this type of recruitment, as well as half of the Roman Catholics.[16] Mass movements had occurred ever since the sixteenth century, but there was an acceleration of them following the First World War. Nowhere or at any time in India was there a general, or even regional, mass turning of people to Christianity, but in a significant number of villages people of the same ethnic and ancestral group were converted. Writing in 1933, one well-informed observer, commented that it 'would be difficult to overstate the faith-kindling power of this modern apologetic'.[17]

The establishment of the Church of South India (CSI) on 27 September 1947, and its subsequent viable life, contrasted with mass movements in both its character and consequences, being primarily a matter of structures, organizations and forms of church government. Nonetheless, as an extremely public demonstration of Christian unity, it was a further aid to the propagation of the Christian faith. It united three religious bodies in the area: the (Anglican) Church of India, Burma and Ceylon, the South India Province of the Methodist Church, and the South India United Church, which itself was the result of previous organic union between the Presbyterians, the Congregationalists, the Dutch Reformed bodies and the Basel Mission, and which drew its members from Lutheran and Reformed churches. No reordination of ministers and clergy was involved, but all future ministers were to be episcopally ordained. A 'Pledge' was provided whereby no congregation would be compelled to accept a ministry about which its members objected on grounds of conscience. Underlying the scheme was a concern for Christians in India and the churches to which they belonged to become more Indian. Over the next few decades the CSI scheme, or at least aspects of it, became widely accepted as a plausible model for other schemes throughout the world.

In 1970, a much weaker Church of North India and a Protestant Church of Pakistan were inaugurated. This entailed the coming together of Baptists and Lutherans, along with many Anabaptist and Free Church people, who still retained their separate identities and communities. The same situation applied to the six to ten Syrian and Thomas Christian communions of Kerala.

Mass movements and the Church of South India were hugely important in promoting the Christian faith in the India–Pakistan subcontinent, but they cannot be allowed to attract all the attention, or to detract from the ongoing, often quite routine and prosaic work of local churches and the many Christian institutions throughout the land. These were at the heart of Protestant Christianity and all that it stood for. And they were increasingly

Indian in membership and leadership as missionaries from abroad, with just a few exceptions, almost disappeared.

In addition to the regular life of worship, prayer, evangelism and pastoral work, of the countless, mostly quite small, fellowships of believers, the effect of which was immeasurable, Protestantism in India impacted on the people perhaps most tellingly through the many specialist bodies it established and maintained. Both before and after Indian independence, Christian schools played an important part in the national educational scheme, especially in raising the literacy rate of the depressed masses and in giving such underprivileged people training that enabled many of them to improve their economic lot. By 1930, Protestants maintained thirty-seven arts colleges, six of which were for women. By the mid 1950s they were also providing 266 hospitals and over 200 dispensaries; and more than twenty-four hospitals were training nurses.[18] In addition, Protestants of various denominations were operating fifty institutions for lepers, thirteen tuberculosis sanatoria, ten centres for the blind and deaf, many orphanages and homes for women, and numbers of social and welfare centres.[19] Other spheres of quite extensive Protestant activity included famine relief, help to refugees, the founding and management of co-operative banks and societies, and agricultural settlements, with advice provided through experts in rural reorganization. Such an abundance of humanitarian institutions and organizations substantially helped in the national effort to establish a social service infra-structure after independence, and to set a high standard of care, concern and professional dedication that contributed greatly to the whole character and viability of a new nation.

In addition to such works, undertaken by the Protestants and the Roman Catholics alike, some progress was made by both in spreading the faith in the second half of the twentieth century, especially among the poorer members of society. This probably accounts for the recurrent persecutions and mob violence directed against the churches throughout India, which markedly increased in frequency and seriousness in the last three years of the century. These acts of aggression were most often Hindu inspired, and included personal assaults and even murder, bomb attacks and the destruction of churches. Ad hoc vigilantism was supplemented by demands from some radical Hindu groups for official discrimination against Christianity, and some cities or states banned conversions or erected many legal difficulties for potential converts, such as requiring changes of religion to be registered with local authorities. All of this is a measure of the fact that Christianity was a force worthy of opposition and resistance; it does not indicate that the churches were inactive and ineffectual.

The Philippines

In the Philippines in the twentieth century there was the unusual spectacle of both Roman Catholicism and Protestantism thriving in the same area. The Roman Catholic Church held sway from the sixteenth century until the beginning of the twentieth century. By 1595 Manila had an archdiocesan see, and during the seventeenth century the nation was extensively Christianized by Catholics. From then onwards was a time of consolidation, so that the beliefs and practices of the Roman Catholic Church became deeply ingrained in the culture and society of the nation.

Nonetheless, Protestantism began to prosper in the twentieth century. The number of reported communicants increased from 46,444 in 1914[20] to 334,000 in 1957.[21] If these figure are reasonably accurate, it means that during a period when the population of the country had increased approximately threefold, Protestants had multiplied between seven- and eightfold. Thus, gains were only in part due to an excess of births over deaths; the bulk were a consequence of conversions or accretions, again, as in many other countries of the world, probably mainly from among nominal Roman Catholics, as well as from among the Aglipayans, a group of schismatic Catholics, and to a limited extent from among the animist minorities. American Congregational, Presbyterian, Baptist and Methodist missionaries, as well as those from the Disciples of Christ were very active in the years up to 1939, when the Philippine Federation of Evangelical Churches was formed. By the 1960s Protestantism was moving towards independence. Financial assistance and personnel continued to come from abroad, but many of the churches were self-supporting. Filipino

Protestantism was notable for the manner in which, as in India, it touched the life of the country through a variety of channels, including education, social services of many kinds, and medical care, by means of improving family life, and in raising the status of women, as well as in the way so many people were won to the faith. It was also an outward-looking church, and in the 1950s was sending missionaries to Malaya, Okinawa, Indonesia, Korea and Hawaii.[22]

By the end of the twentieth century, the Protestants comprised about 8 per cent of the population. This is an impressive figure in view of the fact that Islam was strong, and Roman Catholicism had been the dominant form of Christianity for a long period, to the almost total exclusion of Protestantism. Surging Pentecostal groups, such as the Jesus is Lord movement, helped to give drive and animation to this trend.

But the Roman Catholics also made good progress and the country remained overwhelmingly Catholic. By 2003 about 85 per cent of the nation had some degree of identification with the Roman Catholic Church. In absolute terms this meant a Roman Catholic membership of 61 million, a larger number of adherents than to be found in any individual European state, and it was growing swiftly. An average of about 1.7 million baptisms a year – more than the combined totals of the four leading Catholic nations of Europe, France, Spain, Italy and Poland – was swelling the membership, and continues to do so.[23] By 2025, the Filipino Catholics could number 90 million, and by 2050, 130 million. Such growth will help to change even more the shape of global Catholicism.

Once again, as with the Protestants, the Catholics have been fully and effectively engaged in a variety of 'secular' activities. In the case of the Catholics, the church has a distinguished record on social justice issues. In the early twentieth century Catholic priests were to the fore in anti-colonial struggles, and then later in the revolutionary movement that resulted in the overthrow of the dictator Ferdinand Marcos in 1986. The latter campaign, and a subsequent movement to impeach the Philippine leader, President Joseph Estrada, for receiving massive bribes, were given a symbolic national focus in the person of the charismatic Cardinal Jaime Sin.

All this Catholic and Protestant expansion and vitality were taking place within the framework of a country which itself was advancing on the world scene. In the size of its population alone it has assumed global significance. In 1975, it was the fourteenth largest country in the world, with a population of 44 million.[24] By 2050, however, it is calculated that it will rank eleventh, with 154 million inhabitants. Even more impressive from the point of view of the global disposition of Christians, is the fact that in 2000 it possibly ranked fourth in the world in its number of Christians, with only the USA, Brazil, Mexico, and perhaps Russia, ahead of it, and in 2050 it is reckoned that it will be jointly third, together with Mexico.[25]

Japan

The history of the church in Japan in the twentieth century is less dramatic than that of China, India or Korea, which will be described and discussed next, and it has so far produced less sensational results. Yet it is still significant as an example of the Christian penetration of yet another stronghold of well-established ancient religion and culture, in which Buddhism, Taoism, Shinto and Confucianism were embedded in the very fabric of a highly structured and sophisticated society.

By the beginning of the twentieth century, Japan was increasingly becoming a member of the international community of nations. Christianity made steady progress, with a concentration on cities. The Roman Catholic Church increased from 66,134 members in 1912, with 152 foreign priests, 33 Japanese priests, 133 lay brothers and 232 nuns, to 100,491 members, 251 foreign and 73 Japanese priests, 96 foreign and 141 Japanese lay brothers, and 423 foreign and 355 native nuns, in 1933.[26] The Catholics were also reaching out in fresh ways. These included the opening by the Jesuits of a fully fledged university at Sophia, which in 1938 had over a thousand students. A sanatorium was opened on the outskirts of Tokyo, and there was a multiplication in the number of Christian books made available for distribution. The church also made rapid strides towards the indigenization of the episcopate and the church's administration.

In the post-First World War period, the Protestants made valiant efforts to reach the entire nation with the Christian message, most notably and effectively with the Kingdom of God Movement, which enlisted most of the Protestant forces. Its chief leader was the renowned Toyohiko Kagawa. He united a vigorous witness on social questions with an international reputation gained through the widespread sale of his books. A goal of winning 'a million souls' was set before the Christians, but he sought to make the initiative a means of social as well as individual transformation. Regrettably, he was not rewarded with many converts or much evidence of the kind of corporate changes in society for which he longed. This was typical of most of the indigenous and overseas missionary work in the country in the first half of the twentieth century.

Nonetheless, Protestant Christianity in the period between the World Wars was stronger than the statistics of church membership seemed to indicate. This was so partly because it appealed extensively to the professional and civil service groups. Among these, were some men and women who were eminent in the life of the country, regarded themselves as Christians, but did not formally align themselves or affiliate to any Christian organization.[27]

Intense patriotism and focus on loyalty to the emperor were the hallmarks of the totalitarian regime that existed up to and then throughout the Second World War, with an intolerance of Christianity as an essentially non-Japanese religion. The work of foreign missionaries became ever more difficult and restricted. It was some consolation that there was a small but important growth of both the Japanese church and distinctive, authentic and original Japanese theological scholarship. Here, in a quiet and unpublicized way, were signs that the church was establishing itself in a sound and effective, even if small-scale, manner.

Christian workers started to return in the post-Second World War years, during the time of the Occupation, and by 1963 there were 4,000 Protestant missionaries in the country. Although the Christians went through a difficult time trying to repair both the physical and spiritual damage caused by the war, by 1980 there were almost a million Japanese Protestants and 750,000 Roman Catholics in Japan, which was a small proportion of the total population, but nevertheless a quite satisfactory number in view of the historical and contemporary predominance of other major religions. Even so, it was probably the new religious movements such as Soka Gakkai, which were firmly based in the Japanese religious tradition, that achieved the greater long-term gains. By the end of the century, Christianity was still a marginal faith in the land, but also an influential and significant element in the Japanese religious scene.

Korea

In a review of the progress of worldwide Christianity, South Korea is of interest out of all proportion to its size and its political or economic standing. This is because it has been the scene of a remarkable and virtually continuous Christian revival ever since the early years of the twentieth century, with peaks and troughs, and at the end of that century was the scene of one of the most lively and thriving examples of the faith anywhere on earth. This included many large, healthy and extremely active individual churches.

It all began in 1906, in the midst of severe political and social turmoil.[28] A number of missionaries gathered together to pray, and continued to do so on frequent occasions for over a year. A few months later, a Bible class was convened in Pyongyang. It recruited its members mainly from near at hand, but also from other towns and districts. The attendance grew, until it reached about a thousand or more. Some meetings went on all night.

Largely as a consequence of the prayer offered by such groups, some of the intercessors resolved to proclaim the Christian faith to the whole of the country within a year. They raised a large amount of money to facilitate the work of entering areas previously untouched by missionaries. They had a million copies of the Gospel of St Mark printed, and sold 700,000 in a single year. They also sent missionaries abroad. It was in essence a penitential and confessional renewal movement, for those features were prominent from the start. But many converts resulted from the meetings and the energetic witnessing.

With the Communist occupation of North Korea after the Second World War, there was a serious persecution of Christians.

South Korea experienced the agony and devastation of the Korean War between 1950 and 1953 but, despite this, prayer meetings became ever more popular, with some attendances estimated at 10,000, or even in excess of that.

One anecdote helps to capture something of the prevailing atmosphere of devotion and enthusiasm at that time, and in the following years. Rene Monod recounts his experiences during his first visit to the country after the war. On his arrival in Seoul he was invited to address a prayer meeting at 5.00 a.m. It was raining and snowing as he made his way to the church, and he was convinced that the meeting would have been cancelled or, if still on, that there would be very few present. As an additional discouragement, the taxi driver charged him double fare, which was considered reasonable for a night journey. Somewhat pessimistically he entered the church, only to find the whole place was crammed with people. He was informed that it was a regular prayer meeting, that there were almost 3,000 people present, representing nearly the entire congregation, and that there was a similar gathering daily. The participants were eager to pray, and many uttered their prayers aloud and concurrently, but in harmony and without any fanatical zeal, for just under an hour. One of the elders then asked him to give his address, adding, 'a short one, please, not longer than an hour. These people have to go to work at seven o'clock.'

Monod discovered three such groups, and was told at the third that those types of meeting had been held every day for five years. They were supplemented by smaller gatherings of about a hundred members of the congregation, with different people involved on each occasion, which were held in the evenings, with the prayer continuing until dawn. And once a week, from Saturday to Sunday, about a thousand assembled, and prayed all night.[29] Such dedication of time and effort by the believers was matched by their sacrificial giving of money. A common practice traceable to well back in the revival, was for them to give half of what they earned to enable the work to continue in their country, and in order to support missionaries they sent to neighbouring countries.

From its inception, those involved in the Korean revival gave healing a central place in their ministry. A special meeting was typically held once a month, and these were reputedly linked with exceptional cases of cures and restoration of health. It would require a thorough study to authenticate the claims made, but there is no prima facie reason to doubt them.

In view of such commitment and enthusiasm, not just by the few, but by whole, large, congregations, it is of little wonder that the number of Christians in Korea vastly increased during the twentieth century. There were only 300,000 or so of them in the whole of the country in 1920, but this rose to 10 million or 12 million in the following eighty years.[30] By 2000, Protestants outnumbered Roman Catholics by three to one and, as already seen in South America and to an extent in sub-Saharan Africa, this expansion largely resulted from the staggering growth of Pentecostalism.[31] From the time of the Korean War to the early 1980s the nation's Pentecostals increased from a few hundred to almost half a million, and the graph of growth continued to rise steeply and continuously. The scale of this was dazzling for some individual congregations. Outstanding among these was the Full Gospel Central Church in Seoul, which by the end of the century had well over half a million members, thus earning it a place in the *Guinness Book of Records* as the world's largest congregation. And the mainline, Western denominations were not sidelined in this astounding expansion. The Kwang Lim Methodist Church reported 150 members in 1971, but 85,000 by the end of the century; and by 2000 there were almost twice as many Presbyterians in South Korea as in the United States.[32]

In the latter half of the twentieth century Christianity also made rapid progress in the Chinese diaspora of mostly prosperous Chinese communities scattered around the Pacific Rim, in nations such as Malaysia, Singapore and Indonesia. The latter was the scene of especially impressive Christian growth and activity.

Indonesia

Up to the nineteenth century, 'the government-sponsored Church of the Netherlands East Indies went on its steady unimaginative way, ministering to the Dutch, to the increasing community of mixed origin, and to the old Churches which had arisen in the previous centuries'.[33] The situation was transformed in the early nineteenth century with the arrival and work of the Netherlands Missionary Society. This body was one of the products of the European revival movements of the time and of the previous century, and it undertook its task in Indonesia with gusto, determination and clearness of aim. It concentrated largely on the region of Minahassa in the north of the island of Celebes, and its labours were rewarded when the whole population was Christianized by the end of the century.

It was, in fact, in Indonesia that greater progress was recorded than in any other country in South-east Asia in the nineteenth century. The Dutch missions achieved more success in terms of the numbers of converts than any other mission to Muslims. Large churches were established and attained a high level of maturity in Celebes, in Timor and in Halmahera.

The state of the Protestant churches remained healthy as the twentieth century advanced. After independence was declared in December 1949, however, an attempt was made by the new regime to erase anything that could recall the time of Dutch ascendancy. As part of this policy, the new government put such pressure on the Dutch missionaries that they were in effect compelled to withdraw. The churches were left almost entirely to their own devices, under Indonesian leadership. But the Christian work did not stagnate, grind to a halt or contract. It was less than twenty years after independence that the church experienced a revival that added greatly to its numbers, and imparted new zeal and sense of purpose to its members.

This pivotal event was prefaced by a series of evangelistic campaigns on the island of Timor in the summer of 1965.[34] These were immediate followed by manifestations of spiritual concern, followed by many conversions in other islands of Indonesia. What happened was typical of similar phenomena in Europe, Britain and North America in the eighteenth and nineteenth centuries, and in various places throughout the world since then. But a few aspects of this particular manifestation of revival are worthy of comment.

One feature was the extensive burning of images and emblems of traditional cults by members of the native population who were converted during the revival. In many cases, the people involved were members of churches; but, whether nominal Christians, non-Christians, or committed members of a Christian group, this act had very considerable symbolic as well as practical significance, for it represented a personal casting away of any lingering allegiance to another religious tradition. It was a clear repudiation of any attachment to norms and practices that could be construed as alien to the Christianity the converts were embracing in a new or renewed way. The act was frequently performed in public, so it was a highly visible proclamation of dedication to the Christian religion, and the rejection of any competing religious tradition. The destruction of such images and emblems gave tangible form to an inner act of commitment, and by so doing helped both to make the commitment more obviously genuine, real and meaningful, and to give to it a greater measure and sense of finality.

The revival was also noteworthy for the extent to which it resulted in outreach and efforts by the existing Christians and the converts to spread the faith which meant so much to them. This was demonstrated by the emergence of evangelistic teams, mostly of young people. These were organized as a spontaneous response by a number of congregations to the challenge of making the revival message known in other areas, either of the island in which the assembly was situated, or further afield. During the first year seventy-two such evangelistic bands were formed. They travelled about, mainly intent on preaching, both publicly and conversationally, but also, in some instances, with the secondary purpose of healing. Great numbers of fellow Indonesians were converted by this strategy and, as with all such widespread lay participation, it was a means of maximizing the effective use of the available human resources, and of ensuring a high level of membership commitment.

Finally, this particular revival is of special interest because it occurred in a missionary situation, in a society and culture that, on many of the islands, was fundamentally non-Christian. It was distinctive in that a high proportion of the converts were from outside the Christian tradition. In one of the islands it appears that before the revival there were hardly any Christians, the numbers not even reaching treble figures, whereas, by 1970, there were claimed to be 20,000 Christian believers.[35] It seems that between 1964 and 1970 the Muslims, the traditional religionists and the nominal Christians were all touched by the revival. Numerically, the greatest impact was among the nominal Christians who were members of or associated in some way with the existing churches, but the other two categories of the population also accounted for many who committed themselves to the Christian faith.

The repercussions of the revival were felt for decades after the event. The number of Christians steadily increased, and by the 1990s they were a prominent feature in the religious scene, especially associated with the Chinese mercantile community. With the 'success' of the revival came considerable resentment and opposition, and Christians became the target of Islamic aggression. Periodically they were massacred and expelled, and they were used as a scapegoat by the Suharto dictatorship after the economy went into tailspin in 1997.

The Pacific Island churches

The achievement of self-government in the Pacific Island churches came prior to national independence.[36] It began in the central Pacific, in Samoa, Tonga and Fiji, in places where Christianity had been planted in the early nineteenth century. After the Second World War, the process accelerated. In 1948 the Presbyterian Church of the New Hebrides was founded; and during the following thirty years the London Missionary Society, Methodist, Anglican, Lutheran, South Sea Evangelical and French Reformed missions all became autonomous national churches. This helped to ensure that by the end of the century Christianity remained a dominant force in Pacific Island cultures.

After 1960 the quality and effectiveness of the life of the churches was invigorated by the almost complete dissolving of Western denominational divisions, and by the high level of cooperation among the various Protestant churches and organizations, with the creation of some special bodies to promote such unity and united action. But, just as significantly, there was a lively search for 'the Pacific way' in Christianity. 'Both Protestants and Catholics began working towards expressions of worship, theology and art rooted in the traditions and belief-patterns of the Pacific Islanders.'[37]

The task facing such churches was greatly complicated and made more difficult in the closing decades of the century. The former life of Western denominational churches in unified village communities was eroded. At the same time the churches were faced with new challenges as a result of migration to towns, and by such features of 'modernity' as the expansion of tourism, the ever-growing influence of radio and television, and the arrival of new religious movements, mainly from the United States. These and other changes made life more varied and interesting for the local Christians and the Christian churches, but it also brought some confusion and difficulties because there were more options available than ever before, and more voices calling out to be heard. In Fiji, as one example, whereas the Methodist Church once dominated the Christian scene, by the 1990s there were some thirty different religious denominations and evangelical organizations.

Then there were the political changes that took place. These impinged on the life of the churches, especially as their increased indigenization meant that they played an important role in nationalist causes. The Protestants were drawn into independence movements in French Polynesia, New Caledonia and the New Hebrides; the first prime minister of independent Vanuata, Walter Lini, was an Anglican priest; the majority of Fijian Methodists gave support to the military coup in Fiji in 1987; and the Catholic bishop and his clergy played a part in the Bougainville independence movement in the nation of Papua New Guinea. Such political engagement illustrates the maturity of the churches in being able to address complicated issues, but it also 'illustrates the problems inherent in any alliance of Churches with secular political movements'.[38]

Asia – an overview

Asia is part of the remarkable change in the Christian centre of gravity from the north to the south that has taken place, first in a quite gradual, almost entirely unnoticed way, during the first half of the twentieth century, and then with ever greater acceleration during the latter half of that momentous hundred years in the history of Christianity. This points to an even more stupendous era for Asian Christianity as the twenty-first century unfolds. It is already the home for over 315 million professing Christians, and many of the Asian churches are excited about the prospects for future growth, and the promise of a new Christian epoch. There is widespread Christian pessimism in Europe and Britain; but this contrasts with the buoyant optimism in many parts of Asia. One such enthusiastic observer captures the difference. 'Europe', he writes, 'is in the times of Jesus with anti-establishment protests against aging religious institutions tottering under the weight of its wealth, property and privileges. Asia is in the times of Paul, planting a convert church in virgin soil.'[39] The huge church in China is committed to sending out 100,000 missionaries in the next decade or two, and other churches in the region are likewise looking outward and forward with eagerness. For them, the holding of the faith is not a defensive, rearguard exercise; a desperate attempt to halt a demoralizing decline, but a buoyant seizing of opportunities to enlarge their ministries. They are ambitious to propagate the gospel.

What has been briefly described in this chapter does not tell more than a fraction of the story. Christianity is making progress even where the political situation and the circumstances in general are stacked against it. In Vietnam, as an example, despite much Communist opposition, the churches have been resilient. Even official figures say that 9 per cent of the population is Christian, and this excludes Protestant churches that refuse to register with the government. 'The scale of these catacomb churches is open to debate, but internal government documents suggest mushroom growth in some areas, notably those inhabited by tribal minorities like the Montagnards. In the province of Lao Cai, Protestant numbers grew from zero in 1991 to between 50,000 and 70,000 by 1998.'[40] What the future holds for such churches is, of course, unknown, but it is certainly full of boundless promise.

7

An Appraisal

The revivals and awakenings of the eighteenth century in mainland Europe, Britain and North America were remarkable in
themselves but, in terms of the history of global Christianity as a
whole, they were also seminal and stupendous. They were by
way of a preparation for what amounted to a staggering sequel.
The nineteenth-century 'second phase' vibrant Christianity in
Europe, Britain and North America, then provided the source of
vision, manpower and resources to launch and sustain a remarkable, unmatched, globalization of Christianity. Since 1800, the
world has passed through a Christian revolution of gigantic proportions. 'In an astonishing period of 200 years the position of
Christianity in the world has changed out of all recognition.'[1]
What has been charted in the previous chapters represents 'the
most remarkable movement in the Church since the time of the
apostles'.[2]

In 1492 less than 20 per cent of the world's population was
Christian, and over 90 per cent of these lived in Europe. 'For all
its regional, confessional, and ecclesiastical differences,
Christianity bore the imprint of a broadly European cultural
identity. Only a small fraction of the non-Christian population of
the world, estimated at 2 per cent, had come into contact with
Christianity.'[3] This remained essentially the situation until the
late eighteenth century. The paternalistic approach to empire-
building by European powers in the sixteenth, seventeenth and
eighteenth centuries, especially in North America, but also in
Australia and New Zealand, ensured the dependence of the
colonies on their mother countries, so that this extended
Christendom remained Eurocentric and part of 'Western

Christendom'. In any case, the new colonies themselves incorporated comparatively few of the local natives into their society or church life, so that they continued to be essentially European in their language, culture and social mores. They were to all intents and purposes an extension of European Christendom. This reinforced the sense among all concerned that Christianity was fundamentally a European religion, which primarily consisted of Europeans. The Christian faith had the appearance of being first and foremost a religion for the benefit of Europeans. 'Until recently, the overwhelming majority of Christians have lived in White nations, allowing theorists to speak smugly, arrogantly, of "European Christian" civilization.'[4]

The present-day picture is very different indeed. Just over five centuries after Columbus sailed the ocean blue the global disposition of Christianity has changed astoundingly. There are now approximately two billion Christians in the world, about a third of the total population of the planet. Although the largest single bloc of some 560 million are still to be found in Europe, and North America claims about 260 million believers, South America is already close behind Europe with 480 million, Africa has 360 million, and there are 313 million professing Christians in Asia. Extrapolating these figures to the year 2025, and making no allowance for great gains or losses through conversions or apostasies, although in the 'Third Church' there may well be considerable gains, and in Continental Europe and Britain severe losses, the predicted figures indicate that there would be in the order of 2.6 billion Christians, of whom 640 million would be found in South America, 633 million in Africa, 555 million in Europe, and 460 million in Asia.[5] To project even further, by 2050 it seems that only about 20 per cent of the world's three billion Christians will be non-Hispanic Whites.[6] What is more, it was estimated as early as 1992 that 77 per cent of the world's population had come into direct contact with some form of Christianity, and this percentage has increased since then. Even non-Christians, therefore, mostly live in a world that to some extent features Christianity. By any reckoning, such statistics represent a sensational globalization of Christianity. A process has taken place, and is continuing at an ever more furious pace, that demolishes, and indeed makes a mockery of, the kind of glosses and doom-laden portrayals of the situation offered by many Western academics and commentators.

In Continental Europe as a whole, and in Britain, there is still to a degree a clinging on in the collective consciousness to the memories and remnants of a past age when Spain, Portugal, Britain and later Germany, Belgium and Italy were the motherlands of empires great or small, and vast areas of the world were under the sway of one European power or another. But those days are largely in the past. A new world has emerged that is beginning to be recognized and acknowledged in the political and economic spheres, even though some diehards hold on desperately to past glories, and are blind to the inexorable changes that are taking place. But the new order is less acknowledged in the social and, from the point of view of the present work, most notably in the religious sphere. A shattering realignment has occurred and is still taking place that is not congenial to many Westerners. This redisposition is doing nothing less than producing a new map of the Christian world. Soon, 'the phrase "a White Christian" may sound like a curious oxymoron, as mildly surprising as "a Swedish Buddhist"'.[7] It may be recognized that such people can exist, but a slight eccentricity may well be implied. It is a prospect that few could now even contemplate, but it is by no means beyond the realm of possibility within the next hundred years or so.

It needs to be appreciated that the transformation of the worldwide religious scene during the last two centuries has been and still is part of an overall shift of population, and of both political and economic power, on a mega scale. This reached prodigious proportions in the course of the twentieth century, and it is now of unequalled magnitude. It seems likely to become even more pronounced and critical as the third millennium advances. The United Nations has predicted that as soon as 2015 the top ten largest urban concentrations will not include one Western city. It is anticipated that Tokyo will head the list with 28.7 million inhabitants, followed by Bombay/Mumbai with 27.4 million, Lagos with 24.4 million, and then Shanghai (23.4 million), Jakarta (21.2 million), Sao Paulo (20.8 million), Karachi (20.6 million), Beijing (19.4 million), Dhaka (19.0 million) and Mexico (18.8 million).[8] Politically and economically China is poised to become a superpower, and other at present underdeveloped countries will no doubt join the present elite group of leading political and industrial countries in the next hundred years or so, and in some respects will undoubtedly overhaul existing front-runners in that privileged coterie.

One aspect of the revolutionary redrawing of the global religious map, is the new balance of power and influence in the world of the only two great monotheistic, proselytizing faiths, Islam and Christianity. Although it has been suggested that Islam will be dominant in the next quarter or half a century, it appears that by 2020 Christianity will 'have a massive lead, and will maintain its position into the foreseeable future.' By 2050 there should be 'about three Christians for every two Muslims worldwide. Some 34 per cent of the world's people will then be Christian'.[9]

The blossoming of what is variously called militant or fundamentalist Islam is acknowledged quite widely and receives much academic and popular attention. But the other epoch-making movement, the resurgence and transformation of global Christianity, is hardly recognized outside a fairly restricted cluster of informed scholars. Alongside the political, economic, social and technological revolutions, which have been clear for all to see, and which have commanded enormous media attention and coverage, as well as expert analysis and constant comment, there has been this far less trumpeted, but equally important revolution in the status and standing of worldwide Christianity. Few have taken on board what is happening, or have given it the recognition that it deserves. Indeed, almost the only major and sustained headline-grabbing feature of Christianity as a whole, other than such comparatively minor internal wrangles as the ordination of women and the attitude of the churches to homosexuals, has been the dire prediction of many that the institutional forms of the Christian faith are quickly and surely sliding into oblivion, and that there is even an imminent death of God. How wrong can we be in grasping at least the basic facts of what is happening!

The analysis of many scholars and observers has been seriously inaccurate. 'The death of God has often been prematurely reported and the withering of religion confidently predicted. Instead, today, secularism is on the defensive, while religions are back – active powers in the reshaping of a spiritually charged world. Christianity in particular . . . has made an unpredictable comeback.'[10] Thus wrote Filipe Fernandez-Armesto and Derek Wilson in a highly acclaimed work in the latter part of the twentieth century. Philip Jenkins, in a brilliant portrayal of the changes taking place, elaborates on this. He points out that little regard was given during 2000 and 2001, in the usual reflections at the turn of a century and a millennium, to religious matters. 'After all', he writes, 'the attitude seemed to be, what religious change in recent years could possibly compete in importance with the major secular trends, movements like fascism or communism, feminism or environmentalism?' But, he goes on to say that such a diagnosis and such tunnel vision seriously missed the mark in one important respect. He suggests that

> it is precisely religious changes that are the most significant, and even the most revolutionary, in the contemporary world. Before too long, the turn-of-the-millennium neglect of religious factors may come to be seen as comically myopic, on a par with a review of the eighteenth-century that managed to miss the French Revolution. We are currently living through one of the transforming moments in the history of religion worldwide.[11]

The picture portrayed in the foregoing chapters, albeit with the reservation that, due to lack of space and in order to concentrate on the particular purpose of the book, it does not greatly highlight failures and shortcomings, is hardly that of global Christianity in decline. In 1990, one eminent academic observed that, taking an international perspective, the twentieth century had produced 'two truly global movements of enormous vitality. One' he commented,

> is conservative Islam, the other conservative Protestantism. Since the Iranian revolution at least a good deal of attention has been paid to the former in the West. Conservative Protestantism in its world-wide explosion remains, by and large, terra incognita even to otherwise well-informed people in the West. It is high time that this changed, for the potential impact of this religious phenomenon is likely to be very powerful indeed.[12]

Since these words were penned, this prognostication has proved to be accurate. Some attention has been given to it, but pathetically little in proportion to its historical, sociological and theological significance.

Taking the broad sweep of global Christian history, the last 300 years may reasonably be compared with the similar span of time after the death and resurrection of Christ. The earlier period was unique in that it saw the birth and first major expansion of the faith, and in that regard it is clearly unrepeatable and incomparable, but there are parallels with the post-1700 world developments that are neither fanciful nor outrageous. In the case of the early church, the day of Pentecost was succeeded by the wonders of the apostolic age in which a small band of Christians 'turned the world upside-down',[13] and the faith was planted in many parts of the then known world. In the period from about 1700 to the present day, revivals, awakenings and a resurgence of Christianity in Continental Europe, Britain and North America prepared the way for an unprecedented expansion of the faith throughout most of the world. The growth and extension of the early church was facilitated by the existence of the Roman Empire, with its power to exert authority, its unifying effect on previously discrete and 'underdeveloped' territories, its rule of law, and its roads. In the modern era there was the opening up of worldwide avenues for expansion as a result of exploration, the development of trade routes, improvements in transport and various means of communication, and the seemingly unstoppable growth of European empires. To continue the comparison, there was the emergence of at least a measure of local autonomy allowing for the development of local forms of Christianity in the initial period of the faith, and the comparable, gradual formation of new nations in the nineteenth and twentieth centuries, with all the potential for 'indigenization' and the harnessing of local energies that this entailed, which proved to be a potent force for the expression and propagation of the Christian faith in the modern period. The extent to which any such comparison is valid or not is open to debate, but to speak of the two periods together in one breath as commensurate is not outlandish.

Mainland Europe and Britain

Mainland Europe and Britain have been the main areas of interest for those advocating various forms of the secularization thesis, but seen within the framework and span of the last 300 years of Christianity worldwide, these regions can legitimately be regarded as abnormal; as exceptions to what has and is taking place rather than the norm; and, indeed, almost as aberrations. The 'secularization thesis developed within a European framework. For certain stages in Europe's religious development, moreover, there is a convincing fit between the argument and the data.'[14] But the almost total concentration on mainland Europe and Britain has inevitably distorted, and continues to distort, the picture and portrayal when any attempt is made to generalize for worldwide Christianity. Having once set out with this primary, and in many cases almost exclusive, focus, it is difficult to take sufficient account of the global perspective. Some of the proponents of the thesis in one of its variant forms, have been unaware, or insufficiently aware, of what was occurring in the non-Western world, others have undervalued its strength and significance, and still others, one suspects, have not wanted to know. A few may even have had their own agendas and have not been prepared to consider phenomena that were so patently at variance with the thesis they were championing. Even those who have been conscious of the wider scene have mostly been unprepared to acknowledge the extent to which the Continental European and British situations were out of step with the rest of the world. What was applicable to the 'old world' was not necessarily applicable universally. 'Bit by bit, however, the thesis rather than the data began to dominate the agenda. The "fit" became axiomatic, theoretically necessary rather than empirically founded – so much so that Europe's religious life was considered a prototype of global religiosity; what Europe did today everyone else would do tomorrow.'[15] The brief survey provided by this present book makes nonsense of any such presupposition.

Not only so, but the use of the kind of statistical indicators, such as declining church membership and numbers attending Christian places of worship, that are the very grist to the mill of those suggesting that industrialization, urbanization, modernization and

rationalization, particularly since the eighteenth century, have combined to sink Christianity, or at best, from the Christian point of
view, to make a radical redrafting of its theological concepts and
language a requisite for survival, is questionable. Are such numbers
ever a true measure of a live and healthy church? One wonders, for
instance, how the early church, with the handful of disciples and
converts who by anyone's reckoning effectively, and indeed almost
miraculously, laid the foundations for the future church, would
have fared if subjected to the statistical analysis that underpins all
secularization theories. What would have been the result if such a
yardstick had been used for the European church before and after
the Edict of Milan (the so-called 'Peace of the Church') of 313? There
is widespread acceptance that the Church as a whole was more vigorous and full of evangelistic and pastoral energy before that
hugely determinative event than after it, when to believe was
easier and less costly, and conformism did not necessarily mean
deep commitment and dedication as in the days of persecution. Yet
the application of modern statistics might well have shown the very
reverse of this. Applying modern secularization techniques and criteria, the post-313 Church would unquestionably have won, and
would therefore be deemed more 'successful' than the Church prior
to 313.

It is arguable that in certain circumstances, but by no means
always, after many centuries of Christianization, the higher the
membership figures the lower is the vibrancy of the Church. After
all, Christ made it very clear that 'narrow is the gate that leads to
eternal life, and few are they that go through it'.[16] In talking about
'secularization' it may make for greater clarity, precision and
sophistication if it was acknowledged that there are two types of
Christianity: the one that represents a personal, life-transforming,
faith, that is, almost inevitably, and almost by definition, the experience of a small minority of the population; and the other a diffused, pervasive, somewhat amorphous willingness of a large
proportion of the population to align personal belief and practice
somewhat vaguely to what is the local, national, or indeed international religious norm. In the latter case, national and local
institutions clearly function according to explicit Christian standards and values, accepted and acknowledged by most of the
inhabitants at the time, but there are not necessarily many of the

people who are deeply and passionately committed to the Christian faith and life. A high rating for the second, widespread conformist, situation does not of itself show how healthy Christianity is at any one time and in any one place. A large number of people in the second category may be a less accurate gauge of religious vitality and health than a much smaller number in the first category. Quality, commitment and dedication are difficult to measure and quantify, but they are of crucial importance. Allied to this is the hazard of relying too much on certain easily obtainable statistics. To focus almost exclusively upon church membership and attendance is to decide in advance solely in favour of an institutional description and definition of Christianity.

For the Western world in particular, it is helpful to distinguish between 'Christianity' and 'Christendom'.[17] Christendom is a much broader concept than Christianity. It refers to a society that is infused with the beliefs and values of Christianity, where the Church is the dominant, if not monopolistic, religion, and is accorded a central role in corporate life. It is a cultural and social situation in which every sector of the society at least formally accepts the supremacy of the Christian faith as the source of all standards. In mainland Europe and Britain, there was Christianity for at least three centuries before there was what can be clearly identified as Christendom. There are parts of the world, for instance China, 'where there has never been a Christendom, but where there are many millions of Christians. Christendom is no more than a phase in the history of Christianity, and it represents only one out of many possible relationships between church and society. Yet in western Europe this phase lasted for more than a thousand years, and we are still living in its shadow.'[18] Perhaps most of the statistics used to measure secularization in fact measure the demise of Christendom, and not the decline of Christianity. Such a view harmonizes to a degree at least with Bryan Wilson's definition of secularization as the process by which religion loses its social significance.[19] It also accords with the opinions of Steve Bruce. He argues that whereas religion once acted as a binding force, there has been an irreversible trend towards individualism in modern Western societies that has caused religion to fragment. This, he says, leads ultimately to a market situation where each individual chooses what is suitable to his or her own taste, and this then produces a chaos that neutralizes religion as a social force.[20] In offering such a distinction, he may merely be describing the demise of Christendom which, in itself, does not inevitably and unavoidably mean the decline, or even erosion, of Christianity as a vital force.

Finally, it is necessary to bear in mind that statements about secularization should in any case be treated with caution, and especially those that are unqualified, for 'the data are complex, contradictory even, and clear-cut conclusions become correspondingly difficult'.[21] This is the wise and apposite conclusion of the 1981 cross-national European Values Study, subsequently extended to include other countries worldwide.

What has been said in the last few paragraphs is not intended either to dismiss out of hand, or even to denigrate the statistical findings of many polls and surveys, or to discount all secularization theories. But cautionary notes need to be sounded. The statistics and theories that underscore all secularization theses should not be taken as the sine qua non for an appraisal of the past, present and possible future fortunes of Christianity. Some scholars seem to cling to both the 'facts' and the theories of secularization as if they are self-evidently true as a valid appraisal of the well-being of Christianity or, indeed, the only authentic measuring rod. Even if secularization theories 'have largely been abandoned by most of their erstwhile inventors as being inapplicable to most parts of the world except western Europe', and 'all kinds of theories of historical inevitability have taken a fearful pounding'[22] since the 1950s, 'secularization continues to be invoked uncritically'.[23] This is unfortunate.

There may never have been sociologists who believed that religion would disappear without trace. But there are undoubtedly many sociologists, historians, anthropologists, economists, clergy and men and women in the media, who believe that Christianity as it has evolved during the last 300 years, and as it is found in the contemporary world, will survive only in forms that are sectarian and marginal, or fundamentalist, as they frequently term it, and menacing, or internally so secularized that they have ceased to be religious in the true definition of the word. 'It has often been predicted that Europe will become completely secular and that the rest of the world will end up like it.'[24] Such a forecast should not be dismissed as yet one more thoroughly Eurocentric view – as if what happens in Europe today will happen in the rest of the world, meaning, of course, the less developed world, tomorrow – but it is nonetheless too much of a blanket generalization.

Religion in modern Europe in general, and Christianity in particular, needs to be considered sociologically in the light of the observations made in the preceding paragraphs. One general conclusion seems applicable to the continent as a whole. Allowing for variables and some localized exceptions, it seems to be in accordance with all the findings to say that the inhabitants of West European countries are by and large, 'unchurched populations rather than simply secular. For a marked falling-off in religious attendance (especially in the Protestant North) has not yet resulted in a parallel abdication of religious belief. In short, many Europeans have ceased to belong to their religious institutions in any meaningful sense, but so far they have not abandoned many of their deep-seated religious aspirations.'[25]

What is more, despite the undoubted lessening of the influence of the churches since the early eighteenth century, and the diminished membership of mainstream churches and denominations, both of which are almost universally found, all the flow is not entirely in one direction. The churches have begun to fight back. To start with, there is Pentecostalism and the charismatic movement among Catholics as well as Protestants. Various organizations, such as the Roman Catholic Communion and Liberation, have been working to 're-create a Christian society after the "failure of secularism",' and it, as one example, 'mobilized hundreds of thousands of young Italians, while in Eastern Europe, after the collapse of the Soviet Union, social movements and parties were taking shape which, after forty years of state atheism, base their political identity on a reaffirmation of their Catholicism.'[26]

Concurrently, the pontificate of John Paul II was 'marked by a reaffirmation of Catholic values and identity. These are now based upon an a priori break with the principles of secular society, and are intended to restore to the "post-modern" world a meaning, an ethic and an order which, it is claimed, have vanished in the collapse of all its certainties.'[27] So, as it were, the Roman Catholic

Church has been engaged on a two-pronged effort to re-evangelize Europe, from 'below' and from 'above'.

Within Protestantism, it is notably the European evangelicals who have almost invariably displayed the most obvious signs of vibrancy and growth, or at least the most resolute resistance to decline, and this is not confined to Pentecostal and charismatic type expressions of the faith. There have been and continue to be innumerable examples of thriving churches and Christian communities. This element of European church life is further strengthened as a result of its links with the wider, international, fellowship of evangelicals. There are now as never before international, interdenominational and non-denominational dimensions to evangelicalism, which make it a more global, more potent and more powerful force than at any previous time. This is manifested in many ways, not least of all in the form of periodic congresses and conferences. A global network of evangelicals has developed, which offers great moral sustenance to particular individuals, organizations and national bodies, as well as practical help in the form of the exchange of personnel, literature, funding and a host of supportive actions. It all represents a lively and much appreciated sense of fellowship and unity in God-given tasks, with practical outworkings. Tell these European Christians, who are part of this intercontinental fraternity, that the Church, and even Christianity itself, is dead or dying, and they will respond with amazement.

In Britain, allowing for incomplete figures, difficulties of comparability, and a measure of guesswork in interpretation, some overall trends seem to have become evident. There has undeniably been institutional church decline, however measured. From the beginning of the twentieth century until the mid 1960s the mainline Free Church denominations failed to maintain their numbers, the Church of England just about held its membership, and the Roman Catholic population increased. Since then there has been an overall decline in membership, popularity and influence, most marked since the 1990s. A survey conducted in 2000 showed that 44 per cent of the British public claimed no religious affiliation whatever; a figure that had increased from 31 per cent in 1983.[28] In just ten years, between 1989 and 1998, the combined Sunday church attendance for all Christian denominations fell from 4.7 million to 3.7 million.

Nonetheless, small conservative Protestant sects, denominations and churches have shown more resilience, and there has
been a growth in conservative Protestantism in most of the 'old'
mainline denominations. All the Pentecostal churches, including
especially the Assemblies of God and the Elim Foursquare
Alliance, have increased their membership quite substantially, as
have the African and West Indian churches, the house churches
and the Seventh Day Adventist Church. It is worthy of note that
these are the very kinds of church that are foremost in the non-
Western world expansion.

Then there is the question of the beliefs of people irrespective
of their declared denominational identification or membership
position in any church or chapel. This 'religion beyond the
churches' is an important consideration in assessing the state of
Christianity in Britain at the start of the third millennium.[29]
Surveys generally find that less than a quarter of respondents
claim 'no religion'. In the 1991 British Social Attitudes Survey 10
per cent claimed to be atheists and 14 per cent agnostics. This is
a notable leap from the 4 per cent of declared atheists in 1981.
Nevertheless, among the avowed atheists in 1991, 22 per cent
went on to say that they believed in some sort of spirit or life
force, 22 per cent believed in life after death, and 44 per cent
admitted to some Christian denominational attachment.

There is a persistence of 'religious' beliefs. In the 1991 British
Social Attitudes Survey, 46 per cent of those questioned said that
they believed in God and always had, 46 per cent believed in
heaven, 27 per cent in life after death, 24 per cent in the existence
of the devil, and 24 per cent in hell.[30]

The picture that emerges is of the decline of the mainstream
denominations in Britain, when and however measured statisti-
cally, compensated to some degree but not entirely by the greater
success of the more evangelical bodies. Although the latter is
extremely impressive, it has to be conceded that at present, as
throughout the eighteenth, nineteenth and twentieth centuries, 'it
barely dents the mass of the unchurched. Most British people
now have no church connection and are linked to organized religion only by their infrequent attendance at *rites of passage*, by
their residual respect for 'religion' (which they think is a good
thing), and by their nostalgic fondness for church buildings and

hymns.'[31] The population at large is still to some extent 'religious', but their religious concepts are vague and ill formed. The sacred has not disappeared, but there has developed a disjunction between these pervasive but somewhat vacuous beliefs and the practice of religion in a recognizable form. This gulf not only exists, but has been accentuated with every passing generation since the 1960s. The imprecise 'Christian' notions provide the seedbed for alternative versions of belief such as those of the New Age movement. What has become increasingly common in Britain, and indeed throughout Continental Europe, is 'believing without belonging'.[32] There is individual religion without communal expression, exemplified par excellence, for instance, in the popularity of religious broadcasting.

Ever since the eighteenth century, and to an accelerating extent, the 'Christian churches have lost their ability to shape popular thinking. In so far as many people in Britain continue to think that there is more to the world than meets the eye, their images of the supernatural are no longer structured by Christian precepts. They are amorphous and idiosyncratic and have few, if any, behavioural consequences.'[33] But such imprecise aspirations are not to be dismissed or underrated. There may, in fact, be a contemporary upsurge in 'spirituality' in the West generally; a desire to be in touch with the sacred, however that may be perceived and interpreted. There is both statistical and anecdotal evidence that points to a widespread search for personal wholeness, a quest for meaning and purpose in life. 'It is often linked to concerns about sustainability of the eco-system and a longing for peace and harmony in the world. In the bookshops, for example, material about personal development, relationships, meditation and "spiritual" lifestyles far outstrip volumes of conventional piety or theology. This awakening to the spiritual and the sacred stems from a sense of incompleteness, fragmentation and futility.'[34] This represents a challenge and an opportunity for Christians to present to such 'searchers' what they believe to be a message of potential new and meaningful life. In a nutshell, Europe, including Britain, is in Christian terms a missionary area. This may be unpalatable to many who have been nurtured in the belief that their homeland is Christian, and much of South America, sub-Saharan Africa and Asia are 'fields' for missionary endeavour, but the reverse is rapidly becoming a reality.

The state of the Christian religion in Continental Europe and Britain in the early part of the twenty-first century is thus more complex, and perhaps more hopeful for believers, than the prophets of straightforward decline would have us believe. There is widespread 'spiritual' interest and concern, and there are undoubtedly pockets and areas of vitality in both Continental European and British Christianity, although many of these are in unfashionable and not very prominent or well-publicized places.[35] Whether the scales will tip in the direction of revival or further de-Christianization is one of the foremost conundrums facing the churches in those regions at the beginning of the third millennium.

Of course, the situation that has just been described does not apply to the USA. Christianity in that superpower is still a widespread individual, life-transforming, life-enhancing faith, and its teaching remains the single most important determinant of social attitudes and mores. It is integral to, and arguably the foremost element in, the complex mix of inherited values known collectively as the 'American way of life'. The country is clearly an exception to the secularization process as defined by most sociologists and historians who adopt such terminology and champion such a concept. From the point of view of this present work, it can be excluded from the discussion of secularization. The country is self-evidently a centre of lively Christianity, with a large proportion of its citizens endorsing Christian belief and a high percentage attending church or chapel on a regular basis. Some critical commentators express distaste for some aspects of American Christian belief and practice, but none would deny that it is a power to be taken note of in the life of the nation.

A sociological observation on non-Western Christianity

Not only have each of the examples of Christian revitalization in the world in the twentieth century, described in the previous chapters, broadly occurred at the same time, but they have assumed a generally almost identical form.

> How can this global resurgence be explained? Particular causes obviously operated in individual countries and civilizations. Yet it

is too much to expect that a large number of different causes
would have produced simultaneous and similar developments in
most parts of the world. A global phenomenon demands a global
explanation. However much events in particular countries may
have been influenced by unique factors, some general causes must
have been at work.[36]

It is well to recall that this parallelism was also found with the various awakenings and revivals of the eighteenth and nineteenth
centuries and in the first few years of the twentieth century.

Strangely, and rather ironically, today, as throughout the last
sixty years or so, the 'most salient, and most powerful cause of the
global religious resurgence' has been 'precisely what was supposed to cause the death of religion: the processes of social, economic, and cultural modernization that swept across the world in
the second half of the twentieth century'.[37] Theoretically, according
to some sociologists and others, secularization 'was a necessary
part of modernization and as the world modernized it would automatically secularize'.[38] But this has not happened. Indeed, in many
respects the reverse has time and again been found to be the
actual sequence of events. Reanimated Christianity in many areas
has been connected with modernization. It can be interpreted as 'a
reaction against secularism, moral relativism, and self-indulgence,
and a reaffirmation of the values of order, discipline, work,
mutual help, and human solidarity'.[39]

It is worth noting that the eighteenth-century revival in Britain
was largely centred on towns and cities such as London, Bristol,
Bath and Newcastle, and it is the same with the twentieth-century
upsurge of Christianity. Perhaps this is in part because in such
urban environments there is a high level of anomie, dislocation
and personal sense of estrangement, as contrasted with the more
unified, cohesive and protected nature of small-scale rural communities. But it is also true, but apparently to a somewhat more
limited extent, that an altered and disturbed countryside has probably contributed to the success of Christianity in rural areas as
well. The overarching common factor is the sociological old chest-
nut of rapid social and economic change producing discontent,
disorientation, and a severe sense of personal and corporate alienation, so that there is a greater openness to receive what the

Christian faith has to offer. There is a greater disposition to embrace a faith that claims to provide exceptional spiritual comforts and inner peace. In the midst of personal and corporate confusion, an awareness of salvation and an assured eternal blissful destiny represents a powerful cocktail.

Theological issues

One rather peculiar aspect of the resurgence of Christianity in so many parts of the contemporary, mainly non-Western world, is not only the ignorance of it among 'informed' people, and the unwillingness of many critics of Christianity to take it into account, but the inability or reluctance of the Western churches to learn from the example of thriving churches in erstwhile colonies and other Third World nations. After graphically portraying the remarkable zeal, dedication and fruitfulness of the Christians in Singapore and other areas of Asia, one Western Christian leader draws attention to this unfortunate trait. 'We do not', he writes, 'call them "mission churches" any more, and we take pains to be politically correct. But all the same we feel, deep down, just a little superior. We certainly do not tend to emulate them very much.'[40] As the Western Church becomes more adjusted to an ever-shrinking world, and as the days of colonialism recede ever more into the past, there will probably, and hopefully, be an increased willingness to share with former 'subservient people' what they so richly enjoy and have to offer. An acknowledgement of mutual interdependence, and a willingness to put it into practice, together with respect and a preparedness to give and receive help and advice could, surely, prove to be among the fruits of the new age.

The unprecedented shift in the profile of world Christianity, which has been a central theme of this book, should also make the Western Church think carefully before asserting boldly and in an unqualified way what Christians believe, what is the view of the Church on particular matters, or how the Church is changing. 'All too often, statements about "what modern Christians accept" or what "Catholics today believe" refer only to what that ever-shrinking remnant of *Western* Christians and Catholics believe.

Such assertions are outrageous today, and as time goes by they will become ever further removed from reality. The era of Western Christianity has passed within our lifetimes, and the day of Southern Christianity is dawning.'[41]

One feature of much southern Christianity is its 'back to basics' tendency. There is ample evidence of erudite and profound theological thinking both in academic circles and in the churches of these southern countries. The 'new' churches are theologically well equipped and refined. But there is another side of the coin; for this sophisticated scholarly work and Christian reasoning goes hand in hand with a renewed stress on the Bible and what it teaches. 'The history of Christian missions proves that when the Bible, unqualified by "approved" interpretation, "hits" a society the effects can be devastating.' There are startling examples of this in the modern world. For example, the 'massive contemporary expansion of Christianity in Asia owes much to the impact of the Bible unaided by missionary endeavour'.[42] Even in the dark days of fierce oppression and persecution in China, there were tales of Red Guards being converted simply by exposure to the sacred text. It was an experience repeated in countless other circumstances.

Closely associated with this is the almost unanimous acceptance by these southern churches of the divine authority of the whole Bible, Old and New Testaments, and the assumption that the Bible and what it 'literally' teaches, is of ultimate and final importance for Christians, without any gloss, provisos or exceptions. Believers in the southern regions as a whole are baffled and bemused by the characteristic Western teaching that certain parts of the Bible, such as the resurrection, are reckoned to be absolutely literal, although, of course, even this is questioned by some Western theologians and church leaders, while other parts, such as the lives and exploits of the patriarchs and other Old Testament characters are expected to be treated as no more than instructive fables. Who, many of the southern Christians ask, authorized and gave credence to such a capricious and arbitrary distinction? If the Bible is not to be received in total as the supreme authority for determining doctrine and practice, what is to take its place? Surely, most of these believers say, the Church must submit itself to, and live under the authority of, the Bible, and not place human wisdom and rationality above its teaching? It should be accepted *per se.*

Of course such apparent naivety evokes an immediate and often fiercely hostile response from perhaps most refined and well-instructed Western Christians and others. It is a perspective that is frequently and summarily rejected, together with the rather emotional and often quite extrovert forms of worship typical of a large proportion of the southern churches. Nonetheless, there is a consistency, logic and appeal in such a seemingly simplistic approach to the Scriptures, and in the forms the corporate, communal expression of deeply held beliefs take. Unfortunately, there is a flip side to this coin. There is the constant danger of being so clear cut, forthright and definite about theological and moral matters, that where such churches predominate in a society, they will misuse their power, create an unquestioned and unassailable moral dictatorship, or at least monopoly, and will marginalize, and even oppress and persecute, minorities such as homosexuals against whose practices they are so vehemently opposed. But, if used responsibly, those same unambiguous views and practices can be mightily effective in terms of evangelism and pastoral work.

It is therefore clear that as a whole the newer churches of the non-Western world are far more conservative in both their beliefs and moral teaching than is typical in the West, in large measure because of their acceptance of the Bible in its entirety as the final arbiter in all matters of belief and practice. They are stalwartly traditional or even reactionary by the prevailing standards of many of the churches of the more economically advanced nations. This became apparent in the universally discussed issue of homosexuality, and more especially concerning the ordination of practising homosexuals or their elevation to the episcopate, which has so exercised the Anglican Communion in recent years. With one or two notable exceptions, the theologians, church leaders and other southern Christians have been firmly and resolutely opposed to any attitude that they deemed liberal on this or any other matter. They still unambiguously declare that the teaching of the Bible is transparently hostile to the practice of homosexuality, and there the matter rests. Indeed, there are those who might be prepared to secede from the Anglican Church as a consequence of what is seen as its apostasy and lack of adequate discipline in enforcing such teaching.

This particular issue also highlights a further potentially serious difference of perspective between leading Western world churches and southern churches. Many southern Christians in the new churches, whether they are dogmatic about the ordination and elevation in the Church of practising homosexuals or are more tolerant in their views, are agreed that the Western church is far too preoccupied with sexual matters in general. They believe quite passionately that all sexual issues have assumed far too much prominence, and that the Church should be more concerned about poverty, AIDS, and human need in general.

These various and often deeply felt convictions have found institutional expression in the twenty-first century, especially in Africa. Thus, the divisions in the Anglican Communion dominated the communique issued by the Global South leaders meeting in October 2005. 'Our own Anglican Communion', it stated, 'sadly continues to be weakened by unchecked revisionist teaching and practices which undermine the divine authority of the Holy Scripture. The Anglican Communion is severely wounded by the witness of errant principles of faith and practice which in many parts of the Communion have adversely affected our efforts to take the gospel to those in need of God's redeeming and saving love.' The communique also confirmed a move away from many of the presuppositions and orientations of Western theological education, and declared: 'We reject the expectation that our lives should conform to the misguided theological, cultural, and social norms associated with sections of the West.'[43] Such sentiments, and their forceful expression are further signs of a type of Christianity that is alert and keen to get on with the tasks facing it, without any compromise or watering down of its beliefs and practice.

The general ethos of much of the church life in the non-Western world is not easy for many Westerners to stomach. 'These newer churches preach deep personal faith and communal orthodoxy, mysticism and Puritanism, all founded on clear scriptural authority. They preach messages that, to a Westerner, appear simplistically charismatic, visionary, and apocalyptic. In this thought-world, prophecy is an everyday reality, while faith-healing, exorcism, and dream-visions are all basic components of religious sensibility.'[44] Christians conditioned by the cooler approach to church and theological matters so typical of the Western world are sometimes suspicious that all of this, especially in Africa, represents a revival of the pagan practices of traditional societies. The Western world's tolerance is further tested as a result of the frustratingly common schismatic tendencies evident especially in the churches of the southern hemisphere. Fragmentation quite frequently occurs for what appear to be minor differences of belief or practice, or unfortunate clashes of personality, and this ready triggering of division largely accounts for the 34,000 or so independent denominations into which Christianity worldwide has split.

Many members of Western world churches are especially perplexed by so-called faith or spiritual healing. In the West, this is associated in many people's minds with special, often somewhat bizarre, gatherings and highly questionable claims. In the kind of churches that have been described in South America, sub-Saharan Africa and some countries of Asia, however, healing is an accepted part of the normal Christian ministry, alongside evangelism, pastoral and social work. It is healing through spiritual means that has had the greatest impact in practice in many southern communities. It is also a theme that has a particularly powerful unifying effect among the believers of the new churches. There is a holism about the approach to Christian healing that is unconsciously, but strikingly, in accord with modern medical trends. What Andrew Walls has to say specifically about the African experience has wider application.

> Healing is being addressed to the person, as the centre of a complex of influences. It is addressed to the person as target of outside attack, as sufferer from unwanted legacies, as carrier of the sense of failure and unfulfilled duty. It is the long established African understanding of the nature and purpose of healing that is at work. What distinguishes its Christian phase is that the central Christian symbol of Christ is identified as the source of healing.[45]

Healing is more central to the theology and practice of the newer churches than is often appreciated. It is vital and indispensable as part of the witness and evangelism of these churches. It is 'the key element that has allowed Christianity to compete so successfully with its rivals outside the Christian tradition, with traditional religion in Africa, with various animist and spiritist movements of African origin in Brazil, with shamanism in Korea.'[46] It is often combined with exorcism, which itself has deep roots in many of the traditional religions of the southern countries.

The more extreme radical theologians of the Western world find such an orientation not only unacceptable but incomprehensible. With their eyes and minds firmly fixed on what they regard as a dying faith and church, confirmed by their own experience of the scantily occupied pews of the church around the corner, and with a conviction that the fundamental problem is the church's unintelligible and unbelievable teachings concerning supernaturalism, they endlessly devise new ways of expressing their demythologized form of belief that, they think, will win over post-modern men and women. But they are out of step with most of the world's Christian community. 'Viewed from Cambridge or Amsterdam, such pleas may make excellent sense, but in the context of global Christianity, this kind of liberalism looks distinctly dated.'[47]

There is, however, a yet further aspect of the non-Western world evangelical Christianity of which the Western world is little aware, and which helps to make the portrayal of a dead or dying church even more absurd. To the typical concern with founding churches, evangelism, pastoral work, the provision of Bibles in the vernacular and the exercise of the gifts of the Spirit, the younger churches, especially in recent years, have added a social dimension. 'Modern thinking on mission, especially from the younger Churches, includes dealing with evil not only in people but in social organization, not only the transformation of people but the transformation of the community. Salvation is seen as something more than individual experience'; it 'includes the release from all that dehumanises and oppresses.'[48]

In many of the churches of South America, sub-Saharan Africa and parts of Asia, there is a profound and heartfelt concern to address social problems as well as, and in conjunction with, a clear and unambiguous proclamation of the 'good news' verbally and by individual and corporate testimony. Indeed, in countless cases, the very idea of distinguishing between these two spheres of operation is hardly contemplated. They are but two parts, or facets, of the one integrated gospel. Faith and works are inextricably interwoven. The close identity of the spoken word, and its expression in social action, is viewed as an evident and unavoidable New Testament obligation laid upon individual Christians and upon the Church as a whole. The necessity for linking words to works is immeasurably heightened by the constant, immediate, very obvious poverty, depredation and ill health of the people among whom a large proportion of these non-Western world Christians live. They are surrounded every day of their lives by the pressing material needs of fellow human beings, and to restrict the good news to words alone would be a manifest error and, not to overstate the situation, a blasphemy. The churches know this, and many of them strive to ensure that such an unacceptable dichotomy does not occur.

Christianity and other world faiths

In the last 300 years in the West generally there has been a transformation from living mainly in rural villages to being part of a global village. Immigration, visits abroad, television and the other modern media and channels of communication, have all combined to make Westerners very much aware of the existence of other world faiths.

The emergence of Christianity as a world faith for the first time, the opening up of the world, and the breaking down of barriers between different peoples and cultures have meant that the world religions have encountered each other face to face as never before. Among the unforeseen consequences of this has been the confrontation of Islam and Christianity in a hitherto unknown way. Of course there had been the advance of Islam into Spain in the eighth century, checked by the decisive victory of Charles Martel at Tours in 732, and there were the centuries of the Crusades. But both of these were very geographically confined and largely restricted to military encounters. Also, there was not in those far off days any equivalent of the modern evangelical, Pentecostal and charismatic movements among the Christians, nor, to the same extent as recently, the 'fundamentalist' element in Islam.

The type of Christianity that has been the focus of attention in this book has affinities with movements and trends in the two other main world monotheistic faiths. There 'is a world-wide growth of religious conservatism in Judaism, and in Islam, as well as in Christianity. A balance once supposed to be tipping automatically towards liberalism is now tipping the other way.'[49]

The confrontation, and in many cases the clash, of Islam and Christianity, either just ideologically or with knock-on physical or military accompaniments, is a fact of twenty-first-century life. These are the only world, monotheistic, proselytizing faiths, and as such, with their clear differences as well as similarities, friction at times and in some places is almost inevitable. This is already a global issue in the political, economic and social as well as religious realms, and it is likely to become more so in the future. Forthcoming epochal demographic changes will shift the concentration of much of the world's population very firmly to just those regions of the world where Islam and Christianity will probably prosper most fully, and where they will find themselves in head-to-head situations and even in conflict. Indeed, this fraught situation already exists in some areas of the world. But there is the very real potential for friction and aggression to become more frequent and serious, especially where more populous Muslim and Christian countries are adjacent to each other, or where strong Muslim and Christian communities are to be found in the same country. Rivalry may well be intensified in nations such as Nigeria, Indonesia, the Sudan and the Philippines, as the earnest struggle for converts becomes more pronounced and acute, or where attempts are made to enforce moral codes by means of religiously inspired and motivated civil law. It is all too easy for religious zeal to turn into fanaticism, whether that be Muslim or Christian, or both.

As a postscript to these brief comments on Christianity and Islam, it is of note that official national policies can and often have aggravated rather than lessened the religious tension and hostility. This is frighteningly demonstrated by the posture adopted both in the West and in the Muslim world by certain governments. It has recently and most notably surfaced with the USA and a number of the more militant Islamic regimes.

The political leaders of the United States have tended to exacerbate an already tense situation. Such an outcome may not have been consciously and explicitly intended, but it has happened nonetheless. The policies and actions of the world's only super-power can far too readily be regarded by neutrals and by many in the Muslim world as encouraging a simplistic polarization in which the good is perceived as essentially 'Christian' and much of the evil as essentially 'Muslim'. Whenever and wherever there is any form of trouble that can be viewed in religious terms, this seems to many observers to be the automatic way events are inter-preted. All too frequently, the United States seems to some commentators and nations to be engaging on a self-conscious, self-appointed crusade in which the supposedly almost unquestioned merits of 'Christendom and democracy' are pitched in stark con-trast against 'Islam and evil dictatorships'. This is not the place to discuss all of the ramifications of the political, economic and mili-tary programmes of the USA that are based on such an implicit or declared presupposition, but it clearly, and sometimes disast-rously, impinges on the relationship of Christians and Muslims all over the world. The religious dimension of such a policy is made even more evident if behind that way of thinking there is seen to lurk the conservatism of the evangelical right, which is still mani-fested as an important pressure group, despite its somewhat diminished power in recent decades.

The US leaders themselves would, with much justification, say that they have assumed the kind of stance just depicted because of the actions of Muslims themselves. After all, they can point to Muslim countries whose governments have persecuted Christians in a most vicious and sustained way, and who have a poor, and sometimes, deplorable, record of human rights abuse. There are also the horrific acts of terrorists who are self-declared Muslims. It is of little surprise that this all amounts to immense and intense provocation from the point of view of Western governments. Western leaders can claim that they are driven into a corner by what they perceive as barbaric, warlike behaviour, and that what they do in response is merely to uphold civilized, 'Christian' val-ues. On the other hand, the Muslim governments and individual Muslims can assert that all they are doing is resisting 'Western' aggression, and trying to counter attempts by the West to use political, economic and military might to impose uncongenial, unwelcome and unwanted beliefs, modes of government and lifestyles on other people who sometimes demonstrate, perhaps in a violent manner, that they are unsympathetic to what is being foisted on them.

It is a complicated and tangled situation, and there are no easy answers, but it creates an atmosphere in the midst of which the laudable evangelistic, pastoral and social work of largely indigenous churches in South America, sub-Saharan Africa and some of the countries of Asia is made much more difficult than it might otherwise be. We live in a world in which the opposition of Christianity and Islam is a vital component, and for many Christian believers the policies and practices of 'Christian' governments and of the more extreme, militant, upholders of the Muslim faith, have immediate and painful consequences.

The day of martyrs and of Christians who have to endure prejudice, harassment, oppression, and not infrequently pain, physical assault, torture and death has most definitely not passed. In case after case the Church has withstood such assaults and it has emerged stronger out of its ordeal. No feeble, fragile, hesitant, unsure company of believers would measure up to such trials. The faith of the believers has to be firmly grounded and resolute. They need to be confident in what they believe, and bold in their witness. The churches have to be like rocks amid the storm, and they have almost invariably proved to be so. A countless host of Christian witnesses all over the world have, since the eighteenth century, demonstrated such a calibre of Christian life and witness. For them God has been a living and sustaining presence.

The universal Church that has resulted from the astonishing expansion of Christianity has repeatedly shown that it does not consist of believers whose faith is shallow and merely conventional or conformist. The globalization of Christianity has not only been quantitatively impressive. It has produced churches and believers whose quality of life is profound. Millions of ordinary believers going about their daily, often hard, poverty-stricken, troubled and demanding lives have found new life and fulfilment not in some quirky variant of the Christian faith, but in genuine, life-transforming, traditional Christian belief and practice as handed down from the age of the Apostles.

Conclusion

The doom-laden pronouncements of some atheists and agnostics, theories of Christian atrophy and irrelevance, and theological declarations of the death of God or the need for a new agenda and conceptual framework to meet the needs of 'post-Christian' men and women, seem somewhat arid, cerebral, inappropriate and hollow in the face of the kind of resurgence of Christianity encountered since 1700, and evident throughout much of the contemporary world. Armchair academics and media pundits may cavalierly, or after much reflection, dismiss the kind of post-1700 Christianity that has been traced in this book as an aberration, or even as an insubstantial, temporary phenomenon. They may pour scorn on the various forms of the faith currently adopted by countless million of believers from many nations and cultures, as overly emotional, unsophisticated and/or of no great consequence. What such critics cannot do is to deny what has taken place during the last 300 years, or the reality of what exists today. Both are facts of history or current affairs to be observed and dissected, but not ignored or discounted. The globalization of Christianity is manifestly impressive. The historical and contemporary robust religious movements and life of worldwide churches are not of merely passing interest. They are central to the history and present state of both Christianity and the future of countless countries. Many millions of Christian people in the course of three centuries have felt the touch of God, and have testified that their hearts have been strangely warmed. They have claimed that divine intervention has transformed their lives for eternity. This has happened on a gigantic, global, scale, and it deserves close examination.

The extraordinary transformation of the world Christian profile in the last two centuries, in the last hundred years in particular, and in an especially dramatic way in recent decades, is raising questions of fundamental importance for those prepared to examine the evidence impartially. This is vividly encapsulated in a comment by Harvey Cox, one of the core exponents of the radical 'death of God' theology of the 1960s. Thirty years after that theologically iconoclastic decade, in 1996, he honestly, openly and bravely retracted his former views, and drew attention to a religious revolution that had taken place in the interim. His statement was short and to the point: 'Nearly three decades ago I wrote a book, *The Secular City*, in which I tried to work out a theology for the "post-religious" age that many sociologists had confidently assured us was coming. Since then, however, religion – or at least some religions – seems to have gained a new lease of life. Today it is secularity, not spirituality, that may be headed for extinction.'[50] And in this stunning transmutation, a prime component has been a reinvigorated, expansive, worldwide Christianity.

The globalization of Christianity is well advanced and is accelerating. The risen Jesus Christ once said to his disciples, and through them to succeeding generations of Christians, that they would be his witnesses 'to the ends of the earth'.[51] Almost two thousand years later, much remains to be done, but the achievement of the goal is well on its way.

Notes

Introduction

[1] Kennedy, *All in the Mind*, p. 163. This is a book to which this section is greatly indebted.

[2] Gauchet, *The Disenchantment of the World*, p. ix.

[3] Peter Berger, *The Sacred Canopy*, New York: Doubleday, p. 107.

[4] Masterson, *Atheism and Alienation*, p. 4.

[5] See Max Weber, *The Sociology of Religion*, Boston: Beacon Press, 1963.

[6] Gauchet, *The Disenchantment of the World*, p. 3.

[7] Armstrong, *The Battle for God*, p. 66.

[8] Op. cit., p. 67.

[9] Chadwick, *The Secularization of the European Mind*, p. 21.

[10] J. Gascoigne, *Cambridge in the Age of the Enlightenment*, Cambridge: Cambridge University Press, 1989, p. 2.

[11] Quoted in Blanchard, *Does God Believe in Atheists?*, p. 68

[12] Buckley, *At the Origins of Modern Atheism*, p. 27.

[13] James R. Moore, 'Freethought, secularism, agnosticism: the case of Charles Darwin', in Gerald Parsons (ed.), *Religion in Victorian Britain*, vol. 1, *Traditions*, p. 308.

[14] Lightman, *Origins of Agnosticism*, p. 131.

[15] See Nietzsche, *The Gay Science*.

[16] These examples, and this whole section, are much indebted to Blanchard, *Does God Believe in Atheists?*, pp. 127-139.

[17] Ogletree, *The 'Death of God' Controversy*, p. 13.

[18] Altizer, *The Gospel of Christian Atheism*, p. 15.

[19] Ogletree, *The 'Death of God' Controversy*, p. 21.

[20] Ibid.

21 Paul A. Welsby, *A History of the Church of England 1945–1980*, Oxford: Oxford University Press, 1984, p. 115.

22 Haynes and Roth (eds.), *The Death of God Movement and the Holocaust*, p. 71.

23 See Will Herberg, 'The Death of God Theology', *National Review*, August 9, 1966, p. 771.

24 Altizer, *The Gospel of Christian Atheism*, p. 23.

25 Ogletree, *The 'Death of God' Controversy*, p. 22.

26 Roger Lloyd, *The Church of England 1900–1965*, SCM Press, 1966, p. 597.

27 John T. Robinson, *Honest to God*, SCM Press, 1963, p. 7.

28 Paul Avis, 'The Church's One Foundation', *Theology*, 89, 1986, p. 259.

29 Paul Badham (ed.), *Religion, State, and Society in Modern Britain*, Lampeter: Edwin Mellen Press, 1989, p. 4.

30 Cupitt, *Radicals and the Future of the Church*, p. 1.

31 Op. cit., p. 14.

32 Op. cit., p. 16.

33 Brierley, *'Christian England'*, p. 58.

34 Figures quoted in Wilson, *Religion in Secular Society*, p. 29.

35 Gilbert, *The Making of Post-Christian Britain*, p. 77.

36 The main texts in the debate on the secularization thesis include: Berger, *The Sacred Canopy*; Peter L. Berger, *A Rumour of Angels: Modern Society and the Rediscovery of the Supernatural*, Penguin Books, 1969; Peter L. Berger, *The Social Reality of Religion*, Penguin Books, 1973; Peter L. Berger, *Facing Up To Modernity*, Penguin Books, 1979; Steve Bruce, *A House Divided: Protestantism, Schism and Secularization*, 1990, Bruce (ed.), *Religion and Modernization*; J. Casanova, *Public Religions in the Modern World*, Chicago: University of Chicago Press, 1994; Davie, *Religion in Modern Europe*; K. Dobbelaere, 'Secularization: A Multi-dimensional Concept', *Current Sociology*, 29, 1981, pp. 3-213; K. Dobbelaere, 'Some Trends in European Sociology of Religion: The Secularization Debate', *Sociological Analysis*, 48, 1987, pp. 107-37; Gill, *Competing Convictions*; Gill, *The Myth of the Empty Church*; Thomas Luckmann, *The Invisible Religion: The Problem of Religion in Modern Society*, Macmillan Publishing Company, 1970; Martin, *The Religious and the Secular*; Martin, *A General Theory of Secularization*; R. Stark, *The Future of Religion: Secularization, Revival, and Cult Formation*, Berkeley: University of California, 1985; Wilson, *Religion in Secular Society*; Bryan R. Wilson, *Contemporary Transformations of Religion*, Oxford:

Oxford University Press, 1976; Bryan R. Wilson, *Religion in Sociological Perspective*, Oxford: Oxford University Press, 1982.

37 Gordon Marshall, *Dictionary of Sociology*, Oxford and New York: Oxford University Press, 1994, 2nd edn. 1998, p. 588.

1 Vibrant Christianity in Europe, Britain and North America

1 The following account of the Continental origins of the evangelical revival is greatly indebted to W.R. Ward, and especially his seminal work, *The Protestant Evangelical Awakening*, and to G.M. Ditchfield, *The Evangelical Revival*.

2 Ditchfield, *The Evangelical Revival*, p. 11.

3 Ward, *The Protestant Evangelical Awakening*, p. 57.

4 Fernandez-Armesto and Wilson, *Reformation*, p. 55.

5 Ward, *The Protestant Evangelical Awakening*, p. 62.

6 Podmore, *The Moravian Church in England*, p. 5.

7 For the life and work of George Whitefield, see Dallimore, *George Whitefield*; Marcus L. Loane, *Oxford and the Evangelical Succession*, Lutterworth Press, 1950; J.C. Ryle, *Christian Leaders of the Eighteenth Century*, reprinted, Edinburgh: The Banner of Truth, 1978; Tyerman, *The Life of George Whitefield*; and *George Whitefield's Journals*. For the life and work of John Wesley, see Frank Baker, *John Wesley and the Church of England*, Epworth, 1970; Nehemiah Curnock (ed.), *The Journal of the Reverend John Wesley*, 8 vols, Epworth, 1938; Hattersley, *A Brand from the Burning*; Thomas Jackson (ed.), *The Works of John Wesley*, 7 vols, Grand Rapids, Michigan: Baker Book House, 1996 ed.; Rack, *Reasonable Enthusiast*; J.C. Ryle, *Christian Leaders of the Eighteenth Century*; John S. Simon, *John Wesley and the Religious Societies*, Epworth Press, 1955 edn., and *John Wesley and the Methodist Societies*, Epworth Press, 1952 edn.; John Telford (ed.), *The Letters of John Wesley*, Epworth Press, 1931 edn.; Luke Tyerman, *The Life and Times of the Rev John Wesley*; and A. Skevington Wood, *The Burning Heart: John Wesley Evangelist*, Exeter: Paternoster, 1967. For the life and work of Charles Wesley, see Dallimore, *A Heart Set Free*; Thomas Jackson, *The Life of the Rev Charles Wesley, 1841*; and Charles Wesley, *Journal*. For the life and work of the Countess of Huntingdon see Schlenther, *Queen of the Methodists*.

8 W.E.H. Lecky, *A History of England in the Eighteenth Century*, 8 vols., New York: Longmans, Green and Co, 1925 edn., vol. 2, p. 627.

9 James Stephen, *Essays in Ecclesiastical Biography*, 1883, p. 445.

10 Quoted in Elliott-Binns, *The Early Evangelicals*, p. 418.

11 See Nuttall, *Howell Harris*, Tudur, *Howell Harris*, and Evans, *Daniel Rowlands*.

12 For contemporary, or near contemporary, accounts, see James Robe, *Narrative of the Revival of Religion*, 1840, and A *Faithful Narrative of the Extraordinary Work of the Spirit of God at Kilsyth and other congregations in the Neighbourhood*, 1742, in Glasgow University Murray Collection, MU 40-f19. For a modern account, see Fawcett, *The Cambuslang Revival*.

13 Gerald F. Moran, 'Christian Revivalism and Culture in Early America: Puritan New England as a Case Study', in Blumhofer and Balmer (eds.), *Modern Christian Revivals*, p. 49.

14 Sweet, *Revivalism in America*, p. 45.

15 Ward, *The Protestant Evangelical Awakening*, pp. 269-70.

16 For the Northampton revival, in addition to the works already quoted, see Tracey, *The Great Awakening* and Edwards, *A Narrative*, p. 60. For the life and works of Jonathan Edwards, see Davidson, *Jonathan Edwards* and Murray, *Jonathan Edwards*.

17 Edwards, *A Narrative*, pp. 65, 68.

18 Moran, 'Christian Revivalism', in Blumhofer and Balmer (eds.), *Modern Christian Revivals*, p. 48.

19 For the life and work of George Whitefield, see note 7.

20 Sweet, *Revivalism in America*, p. 120.

21 This section owes much to Sweet, *Revivalism in America*, and to Bruce, *And They All Sang Hallelujah*, p. 4.

22 Boles, *The Great Revival*, p. 184.

23 These figures are quoted in Boles, *The Great Revival*, pp. 185-86.

24 Sweet, *Revivalism in America*, p. 134.

25 Cowing, *The Great Awakening and the American Revolution*, p. 178.

26 Richard Carwardine, 'The Second Great Awakening in Comparative Perspective: Revivals and Culture in the United States and Britain', in Blumhofer and Balmer (eds.), *Modern Christian Revivals*, p. 86.

27 W.R. Ward, 'The Evangelical Revival in Eighteenth-Century Britain', in Gilley and Shiels (eds.), *A History of Religion in Britain*, p. 252.

28 Eugene Stock, *The History of the Church Missionary Society*, vol. 1, p. 38.

29 John Stoughton, *Religion in England from 1800 to 1850*, 2 vols, Hodder & Stoughton, 1884, vol. 1, p. 114.

30 H.P. Liddon, *Life of E.B. Pusey*, Rivingtons, 1876, 1894 edn., vol. 1, p. 235.

[31] William Ewart Gladstone, *Letters on Church and Religion*, 2 vols, ed. D.C. Lathbury, Macmillan, 1910, vol. 1, p. 8.

[32] S.C. Carpenter, *Church and People, 1789–1889: A History of the Church of England from William Wilberforce to 'Lux Mundi'*, SPCK, 1933, p. 28.

[33] For an account of the 'Clapham Sect' and 'the Saints', see especially James Stephen, *Essays in Ecclesiastical Biography*, 1860; Howse, *Saints in Politics*. For a thorough analysis and critique, see particularly Ian Bradley, *The Call to Seriousness: The Evangelical Impact on the Victorians*, London and New York: Macmillan Publishing Co., 1976; Ian Bradley, 'The Politics of Godliness: Evangelicals in Parliament 1784–1832', Oxford D.Phil, 1974; and F.K. Brown, *Fathers of the Victorians: The Age of Wilberforce*, Cambridge: Cambridge University Press, 1961.

[34] For the life of Thomas Fowell Buxton, see Charles Buxton (ed.), *Memoirs of Sir Thomas Fowell Buxton, Baronet, with Selections from His Correspondence*, J. Murray, 1851.

[35] Key books on the Oxford Movement include, R.W. Church, *The Oxford Movement, 1833–1845*, Chicago: University of Chicago Press, 1970 edn.; S.L. Ollard, *A Short History of the Oxford Movement*, Mowbray, 1915; Yngve Brilioth, *The Anglican Revival: Studies in the Oxford Movement*, Longmans, 1933; Geoffrey Rowell (ed.), *Tradition Renewed*; and Hylson-Smith, *High Churchmanship in the Church of England*.

[36] Lovegrove, *Established Church*, p. 14.

[37] Hempton, *Methodism and Politics*, p. 16.

[38] See Norman McCord, *British History 1815–1906*, Oxford: Oxford University Press, 1991, p. 122; and also Gilbert, *Religion and Society*, ch. 2.

[39] See Hempton and Hill, *Evangelical Protestantism*; and Hill, 'Ulster Awakened'.

[40] See Orr, *The Second Evangelical Awakening*.

[41] For the life of Moody see Pollock, *Moody without Sankey*.

[42] For the lives and beliefs of both William and Catherine Booth, see Hattersley, *Blood and Fire*.

[43] Heasman, *Evangelicals in Action*, p. 15.

[44] For the life and work of Lord Shaftesbury, the main secondary sources are G. Battiscombe, *Shaftesbury: A Biography of the Seventh Earl*, Constable, 1974; E. Hodder, *The Life and Work of the Seventh Earl of Shaftesbury, K.G.*, 3 vols, Cassell, 1886; and Geoffrey B.A.M. Finlayson, *The Seventh Earl of Shaftesbury, 1801–1885*, Eyre and Methuen, 1981.

[45] Latourette, *Christianity in a Revolutionary Age*, vol. 2, p. 431.

[46] See, for example, Butler, *Awash in a Sea of Faith*, ch. 9.

[47] Mark A. Noll, 'Revolution and the Rise of Evangelical Social Influence in North Atlantic Societies', in Noll, Bebbington and Rawlyk (eds.), *Evangelicalism*, p. 118.

[48] See Matthews, 'The Second Great Awakening'.

[49] McLoughlin, *Revivals, Awakenings and Reform*, p. 1.

[50] Sweet, *Revivalism in America*, p. 132.

[51] Richard Carwardine, 'The Second Great Awakening', in Blumhofer and Balmer (eds.), *Modern Christian Revivals*, p. 84.

[52] Johnson, *The Frontier Camp Meeting*, p. xi.

[53] Boles, *The Great Revival*, p. 186.

[54] These four revivals are listed in Fish, *When Heaven Touched Earth*, pp. 29-31.

[55] Compare Orr, *The Light of the Nations*, p. 101.

[56] Articles, 'The Great Awakening', *The Tennessee Baptist*, 24 April 1858, quoting from *Mother's Journal*, New York.

[57] Quoted in Orr, *The Event of the Century*, p. 74.

[58] Orr, *The Light of the Nations*, p. 104.

[59] Samuel S. Hill, 'Northern and Southern Varieties of American Evangelicalism in the Nineteenth Century', in Noll, Bebbington and Rawlyk (eds.), *Evangelicalism*, p. 282. For the holiness movement in general, and its theological character in particular, see Paul M. Bassett, 'The Theological Identity of the North American Holiness Movement', in Dayton and Johnston (eds.), *The Variety of American Evangelicalism*, pp. 72-108.

2 World Mission in the Nineteenth Century

[1] Latourette, *Christianity in a Revolutionary Age*, vol. 3, p. 1.

[2] Ibid.

[3] For the history of the SPCK, see especially W.K. Lowther Clarke, *A History of the SPCK*, SPCK, 1959; and Craig Rose, 'The Origins and Ideals of the SPCK 1699–1716', in Walsh, Haydon and Taylor (eds.), *The Church of England*, pp. 172-90.

[4] Rose, 'Origins and Ideals of the SPCK', in Walsh, Haydon and Taylor (eds.), *The Church of England*, p. 180.

[5] H.P. Thompson, *Into All Lands: The History of the Society for the Propagation of the Gospel in Foreign Parts 1701–1950*, SPCK, 1951, p. 44.

⁶ Op. cit., p. 36.

⁷ Neill, *A History of Christian Missions*, pp. 243, 244.

⁸ Op. cit., p. 253.

⁹ George Smith, *The Life of William Carey*, P.B. Murray, 1887, 1909 edn., p. 12, quoted in Raymond Brown, *The English Baptists of the Eighteenth Century*, The Baptist Historical Society, 1986, p. 117.

¹⁰ Smith quoted in Brown, *English Baptists*, pp. 117, 118.

¹¹ Bebbington, *Evangelicalism*, p. 41.

¹² Elizabeth Elbourne, 'The Foundation of the Church Missionary Society: The Anglican Missionary Impulse', in Walsh, Haydon and Taylor (eds.), *The Church of England*, p. 247.

¹³ Ibid.

¹⁴ Andrew Walls, 'The evangelical Revival, the Missionary Movement, and Africa', in Noll, Bebbington and Rawlyk (eds.), *Evangelicalism*, p. 310. This is an article to which the present section is greatly indebted.

¹⁵ Ibid.

¹⁶ Cf. A.J. Raboteau and D.W. Wills, 'Rethinking American Religious History', *Council of Societies for the Study of Religion Bulletin*, 20, 1991, pp. 57-61.

¹⁷ Andrew Walls, 'The Evangelical Revival', in Noll, Bebbington and Rawlyk (eds.), *Evangelicalism*, pp. 310-11.

¹⁸ Jenkins, *The Next Christendom*, p. 15.

¹⁹ See Bediako, *Christianity in Africa*.

²⁰ See the statistics in Barrett, *World Christian Encyclopedia*, p. 796.

²¹ Jenkins, *The Next Christendom*, p. 15.

²² Balleine, *A History of the Evangelical Party*, p. 127.

²³ See Stock, *History of the Church Missionary Society*.

²⁴ Op. cit., p. 235.

²⁵ Glover, *The Progress of World-Wide Missions*, p. 70.

²⁶ Pickett, *Christian Mass Movements in India*, p. 21.

²⁷ Neill, *Christian Missions*, p. 366.

²⁸ Glover, *The Progress of World-Wide Missions*, p. 147.

²⁹ Neill, *Christian Missions*, p. 280.

³⁰ Op. cit., p. 283.

³¹ Glover, *The Progress of World-Wide Missions*, p. 152.

³² Op. cit, p. 154. For the life and work of Hudson Taylor, see especially Dr and Mrs Howard Taylor, *Hudson Taylor and the China Inland Mission: The Growth of a Work of God*, China Inland Mission, 1934; and

Roger Steer, *J. Hudson Taylor: A Man in Christ*, Minneapolis: Bethany House, 1990.

[33] Glover, *The Progress of World-Wide Missions*, p. 169. This is a work to which the present section is greatly indebted.

[34] Neill, *Christian Missions*, p. 328.

[35] Op. cit., p. 331.

[36] Op. cit., p. 414.

[37] Of the key works on the history of Christianity in Africa, special mention should be made of Hastings, *The Church in Africa 1450–1950*, the most comprehensive and authoritative work on the subject, and one to which this section is greatly indebted.

[38] Hastings, *The Church in Africa*, p. 7.

[39] Op. cit., p. 70.

[40] Op. cit., p. 118.

[41] Op. cit., pp. 180-81.

[42] A.F. Walls, 'A Christian Experiment: The Early Sierra Leone Colony', in G.J. Cuming (ed.), *The Mission of the Church and the Propagation of the Faith (Studies in Church History, 6)*, Cambridge: Cambridge University Press, 1970, p. 108, quoted in Hastings, *The Church in Africa*, p. 181.

[43] A.M. Falconbridge, *Narrative of Two Voyages to the River Sierra Leone, 1793*, p. 201 (reprint, Frank Cass, 1967), quoted in Hastings, *The Church in Africa*, p. 181.

[44] Hastings, *The Church in Africa*, p. 187.

[45] Walls, *The Missionary Movement in Christian History*, p. 104.

[46] Ibid.

[47] Ibid.

[48] Hastings, *The Church in Africa*, p. 208.

[49] Neill, *Christian Missions*, p. 312.

[50] Hastings, *The Church in Africa*, p. 246.

[51] Stock, *History of the Church Missionary Society*, vol. 1, p. 251.

[52] Hastings, *The Church in Africa*, pp. 243-4.

[53] Walls, *The Missionary Movement in Christian History*, p. 105. See also, J.F. Ajayi, *Christian Missions in Nigeria*, pp. 25 seq.

[54] Latourette, *Christianity in a Revolutionary Age*, vol. 1, p. 157.

[55] Op. cit., p. 325.

[56] Hastings, *The Church in Africa*, p. 249.

[57] Jenkins, *The Next Christendom*, p. 35.

[58] Latourette, *Christianity in a Revolutionary Age*, vol. 3, p. 465.

[59] For the explorative, political and economic aspects of the scramble for Africa, see Thomas Pakenham, *The Scramble for Africa 1876–1912*, George Weidenfeld & Nicolson, 1991.

[60] Neill, *Christian Missions*, p. 247.

[61] Latourette, *Christianity in a Revolutionary Age*, vol. 3, p. 465.

[62] Modern lives of David Livingstone include, G. Seaver, *David Livingstone: His Life and Letters*, James Clark, 1957; and T. Jeal, *Livingstone*, Heinemann, 1973.

[63] L.E. Elliott-Binns, *Religion in the Victorian Era*, Lutterworth, 1936, p. 381.

[64] Quoted in Neill, *Christian Missions*, p. 315.

[65] L. Schapera (ed.), *Livingstone's Missionary Correspondence 1841–1856*, Berkeley: University of California, 1961, pp. 301-302, quoted in Brian Stanley, *The Bible and the Flag: Protestant Missions and British Imperialism in the Nineteenth and Twentieth Centuries*, Leicester: Apollos, 1990, p. 73.

[66] For Madagascar, see Sundkler and Steed, *A History of the Church in Africa*, p. 491; and Neill, *Christian Missions*, p. 318.

[67] See Wilson, *The History of the Universities' Mission to Central Africa*, p. 283.

[68] For the history of Buganda, see S.N. Kiwanuka, *A History of Buganda from the Foundation of the Kingdom to 1900*, New York: Africana, 1972.

[69] The remark has been quoted by Archbishop Desmond Tutu.

[70] Neill, *Christian Missions*, pp. 203-204.

[71] Latourette, *Christianity in a Revolutionary Age*, vol. 3, p. 284.

[72] For the early history of the South American Missionary Society, see Phyllis Thompson, *An Unquenchable Flame: The Story of Cpt Allen Gardiner*, Hodder and Stoughton, 1983.

[73] Balleine, *A History of the Evangelical Party in the Church of England*, p. 205.

[74] Neill, *Christian Missions*, p. 320.

[75] Op. cit., p. 321.

[76] See the *Daily News*, 25 April 1885, quoted in Neill, *Christian Missions*, p. 321.

3 The Changing Face of Worldwide Christianity in the Twentieth Century. I: The Western World

1. For a useful summary of the origins of Western Pentecostalism, see Williams, *Tongues of the Spirit*, pp. 46-71.
2. For the history of Pentecostalism, see Harper, *As at the Beginning: The Twentieth Century Pentecostal Revival*; Hollenweger, *The Pentecostals*; and Hollenweger, *Pentecostalism*.
3. Williams, *Tongues of the Spirit*, pp. 46-71.
4. For the use of this term, see H.P. Van Dusen, in *Christian Century*, 17 August 1955; H.P. Van Dusen, 'The Third Force in Christendom', in *Life*, 6 June 1968.
5. *Christian Century*, 17 August 1955.
6. See Horton Davies, 'Pentecostalism: Threat or Promise', *Expository Times*, 76 (6), 1965, pp. 197-99, and 77 (8), May 1966, p. 225.
7. Hollenweger, *Pentecostalism*, p. 1.
8. See Barrett, *World Christian Encyclopedia*; and Cox, *Fire from Heaven*.
9. Scotland, *Charismatics and the New Millennium*, p. 14. This is a book to which the present section is greatly indebted.
10. Edith L. Blumhofer, 'Restoration as Revival: Early American Pentecostalism', in Blumhofer and Balmer (eds.), *Modern Christian Revivals*, p. 145.
11. Williams, *Tongues of the Spirit*, p. 51. This is a work to which the present section owes much.
12. See J.T. Nichol, *The Pentecostals*, Plainfield: Logos International, 1966, p. 40; and Gee, *The Pentecostal Movement*, p. 6.
13. Williams, *Tongues of the Spirit*, p. 61.
14. Gee, *The Pentecostal Movement*, 1967 edn., p. 37.
15. See B.R. Wilson, 'A Study of some Contemporary Groups in Great Britain with Special Reference to a Midland city', London Ph.D, 1955, p. 31.
16. Harper, *As at the Beginning*, p. 72.
17. Mills, *Speaking in Tongues*, p. 7.
18. See Nils Bloch-Hoell, *The Pentecostal Movement: Its Origin, Development, and Distinctive Character*, Allen and Unwin, 1964.
19. For the figures and facts stated in this paragraph, see Philip Richter, 'The Toronto Blessing: Charismatic Evangelical Global Warming', in Hunt, Hamilton and Walter (eds.), *Charismatic Christianity*, pp. 98-99.
20. *The Charismatic Movement in the Church of England*, p. 8.

[21] Gunstone, *Pentecostal Anglicans*, p. 12.

[22] *The Charismatic Movement in the Church of England*, p. 50.

[23] Paul A. Welsby, *A History of the Church of England 1945–1980*, p. 242.

[24] See P. Brierley, *UK Christian Handbook: Religious Trends 1998/99*, Christian Research, 1999, p. 217, Table 2.17.2; Scotland, *Charismatics and the New Millennium*, p. 324; and D. Tomlinson, *Post Evangelical*, Marshall Pickering, 1995, p. 211.

[25] Scotland, *Charismatics and the New Millennium*, p. 28.

[26] See Stephen Hunt, ' 'Doing the Stuff'. The Vineyard Connection', in Hunt, Hamilton and Walter (eds.), *Charismatic Christianity*, p. 77.

[27] David Bebbington, 'Evangelicalism in Its Settings: The British and American Movements since 1940', in Noll, Bebbington and Rawlyk (eds.), *Evangelicalism*, p. 375. See also Hunter, *American Evangelicalism*, p. 52.

[28] Kepel, *The Revenge of God*, p. 107.

[29] Bebbington, 'Evangelicalism in Its Settings'. in Noll, Bebbington and Rawlyk (eds.), *Evangelicalism*, p. 375. See also, Leonard I. Sweet, 'The 1960s: The Crisis of Liberal Christianity and the Public Emergence of Evangelicalism', in Marsden (ed.), *Fundamentalism and American Culture*, p. 44.

[30] See Bruce, *The Rise and Fall of the New Christian Right*.

[31] See Hunter, *Evangelicalism*, p. 125.

[32] Bruce, *The Rise and Fall of the New Christian Right*, p. vii.

[33] Ibid.

[34] Kepel, *The Revenge of God*, p. 120.

[35] See Fred J. Hood, 'Kentucky', and J. Wayne Flint, 'Alabama', in Hill (ed.), *Religion in the Southern States*, pp. 121, 123.

[36] See Leonard, 'Independent Baptists', pp. 514-15.

[37] Bebbington, 'Evangelicalism in Its Settings', in Noll, Bebbington and Rawlyk (eds.), *Evangelicalism*, p. 378.

[38] Kepel, *The Revenge of God*, p. 110.

[39] See Wilson, *Religion in Secular Society*; and Wilson, *Contemporary Transformations of Religion*.

[40] Kelly, *Why Conservative Churches are Growing*, p. xxv.

[41] Kepel, *The Revenge of God*, pp. 110-11.

[42] Kepel, *The Revenge of God*, p. 124.

[43] See Hadden and Shupe, *Televangelism, Religion and Politics*, pp. 82-83, which drew largely on the survey by Rothenberg and Newport, *The Evangelical Votes*.

44 Hadden and Shupe, *Televangelism*, pp. 137-38.

45 Of the many biographies of Billy Graham, mention should be made of Martin, *The Billy Graham Story*; and Pollock, *Billy Graham*.

46 See David Edwin Harrell, Jr., 'American Revivalism from Graham to Robertson', in Blumhorfer and Balmer (eds.), *Modern Christian Revivals*, p. 195.

47 John Stott, 'Obeying Christ in a Changing World', in John Stott (ed.), *Obeying Christ in a Changing World*, Inter-Varsity Press, 1977, vol. 1, p. 15.

48 John Stott (ed.), *Obeying Christ in a Changing World*, vol. 3, p. 12.

49 For an exposition of this approach, see John R.W. Stott, *Christian Mission in the Modern World*, Falcon/IVP, 1975.

50 Latourette, *Christianity in a Revolutionary Age*, vol. 4, p. 20.

51 Kepel, *The Revenge of God*, p. 47.

52 Davie, *Religion in Modern Europe*, p. 8.

53 Ibid.

54 Ibid.

55 This account of the Taizé Community owes much to Latourette, *Christianity in a Revolutionary Age*, vol. 4, p. 378.

56 Latourette, *Christianity in a Revolutionary Age*, vol. 4, p. 379.

57 Op. cit., p. 378.

58 This paragraph is based on James Minchin, 'Australia – the Last of Lands', in Wingate, Ward, Pemberton and Sitshebo (eds.), *Anglicanism*, pp. 153-54.

59 See Stuart Piggin, 'Towards a Bicentennial History of Australian Evangelicalism', *Journal of Religious History*, 15, June 1988, pp. 20-37, and Stuart Piggin, 'The American and British Contributions to Evangelicalism in Australia', in Noll, Bebbington and Rawlyk (eds.), *Evangelicalism*, pp. 290-309.

60 Piggin, 'The American and British Contributions to Evangelicalism in Australia', in Noll, Bebbington and Rawlyk (eds.), *Evangelicalism*, p. 290.

61 See Rawlyk, *Wrapped up in God*, p. 153.

62 Op. cit., p. 154.

63 George A. Rawlyk, 'Writing about Canadian Religious Revivals', in Blumhofer and Balmer (eds.), *Modern Christian Revivals*, p. 220.

4 The Changing Face of Worldwide Christianity in the Twentieth Century. II: South America

1 Latourette, *Christianity in a Revolutionary Age*, vol. 5, p. 162.
2 See William J. Coleman, *Latin American Catholicism: A Self-Evaluation*, Maryknoll, NY: Maryknoll Publications, 1958, pp. 20-22; and also Yorke Allen, *A Seminary Survey*, New York: Haprer, 1960, p. 461.
3 See John J. Considine, *Call for Forty Thousand*, New York: Longmans, Green and Co 1946, pp. 9-11; and Allen, *Seminary Survey*, p. 463.
4 See *The Catholic Historical Review*, vol. 26, p. 65.
5 See *The Catholic Historical Review*, vol. 26, pp. 215-21; and Margaret Bates (ed.), *The Lay Apostolate in Latin America Today: Proceedings of the 1959 Symposium held under the auspices of the Intstituteof Ibero-American Studies of the Catholic University of America*, Washington: Charles County Public Library, 1960, pp. 27-31.
6 See *The Catholic Historical Review*, vol. 26, pp. 215-21; and John J. Considine, *New Horizons in Latin America*, pp. 193-201.
7 See Considine, *New Horizons*, pp. 231-32.
8 See Considine, *New Horizons*, p. 233, and Bates (ed.), *The Lay Apostolate*, pp. 8-13.
9 Considine, *New Horizons*, p. 233.
10 Latourette, *Christianity in a Revolutionary Age*, vol. 5, p. 165.
11 Quoted in Neill, *Christian Missions*, p. 506.
12 See Mariz, *Coping with Poverty*, p. 12. This is a book to which the present section is greatly indebted.
13 Jenkins, *The Next Christendom*, p. 145. The whole thesis of the work by Jenkins is at the heart of what is argued in the present work.
14 Op. cit., p. 146.
15 Mariz, *Coping with Poverty*, p. 16.
16 This paragraph owes much to Lehmann, *Struggle for the Spirit*, pp. 54-55.
17 Faustino Luiz Couto Teixeira, 'Base Church Communities in Brazil', in Dussel (ed.), *The Church in Latin America*, p. 403.
18 Mariz, *Coping with Poverty*, p. 153.
19 Martin, *Tongues of Fire*, p. 291.
20 Jenkins, *The Next Christendom*, p. 57.
21 Westmeier, *Protestant Pentecostalism in Latin America*, p. 13.
22 David Stoll, 'A Protestant Reformation in Latin America', *Christian Century*, 17 January 1990, pp. 45-46. The full article was pp. 44-48, and in the same year Stoll published, *Is Latin America Turning Protestant?*

23 See, for example, C. Peter Wagner, 'The Greatest Church Growth is Beyond Our shores', *Christianity Today*, 18 May 1984, pp. 27-28.
24 Martin, *Tongues of Fire*, p. 49.
25 Op. cit., p. 50.
26 See E.J. Bingle and Kenneth Grubb (eds.), *World Christian Handbook*, World Dominion Press, 1957, pp. xii, 312.
27 The figures are quoted in Stoll, *Is Latin America Turning Protestant?* Appendix 3, pp. 337-38. They are based on denominational membership totals in Barrett, *World Christian Encyclopedia*, and other sources.
28 The details in this paragraph are culled from Glover, *The Progress of World-Wide Missions*, pp. 366-69.
29 Figures quoted in Corten, *Pentecostalism in Brazil*, p. 47.
30 See Bingle and Grubb (eds.), *World Christian Handbook*, pp. 115-49.
31 Everett Wilson, 'Revival and Revolution in Latin America', in Blumhofer and Balmer (eds.), *Modern Christian Revivals*, p. 186.
32 See William R. Read, Victor M. Monterroso and Harmon A. Johnson, *Latin American Church Growth*, Grand Rapids, MI: Eerdmans, 1969.
33 Everett A. Wilson, 'Revival and Revolution in Latin America', in Blumhofer and Balmer (eds.), *Modern Christian Revivals*, p. 181.
34 Neill, *Christian Missions*, p. 509.
35 Op. cit., p. 183.
36 Op. cit., p. 184.
37 Hannah W. Stewart-Gambino and Everett Wilson, 'Latin American Pentecostals', in Cleary and Stewart-Gambino (eds.), *Power, Politics and Pentecostals in Latin America*, pp. 228-29.
38 Edward L. Cleary, 'Introduction: Pentecostals, Prominence, and Politics', in Cleary and Stewart-Gambino (eds.), *Power, Politics and Pentecostals*, p. 4.
39 Paul Freston, 'Charismatic Evangelicals in Latin America: Mission and Politics on the Frontiers of Protestant Growth', in Hunt, Hamilton and Walter (eds.), *Charismatic Christianity*, p. 185.
40 Corten, *Pentecostalism in Brazil*, p. 55.
41 Ibid.
42 Martin, *Tongues of Fire*, p. 52.
43 See Chesnut, *Born Again in Brazil*, p. 3.
44 See Jenkins, *The Next Christendom*, p. 64.
45 Op. cit., p. 158.
46 Edward L. Cleary, 'Introduction', in Cleary and Stewart-Gambino (eds.), *Power, Politics and Pentecostals*, p. 1.

⁴⁷ For these details, see Hannah W. Stewart-Gambino and Everett Wilson, 'Latin American Pentecostals', in Cleary and Stewart-Gambino (eds.), *Power, Politics and Pentecostals*, p. 234.
⁴⁸ Martin, *Tongues of Fire*, p. 52.
⁴⁹ Hocken, *The Glory and the Shame*, p. 69.
⁵⁰ Martin, *Tongues of Fire*, p. 290.
⁵¹ Chesnut, *Born Again in Brazil*, p. 4.
⁵² Edward L. Cleary, 'Introduction', in Cleary and Stewart-Gambino (eds.), *Power, Politics and Pentecostals*, p. 12.
⁵³ Ibid.
⁵⁴ Op. cit., p. 13.
⁵⁵ Ibid.
⁵⁶ Chesnut, *Born Again in Brazil*, p. 3.
⁵⁷ Stoll, *Is Latin America Turning Protestant?*, p. 337, quoted in Chesnut, *Born Again in Brazil*, p. 3.
⁵⁸ Adrian Hastings, 'Latin America', in Hastings (ed.), *A World History of Christianity*.

5 The Changing Face of Worldwide Christianity in the Twentieth Century. III: Africa

¹ Isichei, *A History of Christianity in Africa*, p. 1.
² Sundkler and Steed, *A History of the Church in Africa*, pp. 627, 906.
³ Barrett, *The World Christian Encyclopedia*, p. 4, Global Table 2, cited, with rounded figures, in Isichei, *History of Christianity in Africa*, p. 1.
⁴ See Jenkins, *The Next Christendom*, pp. 37-38, and Barrett, *The World Christian Encyclopedia*.
⁵ J.O. Mills, 'Comment', *New Blackfriars*, January 1984, p. 3, quoted in Isichei, *History of Christianity in Africa*, p. 1.
⁶ See Allen Anderson, 'African Anglicans and/or Pentecostals', in Wingate, Ward, Pemberton and Sitshebo (eds.), *Anglicanism*, p. 36.
⁷ Jenkins, *The Next Christendom*, p. 48.
⁸ Op. cit., p. 53.
⁹ Neill, *Christian Missions*, p. 492.
¹⁰ Quoted in W.J. Platt, *An African Prophet*, SCM, 1934, p. 59.
¹¹ Neill, *Christian Missions*, p. 592. See also Sundkler and Steed, *History of the Church in Africa*, pp. 198-99; Hastings, *The Church in Africa*, pp. 443-45, 505-507; Haliburton, *The Prophet Harris*; and Sheila S. Walker,

The Religious Revolution in the Ivory Coast, Chapel Hill: University of North Carolina Press, 1983.

[12] Neill, *Christian Missions*, p. 493.

[13] Wilson, *Magic and Millennium*, p. 368. This is a book to which the present section on Kimbangu and Kimbanguism is greatly indebted.

[14] See Efraim Andersson, *Messianic Popular Movements in the Lower Congo*, pp. 52ff.

[15] Op. cit., pp. 63-66 for a full account of these episodes.

[16] Sundkler and Steed, *History of the Church in Africa*, p. 1033.

[17] Ibid.

[18] The following account of Aladura depends heavily on Hastings, *The Church in Africa*, pp. 514-18. But see also Isichei, *History of Christianity in Africa*, pp. 279-83; Sanneh, *West African Christianity: The Religious Impact*, New York: Orbis Books, 1983, pp. 168-209; *Afe Adogame and Akin Omyajowo*, 'Anglicanism and the Aladura Churches in Nigeria', in Wingate et al. (eds.), *Anglicanism*, pp. 90-97; and Peel, *Aladura*.

[19] Hastings, *The Church in Africa*, p. 515.

[20] See Jenkins, *The Next Christendom*, p. 50.

[21] Sundkler and Steed, *History of the Church in Africa*, p. 1033.

[22] Neill, *Christian Missions*, p. 500.

[23] Jenkins, *The Next Christendom*, p. 68.

[24] Op. cit., pp. 68-69.

[25] G.O.M. Tasie, 'The Prophetic Calling: Garrick Sokari Braide of Bakana (d. 1918)', in Isichei (ed.), *Varieties of Christian Experience in Nigeria*, Macmillan, 1982, p. 99.

[26] For the East African Revival and the balokole, see Hastings, *The Church in Africa*, pp. 596-600; Isichei, *History of Christianity in Africa*, pp. 241-44; Amos Kasibante, 'Beyond Revival', in Wingate et al. (eds.), *Anglicanism*, pp. 363-68; and Allan Anderson, 'African Anglicans and/or Pentecostals', in Wingate et al. (eds.), *Anglicanism*, pp. 34-40. A distinction should, perhaps, be made between 'renewal', when newness of life takes place within the Church itself, and 'revival', where there is such renewal, but the prominent, and in most cases overwhelming, feature is the conversion of many nominal Christians, fringe members of the Church, or complete outsiders. But, which-ever is the more appropriate term for the Balokole movement, it is by now so widely, and indeed probably unanimously, labelled as a revival, that to attempt a relabelling would be pernickety and overly academic.

²⁷ The story of Yona Kanamuzeyi is culled from Guillebaud, *Rwanda*, pp. 155-59. This whole section is greatly indebted to Guillebaud's book.
²⁸ Op. cit., p. 157.
²⁹ Marc Nikkel, 'Death has come to reveal the faith. Spirituality in the Episcopal Church of the Sudan amidst civil conflict', in Wingate et al. (eds.), *Anglicanism*, p. 73.
³⁰ Ibid., p. 73.
³¹ Op. cit., p. 74.
³² Op. cit., p. 77.
³³ See Thompson, *Life out of Death*.
³⁴ Hastings, *The Church in Africa*, p. 568.
³⁵ Adrian Hastings, *A History of African Christianity 1950–1975*, Cambridge: Cambridge University Press, p. 22.
³⁶ Op. cit., p. 22.
³⁷ Op. cit., p. 23.
³⁸ John S. Peart-Binns, *Ambrose Reeves*, Victor Gollancz, 1973, p. 71. This is a book on which the present account of Reeves is based.
³⁹ Op. cit., p. 202.
⁴⁰ Trevor Huddleston, *Naught for Your Comfort*, Doubleday, 1956, p. 16.
⁴¹ Hastings, *History of African Christianity*, p. 26.
⁴² For the life of Desmond Tutu, see DuBoulay, *Tutu*.
⁴³ See Stephen Hayes, *Black Charismatic Anglicans: The Iviyo loFakazi bakaKristu and Its Relations with Other Renewal Movements*, Pretoria: University of South Africa, 1990.
⁴⁴ Anderson, 'African Anglicans and/or Pentecostals', in Wingate et al. (eds.), *Anglicanism*, p. 35. The present work is greatly indebted to this most useful article.
⁴⁵ H.W. Turner, *Religious Innovation in Africa*, Boston, MA: G.K. Hall & Co, 1979, p. 210.
⁴⁶ Allen Anderson, 'African Anglicans and/or Pentecostals', in Wingate et al. (eds.), *Anglicanism*, p. 37.
⁴⁷ F.B. Welbourn and B.A. Ogot, *A Place to Feel at Home*, Oxford: Oxford University Press, 1966.
⁴⁸ Anderson, 'African Anglicans and/or Pentecostals', in Wingate et al. (eds.), *Anglicanism*, p. 37.
⁴⁹ Ibid., p. 37.
⁵⁰ Matthews A. Ojo, 'Charismatic Movements in Africa', in Fyfe and Walls (eds.), *Christianity in Africa*, p. 109.

51 Op. cit., pp. 109-10.

52 See Jenkins, *The Next Christendom*, p. 37.

53 See Aylward Shorter, 'The Roman Catholic Church in Africa Today', in Fyfe and Walls (eds.), *Christianity in Africa*, p. 23. The estimates are based on information supplied by the Catholic Missionary Education Society, London.

54 See Jenkins, *The Next Christendom*, pp. 58-59.

55 See Neill, *Christian Missions*, p. 457.

56 See Jenkins, *The Next Christendom*, p. 59.

57 Op. cit., pp. 58-59.

58 Ibid., pp. 58-59. Cf. Vatican Statistical Yearbook for 1989. for that year there were 20,484 Catholic priests present in Africa, and 700 ordinations to the priesthood took place. This did not include the growing number of ordinations of priests belonging to religious congregations and societies.

59 Jenkins, *The Next Christendom*, pp. 58-59. Cf. *Status Seminariorum in Terra Missionum Existentium, Rome 1988–1989*, p. 172, where it is stated that Nigeria had 2,033 major seminarians in 1988–1989; Zaire, 2,292; Kenya, 741; Tanzania, 579; and Uganda, 522. In addition, Nigeria had 8,451 minor seminarians.

60 Ibid., pp. 194-95.

61 Aylward Shorter, 'The Roman Catholic Church in Africa Today', in Fyfe and Walls (eds.), *Christianity in Africa*, p. 23. The Vatican Statistical Yearbook for 1989 stated that there were 2,663,294 baptisms in Africa in 1989, 21 per cent of which were adult baptisms.

62 See Jenkins, *The Next Christendom*, p. 195.

63 Op. cit., p. 12.

64 See Aylward Shorter, 'The Roman Catholic Church in Africa Today' in Fyfe and Walls (eds.), *Christianity in Africa*, p. 24.

65 Op. cit., p. 24.

66 Op. cit., p. 24.

67 Aylward Shorter, 'The Roman Catholic Church in Africa Today' in Fyfe and Walls (eds.), *Christianity in Africa*, p. 24; J.B. Metz, 'Unity and Diversity: problems and prospects for inculturation', *Concilium*, no. 204, 1989, p. 80.

6 The Changing Face of Worldwide Christianity in the Twentieth Century. IV: Asia

1   Daniel H. Bays, 'Christian Revival in China', in Blumhofer and Balmer (eds.), *Modern Christian Revivals*, p. 162. This is an article to which the present section owes much.

2   See Daniel H. Bays, *China Enters the Twentieth Century*, Ann Arbor: University of Michigan Press, 1978.

3   Bays, 'Christian Revival in China', in Blumhofer and Balmer (eds.), *Modern Christian Revivals*, p. 162.

4   D. MacGillivray (ed.), *A Century of Protestant Missions in China, 1807–1907*, Shanghai: American Presbyterian Mission Press, 1907, p. 669.

5   See Bays, 'Christian Revival in China', in Blumhofer and Balmer (eds.), *Modern Christian Revivals*, p. 166.

6   The following account of Christianity in China in the period from 1949 to 2000 rests heavily on Lambert, Paterson and Pickard, *China's Christian Millions*.

7   For the figures quoted, see Tony Lambert, *China Insight*, OMF International, November/December 2000.

8   The figures quoted in this and the following paragraphs are extracted from Latourette, *Christianity in a Revolutionary Age*, vol. 5, pp. 306-307.

9   See Carolus Streit, *Atlas Hierarchicus*, Paderborn: Sumpt. Typographiae Bonifacianiae, 1913, p. 99.

10 See *Catholic Directory of India*, 1918.

11 See Fides *News Service*, 18 April 1936. The figures given are for both India and Ceylon.

12 See *Worldmission Fides Service*, 6, 13, August 1960, and 26 April 1961; and *Worldmission*, vol 11, Fall 1960, p. 12.

13 See *Worldmission*, vol. 11, Fall 1960, p. 12.

14 For the life, work and beliefs of Mother Teresa, see Spink, *Mother Teresa*.

15 See *World Christian Handbook*, New York: Harper, 1957, pp. 31-38.

16 See Pickett, *Mass Movements*, p. 5.

17 Op. cit., p. 21.

18 See *The Christian Handbook of India, 1954, 1955*, pp. 248-55.

19 Op. cit., pp. 255-67.

20 See Harlan P. Beach and Burton St John (eds.), *World Statistics of Christian Missions*, New York: Committee of Reference and Counsel of the Foreign Missions, 1916, p. 67.

21 *World Christian Handbook*, 1957, p. 59.

22 See William Richey Hogg, *One World, One Mission*, New York: Friendship Press, 1960, pp. 147, 148.

23 *The Official Catholic Directory*, 1999. For the thorough permeation of Filipino life and culture by vernacular Christianity, see Fenella Cannell, *Power and Intimacy in the Christian Philippines*, Manila: Ateneo de Manila University Press, 1999.

24 For these demographic and Christian community figures, see tables 5.1 and 5.2 in Jenkins, *The Next Christendom*, pp. 84 and 90.

25 See Jenkins, *The Next Christendom*, p. 90, and Barrett et al., *World Christian Encyclopedia*, 2001, pp. 594-601.

26 Figures quoted in Latourette, *History of the Expansion of Christianity*, vol. 6, p. 380.

27 Op. cit., p. 389.

28 The following account of the Korean revival is based on Monod, *The Korean Revival*. But see also Donald N. Clark, *Christianity in Modern Korea*, Lanham, MD: University Press of America, 1986; Cox, *Fire from Heaven*, pp. 213-42; and Huntingdon, *Clash of Civilizations*, pp. 96-99.

29 Monod, *The Korean Revival*, pp. 32f.

30 For comments on the growth in numbers and the types of Korean Pentecostalism that emerged, see Hollenweger, *Pentecostalism*, pp. 100f.

31 For an informed, perceptive account of this, see Cox, *Fire from Heaven*.

32 See Jenkins, *The Next Christendom*, p. 71.

33 Neill, *Christian Missions*, p. 291.

34 See Koch, *The Revival in Indonesia*.

35 Op. cit., p. 159.

36 The following account of the Pacific Island churches is greatly indebted to David Hilliard, 'Australasia and the Pacific', in Hastings (ed.), *A World History of Christianity*, pp. 508-35.

37 Op. cit., pp. 530-31.

38 Op. cit., p. 531.

39 Dickson Kazuo Yagi, 'Christ for Asia', *Review and Expositor* 88/4 (1991), p. 375, quoted in Jenkins, *The Next Christendom*, p. 69.

40 Jenkins, *The Next Christendom*, p. 71.

7 An Appraisal

1 Kendall, *The End of an Era*, p. 1.
2 Ibid.
3 Chidester, *Christianity*, p. 579. This is a work to which the present book owes much.
4 Jenkins, *The Next Christendom*, pp. 1-2.
5 See Barrett et al., *World Christian Encyclopedia*, 2001, pp. 12-15.
6 See Jenkins, *The Next Christendom*, chapter 1, note 3, pp. 223-24.
7 Op. cit., p. 3.
8 Source: United Nations projections.
9 Jenkins, *The Next Christendom*, p. 5.
10 Fernandez-Armesto and Wilson, *Reformation*, p. ix.
11 Jenkins, *The Next Christendom*, p. 1.
12 Martin, *Tongues of Fire*, p. vii.
13 Acts, 17:6.
14 Davie, *Religion in Modern Europe*, p. 26.
15 Ibid.
16 Matthew 7:14.
17 For this distinction, see Hugh McLeod, 'Introduction', in McLeod and Ustorf (eds.), *The Decline of Christendom in Western Europe*.
18 Op. cit., p. 2.
19 See Bryan R. Wilson, *Religion in Secular Society*.
20 See Bruce, *Religion in the Modern World*, p. 233 and *passim*. See also, Bruce, *God is Dead*.
21 Davie, *Religion in Modern Europe*, p. 8.
22 David Hempton, 'Established Churches and the Growth of Religious Pluralism: A Case Study of Christianisation and Secularisation in England since 1700', in McLeod and Ustorf (eds.), *Decline of Christendom*, p. 81.
23 Jeffrey Cox, 'Master Narratives of Long-term Religious Change', in McLeod and Ustorf (eds.), *Decline of Christendom*, p. 201.
24 Edwards, *The Futures of Christianity*, p. 285.
25 Davie, *Religion in Modern Europe*, p. 8.
26 See Kepel, *The Revenge of God*, p. 47.
27 Ibid.
28 See Stephen Bates, 'Decline in Churchgoing Hits C of E Hardest', *Guardian*, 14 April 2001.
29 The figures quoted, and the comments made in this section, owe much to Bruce, *Religion in Modern Britain*, especially pp. 46-71.

[30] Davie, *Religion in Britain Since 1945*, p. 121.

[31] Bruce, *Religion in Modern Britain*, p. 70.

[32] This is a useful phrase used by Davie in her helpful book, *Religion in Britain Since 1945*.

[33] Bruce, *Religion in Modern* Britain, p. 71.

[34] Paul Avis, 'Editor's Foreword', in Avis (ed.), *Public Faith?*, p. vii.

[35] For a helpful summary of statistical and other information, with judicious comments, see Terence Thomas (ed.), *The British, Their Religious Beliefs and Practices 1800–1986*, London and New York: Routledge, 1988.

[36] Huntingdon, *The Clash of Civilizations*, p. 97. This is a work to which the present section is greatly indebted.

[37] Ibid.

[38] Davie, *Religion in Modern Europe*, p. 26.

[39] Huntingdon, *The Clash of Civilizations*, p. 98.

[40] Green, *Asian Tigers for Christ*, p. 115.

[41] Jenkins, *The Next Christendom*, p. 3.

[42] Fernandez-Armesto and Wilson, *Reformation*, p. 36.

[43] Further information on the Global South communique is obtainable from Bishop John Chew at johnchew@anglican.org.sg

[44] Jenkins, *The Next Christendom*, p. 8.

[45] Andrew F. Walls, in Fyfe and Walls (eds.), *Christianity in Africa in the 1990s*, p. 13.

[46] Jenkins, *The Next Christendom*, p. 126.

[47] Op. cit., p. 9.

[48] Kendall, *The End of an Era*, p. 7.

[49] Martin, *Tongues of Fire*, p. 293.

[50] Cox, *Fire From Heaven*, p. xv.

[51] Acts 1:8 NRSV.

Bibliography

Unless otherwise stated, the place of publication is London:

Ajayi, J.F. Ade, *Christian Missions in Nigeria 1841–1891: The Making of a New Elite*, Evanston: Northwestern University Press, 1969.

Alden, Karl, 'The Prophet Movement in the Congo', *International Review of Missions* 25, 1936, pp. 347-53.

Alexander, Archibald, *The Log College: Biographical sketches of William Tennent and his students together with an account of the revivals under their ministries*, 1851, Banner of Truth Trust, 1968.

Altizer, Thomas J.J., *The Gospel of Christian Atheism*, Philadelphia, PA: The Westminster Press, 1967.

Altizer, Thomas J.J. and Hamilton, William (eds.), *Radical Theology and the Death of God*, Penguin Books, 1966.

Andersson, Efraim, *Messianic Popular Movements in the Lower Congo*, Uppsala: Studia Ethnographica, Upsalicusia XIV, 1958.

Anker-Petersen, R., 'A study of the spiritual roots of the East African revival movement', M.Th., Edinburgh Centre for the Study of Christianity in the Non-Western World, 1988.

Armstrong, Karen, *A History of God. From Abraham to the Present: the 4000-year Quest for God*, New York: Canongate US, 1993.

——, *The Battle for God: Fundamentalism in Judaism, Christianity and Islam*, New York: Knopf, 2000.

Avis, Paul (ed.), *Public Faith? The State of Religious Belief and Practice in Britain*, SPCK, 2003.

Baeta, C.G., *Prophetism in Ghana: A Study of some 'Spiritual' Churches*, SCM, 1962.

Balleine, G.R., *A History of the Evangelical Party in the Church of England*, Longmans, Green, and Co., 1908.

Balmer, Randall, *Mine Eyes Have Seen the Glory: A Journey into the Evangelical Subculture in America*, New York: Oxford University Press, 1989.

Barber, Benjamin R., *Jihad Vs McWorld*, New York: Times Books, 1995.

Barber, Bernard, 'Acculturation and Messianic Movements', *American Sociological Review* 6, October 1941, pp. 663-68.

Barker, E. (ed.), *New Religious Movements: A Practical Introduction*, New York and London: Garland Press, 1989.

Barrett, David B., *Schism and Renewal in Africa: An Analysis of Six Thousand Contemporary Religious Movements*, Nairobi: Oxford University Press, 1968.

—— (ed.), *The World Christian Encyclopedia: A Comparative Survey of Churches and Religions in the Modern World*, New York: Oxford University Press, 1982.

——, 'The Twentieth-Century Pentecostal/Charismatic Renewal in the Holy Spirit, with its Goal of World Evangelisation', *International Bulletin of Missionary Research*, July 1988, pp. 118-29.

——, George T. Kurian and Todd M. Johnson, *World Christian Encyclopedia*, 2nd edn., New York: Oxford University Press, 2001.

Bays, Daniel H. (ed.), *Christianity in China from the Eighteenth Century to the Present*, Stanford University Press, 1996.

Bebbington, D.W., *Evangelicalism: A History from the 1730s to the 1980s*, Unwin Hyman, 1989.

Bediako, Kwame, *Christianity in Africa: The Renewal of a Non-Western Religion*, Edinburgh: Edinburgh University Press, 1995.

Bennett, D., *Nine O'Clock in the Morning*, Logos, Fountain Trust, 1970.

Bergman, Susan (ed.), *A Cloud of Witnesses: 20th Century Witnesses*, Harper Collins, 1997.

Beyer, Peter, *Religion and Globalization*, Thousand Oaks, CA: Sage Pub., 1994.

Blanchard, John, *Does God Believe in Atheists?*, Darlington: Evangelical Press, 2000.

Blumhofer, Edith L. and Balmer, Randall (eds.), *Modern Christian Revivals*, Urbana and Chicago: University of Illinois, 1993.

Boles, John B., *The Great Revival, 1787–1805: The Origins of the Southern Evangelical Mind*, Lexington: University Press of Kentucky, 1972.

——, *The Great Revival Beginnings of the Bible Belt*, Lexington: University Press of Kentucky, 1996.

Brierley, Peter, *'Christian England': What the English Church Census Reveals*, MARC Europe, 1991.

Brooke, R and C., *Popular Religion in the Middle Ages: Western Europe 1000–1300*, Thames & Hudson, 1984.

Brown, Peter, *The Rise of Christendom*, Oxford: Blackwell Publishers, 1996.

Brown-Lawson, A., *John Wesley and the Anglican Evangelicals of the Eighteenth Century*, Edinburgh: Pentland Press, 1994.

Bruce, Dickson D., Jnr, *And They All Sang Halleluyah: Plain-Folk Camp Meeting Religion, 1800–1845*, Knoxville: University of Tennessee Press, 1974.

Bruce, Steve, *The Rise and Fall of the New Christian Right: Conservative Protestant Politics in America 1978–1988*, New York: Oxford University Press, 1990.

——, *Religion and Modernization: Sociologists and Historians Debate the Secularization Thesis*, Oxford: Oxford University Press, 1992.

——, *Religion in Modern Britain*, Oxford: Oxford University Press, 1995.

——, *Religion in the Modern World: From Cathedral to Cults*, Oxford: Oxford University Press, 1996.

——, *God is Dead: Secularization in the West*, Oxford: Blackwell, 2002.

Buckley, Michael, *At the Origins of Modern Atheism*, New Haven: Yale University Press, 1987.

Burgess, Stanley M., Gary B. McGee, and Patrick Alexander (eds.), *Dictionary of Pentecostal and Charismatic Movements*, Grand Rapids. MI: Zondervan, 1988.

Butler, Jon, *Power, Authority and the Origins of American Denominational Order: The English Churches in the Delaware Valley, 1680–1730*, Philadelphia: American Philosophical Society, 1978.

——, *Awash in a Sea of Faith: Christianizing the American People*, Cambridge, MA: Harvard University Press, 1990.

Cairns, Earle E., *An Endless Line of Splendor: Revivals and Their Leaders from the Great Awakening to the Present*, Wheaton, Illinois: Tyndale House, 1986.

Campbell, T.A., *The Religion of the Heart: A Study of European Religious Life in the Seventeenth and Eighteenth Centuries*, Columbia: University of Columbia, 1991.

Caplan, Lionel (ed.), *Studies in Religious Fundamentalism*, Albany, NY: State University of New York Press, 1988.

Carson, John S., *God's River in Spate*, Belfast: Church House, 1958.

Carwardine, Richard, *Transatlantic Revivalism: Popular Evangelicalism in Britain and America, 1790–1865*, Westport, CT: Greenwood Press, 1978.

Chadwick, Owen, *The Secularization of the European Mind in the Nineteenth Century*, Cambridge: Cambridge University Press, 1975.

The Charismatic Movement in the Church of England, CIO Publishing, 1981.

Chesnut, R. Andrew, *Born Again in Brazil: The Pentecostal Boom and the Pathogens of Poverty*, New Brunswick, NJ: Rutgers University, 1997.

Chidester, David, *Christianity: A Global History*, San Francisco: Harper San Francisco, 2000.

Church, J.E., *Quest for the Highest: An Autobiographical account of the East African Revival*, Exeter: Paternoster Press, 1981.

Cleary, Edward L and Hannah W. Stewart-Gambio (eds.), *Power, Politics and Pentecostals in Latin America*, Boulder, CO: Westview, 1997.

Coalter, Milton J., Gilbert Tennent, *Son of Thunder: A Case Study of Continental Pietism's Impact on the First Great Awakening in the Middle Colonies*, Westport, CT: Greenwood Press, 1986.

Coleman, Simon, *The Globalisation of Charismatic Christianity: Spreading the Gospel of Prosperity*, Cambridge: Cambridge University Press, 2000.

Considine, John J., *New Horizons in Latin America*, New York: Dodd, Mead & Co., 1958.

Corten, Andre, *Pentecostalism in Brazil: Emotion of the Poor and Theological Romanticism*, New York: St Martin's, 1999.

Cowing, Cedric B., *The Great Awakening and the American Revolution: Colonial Thought in the 18th Century*, Honolulu: Rand McNally, 1970.

Cox, Harvey, *The Secular City. Secularization and Urbanization in Theological Perspective*, New York and London: Collier Books, 1965.

——, *Fire from Heaven: The Rise of Pentecostal Spirituality and the Re-Shaping of Religion in the Twenty-First Century*, Reading, MA: Addison-Wesley, 1995.

Craig, Mary, *Candles in the Dark: Six Modern Martyrs*, Hodder & Stoughton, 1984.

Craston, Colin, *The Charismatic Movement in the Church of England*, CIO Publishing, 1981.

Crawford, Michael, 'Origins of the Eighteenth Century Evangelical Revival. England and New England compared', *Journal of British Studies*, 26, 1987, pp. 361-97.

——, *Seasons of Grace: Colonial New England's Revival Tradition in its British Context*, New York: Oxford University Press, 1991.

Cupitt, Don, *Radicals and the Future of the Church*, SCM, 1989.

——, *After God: The Future of Religion*, New York: Basic Books, 1997.

Currie, R., A. Gilbert and L. Horsley, *Churches and Churchgoers: Patterns of Church Growth in the British Isles Since 1700*, Oxford: Clarendon Press, 1977.

Curtis, Richard K., *They Called Him Mr. Moody*, Grand Rapids, MI: W.B. Eerdmans, 1962.

Dallimore, Arnold A., *George Whitefield: The Life and Times of the Great Evangelist of the Eighteenth-Century Revival*, The Banner of Truth, vol. 1 1970, vol. 2, 1980.

——, *The Life of Edward Irving, the Fore-runner of the Charismatic Movement*, Edinburgh: The Banner of Truth, 1983.

——, *Spurgeon: A New Biography, Chicago 1984*, Edinburgh: The Banner of Truth, 1985 edn.

——, *A Heart Set Free: The Life of Charles Wesley. Evangelist, Hymn-writer Preacher*, Wheaton, IL: Crossway Books, 1988.

Davidson, Edward H., *Jonathan Edwards: The Narrative of a Puritan Mind*, Boston: Houghton Mifflin Co., 1966.

Davie, Grace, *Religion in Britain Since 1945: Believing Without Belonging*, Oxford: Blackwell, 1994.

——, *Religion in Modern Europe: A Memory Mutates*, Oxford: Oxford University Press, 2000.

Davies, A., *The Moravian Revival of 1727 and Some of its Consequences*, Evangelical Library, 1977.

Davies, G.C.B., *The Early Cornish Evangelicals 1735–1760. A Study of Walker of Truro and Others*, SPCK, 1951.

Davies, Owen, *Witchcraft, Magic and Culture 1736–1951*, Manchester: Manchester University Press, 1999.

Davies, Rupert E., Gordon Rupp and A. Raymond George (eds.), *A History of the Methodist Church in Great Britain*, 4 vols, Epworth Press, 1965-88.

Davis, George T.B., *Torrey and Alexander: The Story of a World-Wide Revival*, New York: Fleming H Revell, 1905.

Dayton, Donald W. and Robert K. Johnston (eds.), *The Variety of American Evangelicalism*, Downers Grove, IL: Inter Varsity Press, 1991.

de Ste Croix, G.E.M., 'Why were the Early Christians Persecuted?', *Past and Present* 26, 1963, pp. 6-31.

——, 'Why were the Early Christians Persecuted – A Rejoinder', *Past and Present* 27, 1964, pp. 28-33.

Dewar, Diana, *All for Christ: Some Twentieth Century Martyrs*, Oxford, New York: Oxford University Press, 1980.

Ditchfield, G.M., *The Evangelical Revival*, UCL Press, 1998.

Dolan, Jay P., *Catholic Revivalism: The American Experience, 1830–1900*, Notre Dame: The University of Notre Dame, 1978.

Drummond, Lewis, *A Fresh Look at the Life and Ministry of Charles G. Finney*, Minneapolis: Bethany House, 1983.

DuBoulay, Shirley, *Tutu: Voice of the Voiceless*, Penguin Books, 1988.

Duffy, E., 'Primitive Christianity Revived: Religious Renewal in Augustan England', *Studies in Church History* 14, 1976, pp. 287–300.

Durden, Susan, 'Transatlantic Communications and Literature in the Religious Revivals, 1735-1745', Ph.D, Hull, 1978.

Dussel, Enrique (ed.), *The Church in Latin America 1492–1992*, Maryknoll, New York: Orbis, 1992.

Edwards, Brian H., *Revival: A People Saturated with God*, Darlington: Evangelical Press, 1990.

Edwards, David L., *The Futures of Christianity: An Analysis of Historical, Contemporary and Future Trends within the Universal Church*, London, Sydney, Auckland, Toronto: Hodder & Stoughton, 1987.

Edwards, Jonathan, *The Works of, 1834, revd and corrected by Edward Hickman*, Edinburgh: Banner of Truth, 1974 edn.

——, *Jonathan Edwards on Revival; A reissue of A Narrative of Surprising Conversions (1736), Distinguishing Marks of a Work of* the Spirit of God (1741) and An Account of the Revival in Northampton in 1740–1742 in a Letter (1743), Edinburgh: The Banner of Truth, 1965.

Elliott-Binns, Leonard E., *The Early Evangelicals: A Religious and Social Study*, Lutterworth Press, 1953.

Evans, Eifion, *The Welsh Revival of 1904*, Bridgend: Bryntirion Press, 1987 edn.

——, *Daniel Rowlands and the Great Evangelical Awakening in Wales*, Edinburgh: The Banner of Truth, 1985.

Fawcett, Arthur, *The Cambuslang Revival*, Banner of Truth, 1971.

Fehderau, Harold W., 'Kimbanguism: Prophetic Christianity in the Congo', *Practical Anthropology* 9, July-August 1962, pp. 157-78.

Fernandez, James W., 'African Religious Movements – Types and Dynamics', *Journal of Modern African Studies* 2, 4, December 1964, pp. 531-49.

——, 'Politics and Prophecy. African Religious Movements', *Practical Anthropology* 12, 2, March-April 1965, pp. 71-75.

Fernandez-Armesto, Felipe and Wilson, Derek, *Reformation: Christianity and the World 1500–2000*, London, Sydney, Toronto and Auckland: Bantam Press, 1996.

Field, Clive D., 'The Social Structure of English Methodism in the Eighteenth to Twentieth Centuries' *British Journal of Sociology* 28, 1977, pp. 199-225.

——, 'The Social Composition of English Methodism to 1830. A Membership Analysis', *Bulletin of the John Rylands Library* 76 (1), 1994, pp. 153-69.

Findlay, G.G. and W.W. Holdsworth, *History of the Wesleyan Methodist Missionary Society*, 5 vols, Epworth Press, 1921-24.

Findlay, James F., Jr, *Dwight L. Moody: American Evangelist, 1837–1899*, Chicago: University of Chicago Press, 1969.

Finney, Charles G., *Memoirs of the Rev Charles G. Finney*, Grand Rapids, MI: Academic Books, 1989 version ed by Garth M. Rosell and A.G. Dupuis.

——, *Lectures on Revivals of Religion*, ed. G. McLoughlin, Cambridge, MA: Harvard University Press, 1966.

Fish, Roy J., *When Heaven Touched Earth: The Awakening of 1858 and Its Effect on Baptists*, Azle, TX: Need of the Times Publishers, 1996.

Fletcher, William C., *Soviet Charismatics: The Pentecostals in the USSR*, New York: P. Lang, 1985.

Frady, Marshall, *Billy Graham: Parable of American Righteousness*, Boston: Little, Brown and Company, 1979.

Frank, Douglas W., *Less Than Conquerors: How Evangelicals Entered the Twentieth Century*, Grand Rapids, MI: William B. Eerdmans, 1986.

Freston, Paul, 'Pentecostalism in Brazil. A Brief History', *Religion* 25, 1995, pp. 119-33.

Freud, Sigmund, *The Future of an Illusion, 1927*, Buffalo, NY: Prometheus Books, 1990 edn.

Friedman, Richard Elliott, *The Disappearance of God: A Divine Mystery*, Boston: Little, Brown and Company, 1995.

Fuchs, Stephen, *Rebellious Prophets: A Study of Messianic Movements in Indian Religions*, New York: Asia Pub. House, 1963.

Fulton, John and Peter Gee (eds.), *Religion in Contemporary Europe*, New York: Edwin Mellen Press, 1994.

Fung, Raymond, *The Isaiah Vision: An Ecumenical Strategy for Congregational Evangelism*, Geneva: CCBI Publications, 1992.

Fyfe, Christopher and Andrew Walls (eds.), *Christianity in Africa in the 1990s*, Edinburgh: Centre of African Studies, 1996.

Garnett, Jane and Colin Matthew (eds.), *Revival and Religion since 1700: Essays for John Walsh*, Hambledon Press, 1993.

Gauchet, Marcel, *The Disenchantment of the World: A Political History of Religion*, Princeton: Princeton University Press, 1997.

Gaustad, Edwin S., *The Great Awakening in New England*, New York: Harper, 1957.

Gee, Donald, *The Pentecostal Movement*, Elim Publishing Co., 1941.

Gilbert, A.D., *Religion and Society in Industrial England: Church, Chapel and Social Change 1740–1914*, Longman, 1976.

——, *The Making of Post-Christian Britain: A History of the Secularization of Modern Society*, Longman, 1980.

Gill, Robin, *Competing Convictions*, SCM Press, 1989.

——, *The Myth of the Empty Church*, SPCK, 1993.

——, *The 'Empty' Church Revisited: Explorations in Practical, Patroral and Empirical Theology*, Aldershot: Ashgate, 2003.

Gill, Sean, Gavin D'Costa and Ursula King (eds.), *Religion in Europe: Contemporary Perspectives*, Kampen: Kok Pharos, 1994.

Gilley, Sheridan and W.J. Shiels (eds.), *A History of Religion in Britain 1750 to the Present*, Oxford: Blackwells, 1994.

Gillies, John, *Historical Collections Relating to Remarkable Periods of the Success of the Gospel*, Kelso 1845, Edinburgh: The Banner of Truth, 1981 edn.

Glover, Robert Hall, *The Progress of World-Wide Missions, revd and enlarged by J. Herbert Kane*, New York: Harper, 1960.

Goen, C.C., *Revivalism and Separatism in New England, 1740–1800. Strict Congregationalists and Separate Baptists in the Great Awakening*, New Haven, CT: Yale University Press, 1962.

Gordon, James M., *Evangelical Spirituality From John Wesley to John Stott*, SPCK, 1991.

Graham, Ysenda Maxtone, *The Church Hesitant: A Portrait of the Church of England Today*, Hodder & Stoughton, 1993.

Green, Michael, *Asian Tigers for Christ: The Dynamic Growth of the Church in South East Asia*, SPCK, 2001.

Guillebaud, Meg, *Rwanda The Land God Forgot?: Revival, Genocide and Hope*, Monarch Books, 2002.

Gunstone, John, *Pentecostal Anglicans*, Hodder & Stoughton, 1982.

Gunter, W. Stephen, *The Limits of 'Love Divine'*, Nashville: Kingswood Books, 1989.

Gutierrez, Gustavo, *A Theology of Liberation: History, Politics and Salvation*, Maryknoll, New York: Orbis, 1971.

Hadden, Jeffrey K. and Anson Shupe, *Televangelism, Religion and Politics on God's Frontier*, New York: Paragon House, 1988.

Haliburton, G.M., *The Prophet Harris: A Study of an African Prophet and His Mass Movement in the Ivory Coast and the Gold Coast, 1913–1915*, Longman, 1971.

Hall, David D., *Worlds of Wonder, Days of Judgement: Popular Religious Belief in Early New England*, Cambridge, MA: Harvard University Press, 1989.

Harbour, Daniel, *An Intelligent Person's Guide to Atheism*, Duckworth, 2001.

Hardman, Keith J., *Charles Grandison Finney 1792–1875. Revivalist and Reformer*, Syracuse: Syracuse University Press, 1987.

Harmelink, Herman, III, 'Another Look at Frelinghuysen and His 'Awakening', *Church History* 37, 1968, pp. 423-38.

Harper, Michael, *As at the Beginning: The Twentieth Century Pentecostal Revival*, Hodder & Stoughton, 1965.

Harrell, David Edwin, Jnr, *Oral Roberts: An American Life*, Bloomington: Indiana University Press, 1985.

——, *Pat Robertson: A Personal, Religious and Political Portrait*, San Francisco: Harper and Row, 1987.

Hastings, Adrian, *The Church in Africa 1450–1950*, Oxford: Clarendon, 1994.

—— (ed.), *Modern Catholicism: Vatican 11 and After*, London and New York: Oxford University Press, 1991.

—— (ed.), *A World History of Christianity*, Cassell, 1999.

Hatch, Nathan O., *The Democratization of American Christianity*, New Haven, CT: Yale University Press, 1989.

Hattersley, Roy, *Blood and Fire: William and Catherine Booth and the Salvation Army*, Little, Brown and Company, 1999.

Hattersley, Roy, *A Brand from the Burning: The Life of John Wesley*, Little, Brown and Company, 2002.

Haynes, Stephen R and John K. Roth (eds.), *The Death of God Movement and the Holocaust: Radical Theology Encounters the Shoah*, Westport, CT: Greenwood Press 1999.

Hayward, V.E.W. (ed.), *African Independent Church Movements*, Edinburgh House Press, 1962.

Hazlett, Ian (ed.), *Early Christianity: Origins and Evolution to AD 600*, SPCK, 1991.

Heasman, Kathleen, *Evangelicals in Action: An Appraisal of their Social Work in the Victorian Era*, Geoffrey Bles, 1962.

Hefley, James and Marti Hefley, *By Their Blood: Christian Martyrs of the Twentieth Century*, Tennessee: Baker Book House USA, 1979.

Heimert, Alan, *Religion and the American Mind from the Great Awakening to the Revolution*, Cambridge, MA: Harvard University Press, 1966.

Hempton, David, *Methodism and Politics in British Society, 1750–1850*, Hutchinson, 1984.

——, 'Methodism in Irish Society 1770–1830', *Transactions of the Royal Historical Society* 36, 1986, pp. 117-42.

——, *The Religion of the People: Methodism and Popular Religion c. 1750–1900*, Routledge, 1996.

—— and Hill, M., *Evangelical Protestantism in Ulster Society 1740–1890*, Routledge, 1992.

Hill, M., 'Ulster Awakened. The '59 Revival Reconsidered', *Journal of Ecclesiastical History*, 41 (3), 1990, pp. 443-62.

Hill, Samuel S. (ed.), *Religion in the Southern States: A Historical Study*, Macon, GA: Mercer University Press, 1983.

Hindmarsh, D.B., *John Newton and the English Evangelical Tradition*, Oxford: Clarendon, 1996.

Hobsbawm, E.J., *Primitive Rebels: Studies in Archaic Forms of Social Movement in the 19th and 20th Centuries*, Manchester University Press, 1959, 1978 edn.

Hocken, Peter, *Streams of Renewal: The Origins and Development of the Charismatic Movement in Great Britain*, Exeter: Paternoster, 1986.

——, *The Glory and the Shame: Reflections on the 20th Century Outpouring of the Holy Spirit*, Guildford: Eagle, 1994.

——, *The Strategy of the Spirit?: Worldwide Renewal and Revival in the Established Church and Modern Movements*, Guildford: Eagle, 1996.

Hoffer, Eric, *The True Believer: Thoughts on the Nature of Mass Movements*, Harper Collins, 1951.

Hollenweger, Walter J., *The Pentecostals: The Charismatic Movement in the Churches*, SCM Press, 1972.

——, *Pentecostalism: Origins and Developments Worldwide*, Peabody, MA: Hendrickson Publishers, 1997.

Hollister, J.N., *Centenary of the Methodist Church in Southern Asia*, Lucknow: Lucknow Pub House, 1956.

Holmes, Janice, *Religious Revivals in Britain and Ireland 1859–1905*, Dublin: Irish Academic Press, 2000.

Hopkins, Hugh E., *Charles Simeon of Cambridge: A Biography*, Hodder & Stoughton, 1977.

Howse, Ernest Marshall, *Saints in Politics: The 'Clapham Sect' and the Growth of Freedom*, George Allen & Unwin Ltd, 1953.

Hunt, S., '"The Toronto Blessing". A rumour of angels?', *Journal of Contemporary Religion* 10 (3), 1995, pp. 257-71.

——, M. Hamilton and T. Walter, *Charismatic Christianity: Sociological Perspectives*, Basingstoke: Macmillan Press, 1997.

Hunter, James Davidson, *American Evangelicalism: Conservative Religion and the Quandary of Modernity*, New Brunswick, NJ: Rutgers University Press, 1983.

——, *Evangelicalism: The Coming Generation*, Chicago: The University of Chicago Press, 1987.

Huntington, Samuel P., *The Third Wave*, Oklahoma: University of Oklahoma Press, 1991.

——, *The Clash of Civilizations and the Remaking of World Order*, New York 1988, New York: Simon & Schuster, 1996.

Hylson-Smith, Kenneth, *The Evangelicals in the Church of England 1734–1984*, Edinburgh: T&T Clark, 1989.

——, *High Churchmanship in the Church of England: From the Sixteenth Century to the Late Twentieth Century*, Edinburgh: T&T Clark, 1993.

Isichei, Elizabeth, *A History of Christianity in Africa: From Antiquity to the Present*, Grand Rapids, MI: Eerdmans, 1995.

Jenkins, Philip, *The Next Christendom: The Coming of Global Christianity*, Oxford: Oxford University Press, 2002.

Johnson, Charles A., *The Frontier Camp Meeting: Religion's Harvest Time*, Dallas: Southern Methodist University Press, 1984.

Jones, Brynmor Pierce., *An Instrument of Revival: The Complete Life of Evan Roberts*, South Plainfield, New Jersey: Bridge Publishing Inc., 1995.

Kay, William K., *Pentecostals in Britain*, Carlisle: Paternoster, 2000.

Kelly, Dean, *Why Conservative Churches are Growing: A study in Sociology of Religion*, New York: Harper and Row, 1972.

Kendall, Elliott, *The End of an Era: Africa and the Missionary*, SPCK, 1978.

Kennedy, Ludovic, *All in the Mind: A Farewell to God*, Hodder & Stoughton, 1999.

Kent, John H.S., *Holding the Fort: Studies in Victorian Revivalism*, Epworth, 1978.

——, *Wesley and the Wesleyans*, Cambridge: Cambridge University Press, 2002.

Kepel, Gilles, *The Revenge of God: The Resurgence of Islam, Christianity and Judaism in the Modern World, 1991*, tr. Alan Braley, University Park, PA: Pennsylvania State University Press, 1994.

Knox, Ronald A., *Enthusiasm: A Chapter in the History of Religion, with special reference to the XVII and XVIII Centuries*, Oxford: Oxford University Press, 1950.

Koch, Kurt, *The Revival in Indonesia*, Grand Rapids, MI: Kregal Publications, 1970.

Lambert, Frank, 'Pedlar in Divinity. George Whitefield and the Great Awakening, 1737–1745', *Journal of American History 77*, 1990, pp. 812-37.

——, 'The Great Awakening as Artifact: George Whitefield and the Construction of International Revival, 1739–1745', *Church History* 60, June 1991, pp. 223-46.

——, *'Pedlar in Divinity'; George Whitefield and the Transatlantic Revivals, 1737–1770*, Princeton: Princeton University Press, 1994.

Lambert, Tony, Ross Paterson and David Pickard, *China's Christian Millions: The Costly Revival*, Monarch 1999.

Latourette, Kenneth Scott, *Christianity in a Revolutionary Age*, 5 vols., Grand Rapids, MI: Zondervan, 1958.

——, *History of the Expansion of Christianity*, 7 vols., New York: Harper, 1937–1945.

Lawrence, Bruce B., *Defenders of God: The Fundamentalist Revolt Against the Modern Age*, New York: Harper, 1989.

Lehmann, David, *Struggle for the Spirit: Religious Transformation and Popular Culture in Brazil and Latin America*, Cambridge, MA: Polity Press/Blackwell, 1996.

Leonard, Bill J., 'Independent Baptists. From Sectarian Minority to "Moral Majority"', *Church History* 56, 1987, pp. 514-15.

Lerrigo, P.H.J., 'The Prophet Movement in the Congo', *International Review of Missions II*, 1922, pp. 270-77.

Lewis, H. Elvet, G. Campbell Morgan, and I.V. Neprash, *Glory Filled the Land: A Trilogy on the Welsh Revival of 1904–1905*, Wheaton, IL: International Awakening Press, 1989.

Lightman, Bernard, *The Origins of Agnosticism: Victorian Unbelief and the Limits of Knowledge*, Chicago and London: University of Chicago Press, 1997.

Lovegrove, D., *Established Church, Sectarian People, Itinerancy and the Transformation of English Dissent 1780–1830*, Cambridge: Cambridge University Press, 1988.

Lovejoy, David S., *Religious Enthusiasm in the New World: Heresy to Revolution*, Cambridge, MA and London: Harvard University Press, 1985.

Maclean, J. Kennedy, *Torrey and Alexander: The Story of their Lives*, London DNK.

McLeod, Hugh and Werner, Ustorf (eds.), *The Decline of Christendom in Western Europe, 1750–2000*, Cambridge: Cambridge University Press, 2003.

McLoughlin, William G, Jnr, *Modern Revivalism: Charles Grandison Finney to Billy Graham*, New York: Ronald Press, 1959.

——, *Revivals, Awakenings and Reform: An Essay on Religion and Social Change in America, 1607–1977*, Chicago: University of Chicago Press, 1978.

Marini, Stephen A., *Radical Sects of Revolutionary New England*, Cambridge, MA: Harvard University Press, 1982.

Mariz, Cecilia, *Coping with Poverty: Pentecostals and Christian Base Communities*, Philadelphia: Temple University Press, 1994.

Marsden, George M. (ed.), *Fundamentalism and American Culture: The Shaping of Twentieth Century Evangelicalism, 1870–1925*, New York: Oxford University Press, 1980.

Marshall, Paul with Lila Gilbert, *Their Blood Cries Out: The Worldwide Tragedy of Modern Christians Who are Dying for Their Faith*, Dallas: Word Publishing, 1997.

Martin, David, *The Religious and the Secular: Studies in Secularization*, Routledge & Kegan Paul, 1969.

——, *A General Theory of Secularization*, Oxford: Blackwell, 1978.

——, *Tongues of Fire: The Explosion of Protestantism in Latin America*, Oxford: Blackwell, 1990.

Martin, M.L., *Kimbangu: An African Prophet and His Church*, Grand Rapids, MI: Eerdmans, 1975.

Martin, William, *The Billy Graham Story: A Prophet With Honour*, New York: P.B. William Morrow and Company, 1991.

Marty, Martin E., *Fundamentalism Comprehended*, Chicago and London: University of Chicago Press, 1995.

—— and R. Scott Appleby, *Accounting for Fundamentalisms: The Dynamic Character of Movements*, Chicago and London: University of Chicago Press, 1994.

Masterson, Patrick, *Atheism and Alienation: A Study of the Philosophic Sources of Contemporary Atheism*, Notre Dame: University of Notre Dame Press, 1971.

Mathews, Donald G., 'The Second Great Awakening as an organizing process, 1780–1830. A hypothesis', *American Quarterly* 21, 1969, pp. 23-43.

Maxson, Charles H., *The Great Awakening in the Middle Counties, 1920*, reprint edn., Gloucester, MA: Peter Smith, 1958.

Mills, Watson, E., *Speaking in Tongues: A Guide to Research on Glossolalia*, Grand Rapids, MI: Eerdmans, 1986.

Moffett, Samuel Hugh, *A History of Christianity in Asia, vol. 1: Beginnings to 1500*, 2nd rev ed, Maryknoll, New York: Orbis, 1998.

Monod, Rene, *The Korean Revival*, Hodder & Stoughton, 1969.

Moody, William R., *The Life of Dwight L. Moody*, New York: Fleming H. Revell, 1900.

Morgan, Derec Llwyd, *The Great Awakening in Wales*, Epworth Press, 1988.

Morgan, P.B., 'A Study of the Work of Four American Evangelists in Britain from 1873 to 1905, and of the Effect upon Organized Christianity of their Work there', B.Litt, Oxford 1958.

Morris, J.N., 'The Origins and Growth of Primitive Methodism in East Surrey', *Proceedings of the Wesley Historical Society*, 48, pt 5, 1992, pp. 133-49.

Moule, Handley C.G., *Charles Simeon*, 1892, Inter-Varsity Press, 1965 edn.

Murchland, Bernard (ed.), *The Meaning of the Death of God: Protestant, Jewish and Catholic Scholars Explore Atheistic Theology*, New York: Random House, 1967.

Murray, Ian, *Jonathan Edwards: A New Biography*, Edinburgh: The Banner of Truth, 1987.

———, *Revival and Revivalism*, Edinburgh: The Banner of Truth, 1994.

Neill, Stephen, *A History of Christian Missions*, Penguin Books, 1964.

Newbigin, Leslie, *Foolishness to the Greeks: The Gospel and Western Culture*, Grand Rapids, MI: Eerdmans, 1986.

Nietzsche, Friedrich, *Thus Spoke Zarathustra: A Book for Everyone and No One*, trans R.J. Hollingdale, Penguin Books, 1961.

———, *The Gay Science*, New York: Vintage, 1974.

Noll, Mark A., *A History of Christianity in the United States and Canada*, Grand Rapids, MI: Eerdmans, 1992.

——— (edn.), *Religion and Politics in America: From the Colonial Period to the 1980s*, New York: Oxford University Press, 1990.

———, David W. Bebbington and George A. Rawlyk (eds.), *Evangelicalism: Comparative Studies of Popular Protestantism in North America, the British Isles, and Beyond, 1700–1990*, New York and Oxford: Oxford University Press, 1994.

Nuttall, G.F., *Howell Harris, the Last Enthusiast*, Cardiff: University of Wales Press, 1961.

O'Brien, Susan, 'A Transatlantic Community of Saints: the Great Awakening and the First Evangelical Network, 1735–1755', *American Historical Review*, 91, 1986, pp. 811-15.

Ogletree, Thomas W., *The 'Death of God' Controversy*, New York: Abingdon Press; London: SCM Press, 1966.

Orr, J. Edwin, *The Second Evangelical Awakening: An account of the Second Worldwide Revival beginning in the Mid-Nineteenth Century*, London and Edinburgh: Marshall Morgan & Scott, 1955.

——, *The Light of the Nations*, Wheaton: Moody Press, 1965.

——, *Evangelical Awakenings Worldwide*, Wheaton, IL: Moody Press, 1975.

——, *Evangelical Awakenings in Africa*, Minneapolis: Bethany Fellowship, 1975.

——, *Evangelical Awakenings in Eastern Asia*, Minneapolis: Bethany Fellowship, 1975.

——, *Evangelical Awakenings in Southern Asia*, Minneapolis: Bethany Fellowship, 1975.

——, *Evangelical Awakenings in Latin America*, Minneapolis: Bethany Fellowship, 1975.

——, *The Eager Feet: Evangelical Awakenings, 1790–1830*, Wheaton: Moody Press, 1975.

——, *The Event of the Century: The 1857–1858 Awakening*, Wheaton: Moody Press, 1989.

Osbourne, H.H., *Fire in the Hills*, Crowborough: Highland, 1991.

Parsons, Gerald, 'Emotion and Piety. Revivalism in Victorian Christianity', in Gerald Parsons (ed.), *Religion in Victorian Britain*, 4 vols, Manchester: Manchester University Press, 1988.

Pedersen, Susan, 'Hannah More Meets Simple Simon: Tracts, Chapbooks, and Popular Culture in Late Eighteenth-century England', *Journal of British Studies* 25, 1986, pp. 84-113.

Peel, J.D.Y., *Aladura: A Religious Movement among the Yoruba*, Oxford: Oxford University Press, 1968.

Penn-Lewis, Jessie, *The Awakening in Wales*, New York: Fleming H. Revell, 1905.

Peters, George W., *Indonesian Revival*, Grand Rapids, MI: Zondervan, 1973.

Pickett, J. Wascom, *Christian Mass Movements in India*, Cincinnati: Pub NK, 1933.

_____, *Christ's Way to India's Heart*, revd edn. Lucknow: Lucknow Publishing House, 1938.

Pirouet, M.L., *Black Evangelists: The Spread of Christianity in Uganda*, 1891–1914, Collins, 1978.

Podmore, Colin John, *The Moravian Church in England, 1728–1760*, Oxford: Clarendon Press, 1998.

Poewe, Karla (ed.), *Charismatic Christianity as a Global Culture*, Columbia: University of South Carolina Press, 1994.

Pollard, Arthur and Hennell, Michael, *Charles Simeon 1759–1836*, SPCK 1964.

Pollock, John, *A Cambridge Movement*, John Murray, 1953.

_____, *The Cambridge Seven: A Call to Christian Service*, Inter-Varsity Fellowship, 1955.

_____, *Moody without Sankey: A New Biographical Portrait*, Hodder and Stoughton, 1963.

_____, *The Keswick Story: The Authorised History of the Keswick Convention*, Hodder & Stoughton, 1964.

——, *Billy Graham: The Authorised Biography*, Hodder & Stoughton, 1966.

Poloma, M.W., 'The "Toronto Blessing". Charisma, Institutionalization, and Revival', *Journal of the Scientific Study of Religion* 36, 1997, pp. 257-71.

Pugh, E. Cynolwyn, 'The Welsh Revival of 1904–1905', *Theology Today* 12 (2), July 1955.

Rack, H.D., *Reasonable Enthusiast: John Wesley and the Rise of Methodism*, Epworth Press, 1989.

Rawlyk, G.A., *Wrapped up in God: A Study of Several Canadian Revivals and Revivalists*, Burlington, Ontario: Welch Publishing Company, 1988.

——, *The Canada Fire: Radical Evangelicalism in British North America 1775–1812*, Montreal and Kingston, Ontario, 1994.

——, and M.A. Noll (eds.), *Amazing Grace: Evangelicalism in Australia, Britain, Canada and the United States*, Macon GA: Mercer University Press, 1993.

Riss, R.M., *A Survey of 20th Century Revival Movements in North America*, Peabody, MA: Hendrickson Publishers, 1997.

Robbins, Keith (ed.), *Protestant Evangelicalism: Britain, Ireland, Germany and America c.1750–c.1950. Essays in Honour of W.R. Ward*, Oxford: Blackwell, 1990.

Robert, Dana L., 'Shifting Southward', *International Bulletin of Missionary Research* 24 (2), 2000, pp. 50-58.

Roberts, D., *The 'Toronto' Blessing*, Eastbourne: Kingsway, 1994.

Rosell, G.M. and A.G. Dupuis (eds.), *The Memoirs of Charles G. Finney: The Complete Restored Text*, Grand Rapids, MI: Zondervan, 1989.

Rowell, Geoffrey, *Tradition Renewed: The Oxford Movement Conference Papers*, Darton, Longman & Todd Ltd, 1986.

Rubenstein, Richard L., *After Auschwitz: History, Theology and Contemporary Judaism, 1966*, 2nd edn. Baltimore and London: John Hopkins University Press, 1992.

Rudnick, Milton, *Speaking the Gospel Through the Ages: A History of Evangelism*, St Louis: Concordia, 1984.

Ruttenburg, Nancy, 'George Whitefield, Spectacular Conversion, and the Rise of Democratic Personality', *American Literary History* 5, 1993, pp. 429-58.

St John, Patricia, *Breath of Life: The Story of the Ruanda Mission*, Norfolk Press, 1971.

Schlenther, B., *Queen of the Methodists: The Countess of Huntingdon and the Eighteenth-Century Crisis of Faith and Society*, Bishop Auckland: Durham Academic Press, 1997.

Schmidt, L.E., *Holy Fairs: Scottish Communions and American Revivals in the Early Modern Period*, Princeton: Princeton University Press, 1989.

Schwarz, Christian A., *Natural Church Development*, St Charles, IL: Church Smart Resouces, 1996.

Scotland, Nigel, *Charismatics and the New Millennium: The Impact of Charismatic Christianity from 1960 into the New Millennium*, Hodder and Stoughton, 1995, Guildford: Eagle edn., 2000.

Scruton, Roger, *The West and the Rest: Globalization and the Terrorist Threat*, London and New York: ISI Books, 2002.

Semmel, Bernard, *The Methodist Revolution*, London: Heinemann Educational, 1974.

Shank, D.A., 'William Wade Harris: a prophet of modern times', Aberdeen Ph.D, 1980.

——, 'The Legacy of William Wade Harris', *International Bulletin of Missionary Research* 10, 1986, pp. 170-76.

Sharpe, John, 'Juvenile Holiness. Catholic Revivalism in Victorian Britain', *Journal of Ecclesiastical History* 35 1984, pp. 220-38.

Shepperson, George A., 'Ethiopianism and African Nationalism', *Phylon* 14, 1953, pp. 9-19.

Smail, Tom, Andrew Walker and Nigel Wright, *Charismatic Renewal: The Search for a Theology*, SPCK, 1993.

Smith, Stanley A.C., *Road to Revival: The Story of the Ruanda Mission*, Church Missionary Society, 1946.

Smith, Timothy L., *Revivalism and Social Reform in American Protestantism on the Eve of the Civil War*, Baltimore: Johns Hopkins University Press, rev edn. 1980.

Smout, T.C., 'Born Again at Cambuslang. New Evidence on Popular Religion and Literacy in Eighteenth Century Scotland', *Past and Present* 97, 1987, pp. 114-27.

Sordi, Marta, *The Christians and the Roman Empire*, tr. Annabel Bedini, Routledge, 1994.

Spickard, Paul R and Kevin M. Cragg, *A Global History of Christians*, Grand Rapids, MI: Baker, 1994.

Spink, Kathryn, *Mother Teresa: An Authorized Biography*, San Francisco: Harper, 1997.

Sprague, William B., *Lectures on Revivals of Religion*, Edinburgh: The Banner of Truth, 1959 edn.

Spurgeon, *Autobiography*, 2 vols, Edinburgh: The Banner of Truth, 1962 edn.

Stanley, Brian, *The Bible and the Flag: Protestant Missions and British Imperialism in the Nineteenth and Twentieth Centuries*, Leicester: Apollos, 1990.

Stanton, W.A., *The Awakening in India*, Portland, 1910.

Stock, Eugene, *History of the Church Missionary Society*, 4 vols, CMS Press, 1899-1916.

Stoeffler, F.E., *The Rise of Evangelical Pietism and German Pietism in the Eighteenth Century*, Leiden: E.J. Brill, 1971, 1973 edn.

Stoll, David, *Is Latin America Turning Protestant?: The Politics of Evangelical Growth*, Berkeley: University of California Press, 1990.

Stott, John R.W., 'Twenty Years after Lausanne: Some Personal Reflections', *International Bulletin of Missionary Research* 19 (2), April 1995, pp. 50-55.

Stout, Harry S., *The New England Soul: Preaching and Religious Culture in Colonial New England*, New York: Oxford University Press, 1986.

——, *The Divine Dramatist: George Whitefield and the Rise of Modern Evangelicalism*, Grand Rapids, MI: Eerdmans, 1991.

Sundkler, Bengt G.M., *Bantu Prophets in South Africa*, 1948, 2nd edn., Oxford: Oxford University Press, 1964.

—— and Steed, Christopher, *A History of the Church in Africa*, Cambridge: Cambridge University Press, 2000.

Sweet, William Warren, *Revivalism in America: Its Origin, Growth, and Decline*, Gloucester, MA: Peter Smith, 1965.

Taylor, J.V., *The Growth of the Church in Buganda*, SCM Press, 1958.

Thomas, George M., *Revivalism and Cultural Change: Christianity, Nation Building, and the Market in the Nineteenth-Century United States*, Chicago: University of Chicago Press, 1989.

Thompson, Phyllis, *Life Out of Death in Mozambique: A Miracle of Church Growth in the Face of Opposition*, Hodder & Stoughton, 1989.

Thornbury, J.F., *God Sent Revival: The Story of Asahel Nettleton and the Second Great Awakening*, Welwyn and Grand Rapids: Evangelical Press, 1977.

Thrupp, S.L. (ed.), *Millennial Dreams in Action*, The Hague: Mouton & Company, 1962.

Tracey, Joseph, *The Great Awakening: A History of the Revival of Religion in the Time of Edwards and Whitefield*, 1842; reissued Edinburgh: The Banner of Truth, 1976.

Tudur, Geraint, *Howell Harris: From Conversion to Separation, 1735–1750*, Cardiff: University of Wales Press, 2000.

Turner, Harold W., 'African Prophet Movements', Hibbert *Journal* 61, 242, April 1963, pp. 112-16.

——, 'A Methodology for Modern African Religious Move-ments', *Comparative Studies in Society and History* 8, 1965–1966, pp. 281-94.

——, 'A Typology for African Religious Movements', *Journal of Religion in Africa* 1, 1967, pp. 1-30.

Tyerman, L., *The Life and Times of the Rev. John Wesley, M.A., Founder of the Methodists*, 3 vols, Hodder & Stoughton, 1870.

——, *The Oxford Methodists*, Lutterworth Press, 1873.

——, *The Life of the Rev. George Whitefield, B.A. of Pembroke College*, 2 vols, Hodder & Stoughton, 1890.

Vahanian, Gabriel, *The Death of God: The Culture of Our Post-Christian Era*, New York: George Braziller, 1961.

Van Buren, Paul M., *The Secular Meaning of the Gospel based on an analysis of its Language*, SCM Press, 1963.

Walker, Andrew, *Restoring the Kingdom: The Radical Christianity of the House Church Movement*, Hodder & Stoughton, 1985.

Walls, Andrew, *The Missionary Movement in Christian History: Studies in the Transmission of Faith*, Maryknoll, NY: Orbis, 1996.

——, 'Eusebius tries again', *International Bulletin of Missionary Research*, 24 (3), 2000, pp. 105-11.

—— and Shenk, W.R. (eds.), *Exploring New Religious Movements: Essays in Honour of H.W. Turner*, Grand Rapids, MI: Eerdmans, 1990.

Walsh, J.D., 'Origins of the Evangelical Revival', in G.V. Bennet and J. Walsh (eds.), *Essays in Modern Church History in Memory of Norman Sykes*, Adam and Charles Black, 1966.

——, 'Religious Societies: Methodist and Evangelical 1738–1800', in W.J. Shiels and Diana Wood (eds.), *Voluntary Religion* (*Studies in Church History* 23), Oxford: Blackwell, pp. 279-302.

——, C. Haydon and S. Taylor (eds.), *The Church of England c.1689–c.1833: From Toleration to Trinitarianism*, Cambridge: Cambridge University Press, 1993.

Ward, W.R., 'The Relations of Enlightenment and Religious Revival in Central Europe and in the English-speaking World', *Studies in Church History*, Subsidia 2, 1979, pp. 281-305.

——, 'Power and Piety. The Origins of Religious Revival in the Early Eighteenth Century', *Bulletin of the John Rylands Library* 63, 1980, pp. 231-52.

——, *The Protestant Evangelical Awakening*, Cambridge: Cambridge University Press, 1992.

——, *Faith and Faction*, SCM Canterbury Press, 1993.

Warren, Max, *Revival. An Enquiry*, SCM, 1954.

Watson, E. Mills, *Speaking in Tongues: A Guide to Research on Glossolalia*, Grand Rapids, MI: Eerdmans, 1986.

Watts, Michael R., *The Dissenters: From the Reformation to the French Revolution*, Oxford: Clarendon Press, 1978.

——, *The Dissenters: The Expansion of Evangelical Nonconformity*, Oxford: Clarendon Press, 1995.

Weisberger, Bernard A., *They Gathered at the River: The Story of the Great Revivalists and their Impact upon Religion in America*, Boston: Little, Brown and Co, 1958.

Welbourn, F.B., *East African Rebels: A Study of Some Independent Churches*, SCM Press, 1961.

Welch, C., *Spiritual Pilgrim: A Reassessment of the Life of the Countess of Huntingdon*, Cardiff: University of Wales Press, 1995.

Westmeir, Kael-Wilhelm, *Protestant Pentecostalism in Latin America: A Study in the Dynamics of Missions*, Madison NJ: Associated University Press, 1999.

White, J.W., 'The Influence of North American Evangelism in Great Britain between 1830 and 1914 on the Origin and Development of the Ecumenical Movement', Oxford D.Phil., 1963.

Whitefield, George, *George Whitefield's Journals*, Edinburgh: The Banner of Truth, 1960 edn.

Whittaker, Colin C., *Seven Pentecostal Pioneers*, Basingstoke: Marshall Pickering, 1983.

Williams, Cyril G., *Tongues of the Spirit: A Study of Pentecostal Glossolalia and Related Phenomena*, Cardiff: University of Wales Press, 1981.

Willis, Avery T., *Indonesian Revival*, South Pasadena, CA: William Carey Library, 1977.

Wilson, Bryan R., *Religion in Secular Society: A Sociological Comment*, C.A. Watts & Co Ltd, 1966.

——, *Magic and the Millennium: A Sociological Study of Religious Movements of Protest among Tribal and Third World Peoples*, Heinemann, 1973.

Wilson, Everett A., 'The Central American Evangelicals. From Protest to Pragmatism', *International Review of Missions 77*, January 1988, pp. 94-106.

Wilson, G. Herbert, *The History of the Universities' Mission to Central Africa*, Universities' Mission to Central Africa, 1936.

Wimber, John, *Power Evangelism: Signs and Wonders for Today*, Hodder & Stoughton, 1985.

Wingate, Andrew, Kevin Ward, Carrie Pemberton and Sitshebo Wilson (eds.), *Anglicanism: A Global Communion*, Mowbray, 1998.

Wolffe, John (ed.), *Evangelical Faith and Public Zeal: Evangelicals and Society in Britain 1780–1980*, SPCK, 1995.

Wood, A. Skevington, *The Inextinguishable Blaze: Spiritual Renewal and Advance in the Eighteenth Century*, Grand Rapids, MI: Eerdmans, 1960.

Wuthnow, Robert, *Christianity in the Twenty-First Century*, New York: Oxford University Press, 1993.

Yates, Timothy, *Christian Mission in the Twentieth Century*, Cambridge: Cambridge University Press, 1994.

Youngs, J. William T., *God's Messengers: Religious Leadership in Colonial New England, 1700–1750*, Baltimore: John Hopkins, 1976.

Zehrer, Karl, 'The Relationship between Pietism in Halle and Early Methodism', *Methodist History* 17, 1979, pp. 211-24